Teachers Talk

TEACHERS
TALK

John Godar

Glenbridge Publishing Ltd.

Contents

FOREWORD

"The time has come the walrus said to talk of many things . . ."
of performance—politics—and personal philosophy!

Teachers Talk reflects the three Ps in a mirrored image of today's educational system. Sensitivities and raw emotions are brought to the surface in John Godar's cross-country interviews of teachers. Presenting both personal statements and dialogue, Godar exposes both the open wounds and the healings; he and his teachers touch sensitive nerves with a universal theme.

Teachers Talk is a powerful statement about today's society, a dysfunctional family with our nation's teachers the enablers. Can our country allow this situation to continue?

Teachers everywhere must learn to speak their truth—not in little hidden closets but in public. Only in this way can teachers be true to themselves and to their students. The teachers in this book bare their souls, and our country needs to listen.

Godar's interviews show public education to be a risk averse institution. Teachers must stop being afraid. Societal and administrative intimidation must be replaced by free and open communication between teachers, school administration, communities, and parents.

After reading *Teachers Talk*, it becomes clear that teachers must refill their "well." Burnout is a spreading disease in the teaching profession at every level. Overwork and classroom stress are claiming the best and brightest of teachers.

Education should be vibrant and life-giving. The child's mind and character are sculpted by the teacher's hand. What the world is going to be like tomorrow depends on what the teachers are doing in the classroom today; society needs to recognize teachers and the educational process as our greatest resource for the future. Godar and his teachers remind us that teaching is the most noble of all professions.

Hopefully, *Teachers Talk* will begin a healing process by encouraging a public awareness of the realities of the issues confronting educators daily.

So prepare yourself for an experience of "shoes—and ships—and sealing wax—of cabbages—and kings . . ." (*Alice in Wonderland*).

Shar Wilkes

Casper, Wyoming; Resource Specialist,
Natrona County School District #1

Preface

After my father died in December of 1985 and my lover broke up with me two months later, I decided to quit my high school English teaching job which I'd held for twelve years and at which I'd been very successful. I wanted to see what it would be like to face the three biggest stress-producing situations all at the same time: losing a parent, losing a lover, and losing a job. Besides, I was burnt out on teaching, due to a new principal who thought he was the second coming, the same old wearying ignorance from central administration — too many boring cohorts and apathetic students involved in a curriculum over which I had no say. In short, I felt I wasn't accomplishing anything.

But I couldn't just sit in my house so I decided to travel the country and sound out other teachers across the nation to find out how many felt as I did, to find out what they thought was wrong with public education, to find out if the majority of teachers were really good or bad . . . to find out if I wanted to go back into teaching again. Part of it was that I'd had enough, and part of it was that I hadn't.

I spent a year interviewing 282 teachers in 10 different states and over 30 different school districts. I talked to elementary teachers, middle school teachers and high school teachers. The districts were rural, inner city, suburban, and combinations of those. I taped what they said and polled them on several issues in public education today.

What I found were some wonderful teachers out there who were "loving them every day" as one told me. What I found were other people with my dedication working for non-professional wages and lacking the power to change things that they knew needed to be changed. What I found were great teachers, often in horrendous working conditions dealing with impossible children, broken by a weak society. And I felt it was time they had their say in the debate over what's wrong with public education.

So here are their interviews, word for word; here's what the professionals in the field of education think is good and bad about public education today. Here's what the teachers think; here's what teachers say when teachers talk.

Here's what convinced me that public education was an impossible job. . . and I wanted back into it. What could be more important than teaching! "There are three things a person is supposed to do in life: have a child, plant a tree... and teach."

I would like to acknowledge a debt of gratitude to the National Education Association that helped me to contact many (though not all) of the people whom I interviewed for this book. There were many people who volunteered their time to organize interviews for me in their school districts. In particular, I'd like to remember Judy Dellamonica, Nancy Demartre, Ken Freed, John Grossman, Margaret Jeffus, Robley Jones, Colleen Lanier, Nick Leon, Jack Patterson, Barbara Pemberton, Louann Reid, Phil Rumore, Charlotte Schipman, Larry Simon, Stephen Sirkin, Jo Ann Valerino, Kathy Warren, and many others.

I would also like to thank Janet Baker, Barb Brough, Deb Dalzell, James A. Keene, Andy Ruffner and all my family and friends for their help in typing, editing, and encouraging.

But most importantly, I would like to thank all of the public school teachers who took the time out of their busy work schedules to talk with me for an hour or two. As a working high school teacher, I know how precious an hour or two can be in a long day of teaching. So I dedicate this book to them and to all of their many peers who are out there working hard in the public schools of this country.

Section 1:

TEACHERS WHO CARE

What makes a good teacher? They have to know their material and then have the ability to communicate it to the level of their students. But most important, they have to care. What matter knowledge; what matter skill, if a person doesn't care to use it? That's the difference between a teacher and so many others: teachers care.

Tape #78

Ms. M. was a New Yorker . . . it showed. What made it stand out was that she was teaching in the South. Her association president told me that they had to put a muzzle on her when she was dealing with the administration. I loved her. She was witty, intelligent, and cared a great deal about teaching. While we chatted, she smoked and tried to stop with each cigarette. She had taught English for ten years, two in horrible classes in New York and the last eight in a very suburban high school in the Southeast. She gestured a lot and thought out each question.

And she had a vulnerable side that she barely let show. When she walked into the room I was using to do my interviews, she first asked, "Do you still want to talk to me?" Yes, a thousand times yes. You and all intelligent, unique educators like you.

"What is a good teacher? Someone who cares.

"Do you believe in callings? Yeah, I believe I was called to be a teacher. All of the things that I have to do in my job are very compatible with my nature and my world view and everything. It's just the perfect job for me. And as a child, I wanted to be a teacher.

"I have so correctly meshed my career . . . I always had a sense that I would be a good teacher. And I knew I would be good with kids. And it's good I'm teaching psychology now because there's always been a tug of war between being a therapist and being a teacher. I would have made more money as a therapist. But God! I *am* a therapist. I have been in family conferences as a teacher and what got accomplished at those conferences would have cost these people eight hundred dollars in psychiatric counseling and taken a month . . . I think many teachers do things like this. I may have a gift for it. And in the classroom my psychology background helps a lot — with behavior mod in discipline problems and very concrete thinkers.

"We had a lot of talk of relevance at one time as though it were some kind of new concept, and it probably got abused. I would say that I acknowledge and recognize that my students bring to literature — very sophisticated and mature literature that we teach them — very limited experience. What have they done? Where have they been? They're only sixteen, though many of them have been through a whole lot more in their sixteen years than I have in my thirty-five. So what do I try to do to get them interested in the literature — a lot of techniques I could tell you about, but I guess basically it boils down to this. Whet their appetite by starting out where they are. They don't know from tragic heroes, you know. That's kind of irrelevant. They don't know about — let's say the theme in literature is family interrelationships and so on. And you've got something as sophisticated as *Sons and Lovers* by D. H. Lawrence. How do they relate to something like that? You start out — I start out where they are. And I build up to more abstract applications. I see the teaching of literature as the planting of a seed. Unfortunately, I'm not usually around to see it sprout. But I take it on faith that I have planted a seed and that it may well grow later on, because they're not necessarily intellectually or emotionally mature enough to appreciate it this week. Down the road —

"Strategy? There will be a story about the Indian culture, housed in this American culture which does a number on the Indians and so on. And this really sounds kind of corny, but the Indian rituals sometimes are pretty grotesque by our standards. And there was one story that I've taught that had a ritual in it that is awful. I almost have to close my eyes when I read it . . . which I manage to do sometimes! So anyway . . . I send them home with a directive reading, with something to look for. On that story I'll throw in: 'By the way, don't prepare a peanut butter and jelly sandwich to eat along with the reading of this story tonight. It will — it will — well, don't.' And they're dying to know what it is. Or I'll say to them: 'When you get to the end of the story, don't blame me for how it ends up; *I* didn't write it.' And I'll say: 'I don't know any more about what happens to this dying Indian than you do; maybe we can figure it out. So when you're reading it, see if you can find any clues to — maybe the author did give us an answer, but he doesn't tell us straight out.' You know, this kind of thing, to get them going.

". . . I never wanted to work at Macy's — I wanted to teach. We're going back to 1973 or '74 when I graduated from college. And up in New York, there were no teaching jobs to be had. I mean, the story was that people were reading the obituaries and if a teacher died, they went and applied for the job the next day. So I didn't have a teaching job and that's how I ended up at Macy's. I had to do something; I had to make a living. And then in February the high school where I student-taught called and there was an opening. I'll never forget these classes. There were two classes that were notorious throughout the system . . . and no one said a word to me. But their names were legendary. (Laughter) Which is just great — it's February and everybody knew who they were. They'd been through three teachers. Now I knew they'd been through three teachers since it was a fact they couldn't hide from me, but they told me one left to take a lead in a play, one got pregnant . . . but the kids let me know the first day I was there. One of them came out from under his desk and said, 'We got rid of the other three; we'll get rid of you.' But then I was excessed — let go because they didn't need as many teachers.

"Of course this is the same school district that put me in with seventh graders who were emotionally disturbed students . . . no one *told* me they were emotionally disturbed. I was sitting there scratching my head thinking — how come my class is half the size of all the others? No one told me! I thought — what, is it me? I've only got *ten* here. This kid's throwing papers and this one keeps hanging himself. No one said anything to me. Finally, I thought now let's see — something's not right. You have to understand I went from high school to junior high so I chalked up some of it to that. I wasn't suited to junior high. The children showed up shorter than I — the first time that had ever happened — with voices like this — way up high! And they couldn't say my name. Finally I went in — I was relentless — 'Somebody tell me what to do here.' And someone said finally — 'They have emotional problems.' And my immediate reaction was — 'Was it me?!' I will go to my grave wondering what that district's logic was for not telling me. Maybe they told me in educationese and it went over my head — I don't know."

(What percentage of teachers nationwide are good teachers?)

"A whole lot more than anybody realizes. A whole lot more — but I want to qualify this — I have personally known teachers who would have been terrific . . . if they hadn't gotten squashed . . . year after year after year. Counting those as competent teachers . . . ok? Counting those — I would say that in spite of everything, eighty percent are good teachers. I mean . . . above average. That leaves maybe ten percent who are mediocre and ten percent who shouldn't be in teaching. I would love to get them out. Where else do they try to educate everybody?

"I think that the reason that we look so bad on paper is that we try so much more than anybody else — the American education system. It takes on the impossible. We don't say at age fourteen, the only thing you can do is be a carpenter . . . and I don't mean to belittle carpenters. A lot of my students will make good carpenters . . . and they will make more money than I do. And — more power to them. Let them be carpenters. But I think we really do try to do more things — just that basic right: everybody is entitled to an education. We care about everybody.

"I think you can talk to anybody and about ninety-five percent of the people will talk about a teacher who made an impact on their life. It may have been their fourth grade teacher; it may have been their science teacher in the eleventh grade; it may very well have been an English teacher. You know the relationship between a teacher and a student is unique; there is nothing like it. You're not a friend; you're not parents; you're not lovers; you're not strangers. You're a little bit of all those things to each other. And anyone who would deny that is a liar. (Laughter)"

Tape #76

Mr. J. was president of his local association and teaching only half a day. He had curly blonde hair and a wonderful Southern accent. He taught eighth grade English in a suburban school district. He was dressed in a coat and tie, and we were speaking in his office where I could see the picture of him with his wife and three children. It was hard to tell by looking at him if he were young or old, but he said he was thirty-five, the same age as I at the time.

And like me and so many of our generation, he had felt impelled to do something for the world, to live his caring.

"I guess my reasons for wanting to teach are rather altruistic. My mother was a teacher as was my grandmother — very strong women. [My mother] just thought education was just the most important thing a child could have and that was instilled in me very early on. And I think I bought the whole '60s stuff about — be a teacher: your country needs teachers; I think I was sort of suckered into that. Because this was the time of teacher shortage, and the post-Sputnik era was one where education was seen as very important. And there was a push to get good teachers. And I came from an upper middle class situation where I had never had to make monetary decisions, and so I guess the salary just wasn't that big of a factor. I think there were mixed signals even then about whether society respected teachers or not, but it was so ingrained in me about respecting education that I really didn't care whether the rest of society respected teaching very much. When I came out of college, my father — he was in insurance — set up some interviews for me because he wanted me to go into that. But it just seemed that education was such an honorable profession. You weren't trying to take anything from anybody. All you were trying to do was to help people live better lives. And I guess I am very altruistic, because that was — important.

"And I think I agree with a lot of the studies that say we need a change in structure. I think the most frustrating thing for not only myself but for many classroom teachers is the number of tasks you have to do that have no relationship to quality instruction. An example? — having lesson plans ready two weeks in advance to turn in to be looked at. And to me, not only is that a waste of *my* time, but it's a waste of the principal's time to be sitting around in the office looking at plans when he could be going around and directly looking at people's instruction so he could be offering suggestions on how people's instruction could be improved. And we need a whole restructuring of the administrator's duties. I think the whole way they deal with teachers needs to be analyzed. It seems like every teacher's treated the same way — and I've worked in several different buildings. And it's . . . you get a memo and everybody has to do exactly the same thing when teachers really are different as individuals. I read an article by a principal that said he had three groups of teachers. One was the group that were doing a poor job and they had to be gotten out of the career, either through counseling or through documenting their job and firing them. Another group were those teachers that were trying and making their best effort, but they had some weaknesses. And you had to identify those weaknesses and try to help them so they could be a better teacher. And then the third group were those that were highly motivated, self-motivated, doing a bang-up job and really, probably were exceeding any expectations as to what the school district could have of the average teacher. They were teachers who cared. And he said you had to treat each of those different groups a different way and that third group — you had to leave them alone. Just get out of their way and let them teach. Realize what you have, that you have a valuable resource.

"But the way schools are run, everybody gets the same memo. Now why in the world would somebody who's doing a bang-up job, and everybody knows it, have to turn in plans two weeks in advance? Caring teachers overplan; caring teachers constantly revise; caring teachers constantly develop new materials, and they may develop new materials in one night. You know — they may go home and say, well, I didn't do very well in that and what's another way to hit it? If you're confined by some two week plan, it just stifles creativity. The Carnegie Report talks about a bureaucracy of mediocrity and how it just encourages the mediocrity. We need people managers — you know running the school district and running the football team are two different things . . . A man who was trained in how to manage people might be able to do a better job. And I think the school administrator's role should be to facilitate. It should be to facilitate education, to encourage education rather than to police.

"And I think salaries have got to be increased. The kids that I have taught over the last ten years, they're not nearly as altruistic as I was . . . as we were. They're looking at how much they're going to make. And we need to recruit minorities. It's so important for those minority kids to have professional role models of their own race. I think a school system needs teachers for both races. It is just essential for these white students to see an able black professional in front of them. There still are vestiges of racism in our society and I can't think of a better way to combat that. Maybe put money into forgivable loans for minority students.

"I also think you need to lower the class size in all academic classes and look at doing it in the others too. I know people argue that the class size doesn't matter, and it isn't important for the kind of education that raises test scores on multiple choice tests. But if you really want to have kids coming out of school with writing ability, then class size is essential because in order to write, you have to write. It's something that you have to practice. You're not going to get better at that by filling in multiple choice answers. That's mass education. And when you give an English teacher 150 kids, you're going to have to go to that kind of teaching. And the writing will get done less. So what is it that we're after? If you're going to talk about class size being important or not important, you have to look at what kind of education you're looking for. Do we want the kind of education that will keep test scores up, which I think ends up being the bottom line a lot of the time. That's how school systems are judged by the public and that's not right. Or do we want people that are going to be thinkers, that are going to be writers, that are going to care?

"I probably would become a teacher again because I can't imagine doing anything else. I like it. I think it's important. I ask myself if I really want to do this for forty years. You look at the way the kids interact with some of the older teachers, and teenagers can be so cruel. They don't cut them any slack. But then I look at what else can I do that's as honorable? What else can I do that — you know, I can't sell insurance! (Laughter) I can't. I don't want to make my living where I feel like part of my earning it is fooling people."

Tape #157

I interviewed Mr. W. amidst his own children. First they came home from school, grade school, and wanted him to see the papers they had brought with them. He did, very enthusiastically. Then they had to be bundled off to soccer practice. Then they came back. Then they wanted to use the computer. Then —

Mr. W. has two young children of his own. He's taught for sixteen years and currently teaches ninth grade science and computers. He is handsome but heading for forty. He also works as a small machines repairman at least one weekend a month and full time in the summer. He teaches in a rural-suburban school district in an eighth-ninth grade building.

He told me he still has dreams about his former students who killed themselves.

"I don't think I planned on teaching until I was a sophomore in college. And it does seem like all the strong role models when I was growing up seem to be teachers. Looking back I can see them influencing me a lot more than I felt at the time. But I've always enjoyed working with people. I put myself through college, farm work, factory work, roofing — it seems like I always liked the people more than the — actual work, if you know what I mean. It seems like all the lines just sort of led the same way. And I did love coaching at the time; I coached for ten, eleven years. I could get a job in a lot of other places right now — especially in computers. But I grew up in a poor family. And compared to the way I grew up, I'm wealthy right now. I guess money just isn't a big motivator for me. I do work part time for a repair place, make probably about five thousand a year. And the guy will just give me a three hundred dollar bonus — just for doing a good job. There are no bonuses in education. You get fifty bucks, and you think WOW! But to me, I get to enjoy my family more. I'm here when the kids come home. You know, my neighbor's a truck driver and he makes pretty good money, but he's gone a lot."

(If someone of college age told you they wanted to go into teaching, would you discourage them or encourage them?)

"I'd inform them. I knew going in what it was like. I'd never seen any teachers driving Porsches. I guess it just depends on what motivates you. It's very fulfilling; it's not something you can hook on a pay scale. No, I wouldn't discourage them, but I'd say to them, 'Look, if you want to live in that 200,000 dollar home, and drive a fancy car and visit the Bahamas, this isn't the place to be . . .'

"But we've got to change. We've got to get teacher-pupil ratios down. I mean, putting thirty people in an English class and saying you're going to teach composition is a contradiction in terms. It becomes an assembly line. What they're trying to do is get us to get more and more specific, and I think as a society we need to get more and more general. We need to turn out well-rounded individuals. I mean, if everybody leaves thinking — I never want to do another math problem again; I never want to write another sentence — I mean, how much back to basics have you done? First graders — they're just dying to learn. My ninth graders — 'Make me learn. You want me to do homework — only if I can get it done here.' Why? They're caught in this huge system. They're stuck in a room of thirty.   You didn't learn? Hey, well — you walk through. We're all stepping in time. Whether you're stepping or not, you're getting dragged. One way or another — you're in the system. And we never get the support we need. It's always band-aid help. I mean if you go into business, you would never send anything out that wasn't first rate. But in education, it's always — what's the bottom line, what's the bare minimum, and that's what you go with. You can't be expected to do an A-1 job with minimal funding. Everything's just geared to the minimum.

"I think the strength of public education is in the teacher's dedication. We're still living on the old teacher's reputation. I mean, when you say teachers, you think of the old down-the-line marm. We've got to carry on that tradition. The strength now is in the diversity of people, the interaction. School is the common ground. We're there for them to interact with. It's a place where kids can be made or broken quickly. And I think we make a lot of kids . . . we don't break many. I think there're a lot of good teachers. I mean, there's a real strong weeding process. Years ago, you could be dead and teach. Now, you have to be motivated to stay in the field. It's kind of survival of the fittest. Teacher trends are up. I feel good about us, but at the same time, the task is harder. Teachers are leaving — money and stress. Maybe stress is the number one reason — I mean, there's no way I can keep this intensity up for thirty years. Computers saved me. Ten years ago, I was starting to hit that — I need to switch. But computers turned me around; I'm on the up. I buck the trend, though. I realize that.

"But I like to deal with people — just sit down and talk to kids. I mean, with computers after school, I can do that. Hey, you got a haircut, right? Yeah, you noticed? Well, you're not in a class of three hundred, I noticed. You look good in pink. When you can actually rub shoulders with them — they don't get that anymore. It helps with the motivating of students too. Right now, I have kids doing a program on the computer. I said I needed twenty-five people to type during the day — I can get you fifty kids; I'd say — 'Hey, we have to stay til — eight o'clock tonight so call your parents, bring a lunch.' I can get those kids to do that. They understand; they appreciate the little niceties. Oh, I've seen it. There are about fifteen teachers at our building and even if they were giving out free ten dollar bills, man, you couldn't get anybody in that room. Let me tell you the personal touch is what we need; it's what this whole world needs, and we kind of get away from it. You know, in the first grade the kids are crying and they pat them on the shoulder. We don't do that.

"How long you been teaching? How many kids have you had commit suicide? I've had — I think I'm up to eight. That's a lot, I know. Now, not during my classroom, but before they've graduated — of the kids I've had in class, I've had eight kill themselves . . . in sixteen years. Now I'll tell you what — one played football for me . . . as a ninth grader. And when he was a junior, he killed himself. I joked with him when I had him; you know . . . he was a good friend of mine. I don't know how personal I was with him . . . but I talked to him . . . in his other classes, no teachers seemed to really know him. He was one of those quieter kids. I always look back . . . I mean — I have dreams about those kids . . . how personal were you, you know? We tend not to be . . . it's easy not to be. I knew him better than a lot of teachers . . . I'm sure I did . . . yet it didn't help him.

"You can't save everybody, but then again — you know, you don't see the family life and all this . . . but I think you've got to be warm. You know you can walk into any school — 'Hey, who do you learn best from?' And you ask any group of kids, and you'll come up with maybe fifteen names

— and they'll just keep recurring. You can write a scenario on those teachers though you've never met them. It doesn't matter what they teach — the shop teacher, the English teacher. It just takes some personal qualities. These are the ones that influenced me the most. I had a couple and if I can ever be like them, buddy . . . I'm set."

(Would you go back into education if you were in college now and you knew then what you know about education?)

"I'd say yes. I'm a product of the '60s and revolution. I can't see myself being an insurance agent. Some of my friends went into that and they're making big bucks. I'm not one of those; I'm not an accountant. I pay the money price, but I enjoy it. I enjoy it. I get up in the morning — boy, I don't have to dread it. I'm *doing* something."

Tape #210

She looked young but she walked maturely — she had an aura of confidence about her without which I think she might have been eaten up, a pretty "girl" who stood in front of the classroom. But she struck me as being a good teacher after I talked with her. And it was only her second year of teaching high school English at a very large, very diverse high school. Its population covered slum areas for both blacks and whites and one of the most exclusive areas in this large Midwestern city.

Yet Ms. W. knew her kids — of all kinds. She got involved with them. She cared. She already had great student stories after only two years of teaching . . . I was impressed.

She was twenty-three and married, blonde and pretty. Her hobbies were photography and writing.

"It's been a rough week here because one of our students committed suicide . . . I'm not allowed to say that because the police investigation isn't finished yet, but — it was apparently a suicide. And that's been difficult for the students. There's been quite a bit of talking about it in several of my classes, my seniors in particular. They went to the funeral last night, and it's been hard to get much out of them today, and I'm not pushing them too much right now.

"Another down was my fourth period class, a sophomore class which is a lower level class; of course we're not grouped, but it's the lowest level that we have! (Laughter) Usually it's a really neat class; it didn't start out that way, but I feel really good about the routine that I've gotten them into.

They've been doing pretty well. Today they weren't paying attention and we were doing something that was slightly challenging for them, a little different from what we usually do. And whenever that happens, there's more tension. It's more difficult. And I got frustrated with them and they were getting frustrated, but I didn't think that they were really paying attention; and they didn't get it right off so they said — well, I can't do this. That was very frustrating; finally by the end of the period I got them back around ok.

"And then fifth period I have a junior class; it's the next level up from low level and it's called college prep . . . college prep is a euphemism because not all those kids are going to college. It's just kind of what we have to have between regular (low level) and advance placement. We were doing Edgar Allen Poe; this class has a fairly low ability level, very, very low effort. I have been on them all year. And they're getting better, but today it was again — just a fight to get them to pay attention. They weren't into Edgar Allen Poe. (Laughter) 'Bells, Bells, Bells' — (Laughter). After we explained it and got on with it, they were ok; it was just the initial getting into; the motivation is not there so I have to be really up — 'we're going to read Edgar Allen Poe today!' And I don't always feel like being that way every day. It's hard to be optimistic and cheerful all the time with some of them. In that class I would like different literature to deal with. I'd like to do a lot more modern things; I'd also like to include a lot more works by women and minorities — that class is American Lit and it's very mainstream. And I get bored with it; and they get bored with it.

"You know, I ended up liking the low level kids more than I thought I would ... I love them. It's just so rewarding, when you get something good out of them. It's a feeling like I've never felt before. For example, I'm doing a poetry unit right now, and these tenth grade regular kids (low level) are recognizing alliteration; they can chart the rhyme scheme of a poem; recognizing assonance, all these things that my college prep kids can't do. And it's just so wonderful. They're also the most loyal personally.

"Discipline is always rough, these two years anyway. It's been really rough at first, more so last year because I didn't know what to do. But once I handled that discipline, I've had relatively few problems. They're very loyal; they'll do anything for Ms. W. I use a sort of modified assertive discipline approach, but fewer rules and fewer steps that you have to go through. And also, I never sit behind my desk, especially in those classes. I'm always up and down and so I'm always in contact with them. I also do a lot of talking to the kids individually, have them in after school or after class. Try to find out what's below the surface behavior. The combination of those things seems to really work for me.

"I had a lot of problems with discipline last year."

(Can you remember what your worst discipline problem had been in the two years?)

"Oh, very easily. (Laughter) I had a student named Vincent — Vince who was terrible. He was in one of my lower level tenth grade classes. He was in a very different class anyway; he was continually out of his seat, always talking while I was; frequently he cussed. He several times got into 'almost fights' — I never actually had a time when somebody hit somebody else, but I did have a time where one kid threatened another kid and they started to fight, but another kid got involved and then he separated them and then — there were three different possible fights and that was one time when I was threatened; because when I stepped in, the kid said, 'I'm going to hit you if you don't get out of my way.' And I — this is so stupid! — I said 'Go ahead!' (Laughter) 'make my day!' The thing was that what happened and what I hoped would happen was that about five kids were out of their seats and they said, 'Don't you touch her.' The loyalty! But this kid Vince was involved in that. He threatened me. He walked by me in the hallway and raised his hand like he was going to hit me, and then he didn't. It was a power trip for him. I would call home and I would send him to his administrator but they never did anything. The parents — well, we'll talk to him. He would do things like — he would throw things. He threw a book across the room once. In the middle of class he started laughing or something and rolled out of his chair onto the floor. It's amazing I'm still teaching after all of this! (Laughter) And finally two things happened. I finally wrote enough referrals and sent him to the office enough times that he got ten days out-of-school suspension, which is the worst thing next to expulsion. Plus, he invited me to one of his basketball games and I went. It was just — the biggest success story that you could come up with. He still visits me this year. Every time he gets a good grade in English he brings it back to me. I had him put into a higher English class, which in a way he didn't quite have the skills for, but he's slowly building them, and it gets him into a different group. He comes and visits me practically every day. When that kid killed himself, Vince grabbed me in the hall and said 'God! I can't believe it!' It's probably why I'm still teaching!

"I've had some sweet moments in teaching. I can think of two others. A boy that I helped with his drug problem called me once and said, 'I don't know where I'd be without you; you changed the whole direction of my life.' And the other incident is another girl who is incredibly bright — failed my class. There were lots of family problems — anorexic. Just you name it — she had the problem. And she graduated last year, and on the last day before graduation she came in and gave me a big hug and said, 'I don't know what I would have done if I hadn't had somebody to talk to.' I don't think the parents even in this community realize [the] extent [of] the problems.

"There are some teachers who would probably make fun of some of the things I do. For example, I get fairly INVOLVED with some of my kids other than — who wrote "Fall of the House of Usher"? An example is that I had this student last year who called me at the beginning of this year. I've talked to him before and I thought he had a drug problem, but I wasn't sure. I talked to him about it and told him if he ever wanted to get help for it to let me know and I'll set you up. He called me and he was very upset and said, 'I have to do something right away and I just don't know what to do.' I said, 'Why don't you talk to your parents and have them take you to a center?' 'I already have,' he said; 'they refuse.' His home situation was terrible, ok? I guess this was not the most correct thing to do for my career, but I said, 'I'll pick you up and I'll take you there.' And I did. And he was admitted; I went and visited him. It caused some problems because his mother is an alcoholic, got resentful of me. She said something to someone who teaches here, that her son and I were having this romantic relationship — (laughter) — just what her son needs. So the principal called me in; and 'we're concerned' — he was very understanding actually. He said, 'I know you; this doesn't seem very likely.' But he had to say something. He said if that were to happen again, 'I would suggest that you not take the kid down yourself.' But I don't know if I'd do it any differently."

(Do you think public education works?)

"Yes and no."

(Would you say more yes or more no?)

"More no."

(Would you become a teacher again?)

"Yes. There's something about the classroom; when something works in the classroom, it's just so wonderful. And when you feel like you've gotten through to them, whether it's about a personal issue, a values issue or whether it's about a work of literature, that's really neat. I don't know if I'll stay in. I figure I'll be here for another five to ten years and then we'll see.

"I see other teachers who are burnt out and ineffective, and I don't ever want to be like that. There are also a lot of other things that I think I'm good at that I can't pursue while I'm teaching and that I'd like to pursue. I enjoy teaching, but I'm afraid there will come a time when I won't."

(Does salary have a role in this decision?)

"No . . . not yet. It may in the future if we decide to have a family, depending on what my husband decided to do. But like I said, I think there are a lot of things I could do well; I wouldn't enjoy it; but I think I could do it. Still, money isn't what I'm looking at to decide if I stay in or not."

Tape #225

When I asked in the office where I would find Ms. B., I was told she was probably in the teacher's lounge. When I asked what she looked like, the secretary smiled and said, "She's a large lady in cords and a tie . . . " She was also wearing gym shoes. Ms. B. was unusual in many ways, but she seemed a very sincere teacher, really trying to work out the problems of inner city education. By the end of the interview she had begun to cry — over the importance of our work.

She was forty-five, single, and had taught at the high school level and the middle school level in social studies and English for nineteen years.

"I had done social work and I found that all of my clients were dying on me and I wanted to start working with somebody at the beginning of their lives rather than at the end of their lives. And now I'm hooked on teaching — because nineteen years later I still get out of bed excited to go to work that day. It's a deeply satisfying job. I don't really care if I go to work every day and make money for some corporation, but I do care if I go to work and help a kid some way . . . .

"We struggle daily with the image that teachers are not much more than primordial slime. And I struggle to maintain my own sense of self respect even with my own closest friends who know what I'm like in the classroom and who know what my commitment is to kids. They think if teachers were in the private sector, ninety percent of us would be fired. They don't think teachers teach. I don't think that's true. I know that there are teachers who are devastating to kids, and if you hurt a child's self image, you will never get anywhere with that kid. If you devastate a child, you have lost that child. And there are some that do that to kids, but the vast majority of teachers are deeply committed to kids and I know what all the extra things the teachers I know do for kids — have Saturday classes on their own; they don't get paid for doing that. I have a friend who teaches math down South and there isn't money to pay for extra time in her accelerated class so she has class on Saturday morning and she tells them they better get their buns out of bed and be there. The friends I have in teaching go that extra mile. But we are seen by people as slime, especially since we are being represented by unions. How can we expect teachers to get five years of college, expect them to teach the kids we have today, become all but surrogate parents, pay them poverty level wages and then expect them to teach the content on top of all that . . . and then treat them like s___? (Laughter) You can't do that to people. But that is what is happening."

(What keeps you teaching?)

"I love kids; I love kids; I love kids. Yesterday when I told the kids I was going to be evaluated, a kid who is killing me because his reading level is so low, an eighth grader reading at third grade level, a kid that I'm so frustrated with because I don't feel like I'm helping him at all, he's just been such a neglected child that he needs more than I can help him with — and he said, 'If they try to mess with my teacher . . . I'll get them.' So — I get hugs, I get kisses, I get lots from the kids. I get a reason to get up in the morning. I get — definite reasons to be able to go to sleep at night!"

(Do you think public education works?)

"Oh, yeah absolutely. How the American people could not be committed to public education is — is — that's what America is all about. It's democracy and for all of the people who have pulled their kids out of public school it's just — what a shame! What a shame! I'm no Mother Theresa or Joan of Arc, but I do what I do well and work very hard at it. And I don't bring my private problems into the classroom, but God knows that society certainly puts its private problems off on me every day with the condition of the kids when they're sent to me and the condition the kids are in when they get to me every day. They are the most damaged and destroyed children.

"I do love teaching, but it's hard . . . because I feel it so deeply."

Tape #260

Ms. L. had been her upstate New York city's teacher of the year last year. She was short, pert, and slightly overweight. At forty-two, she was also single and had taught for twenty years — high school math. She taught in an inner city school, with locked doors during the day to prove it. (I had to go through the "tunnel" and bang on a cafeteria door to get a teacher's attention to get in.)

Ms. L. was the energetic type who took kids to plays, on camping trips and on vacation. She believed, and at the same time had a lot of doubts that she didn't seem to want to admit to. As I sat in a dim little office somewhere in the high school and mused on the symbolism of a dying geranium plant there, she told me that she definitely thought public education worked and that she would go into education again.

Ms. L. was a teacher who cared.

"I think from the time I was a young child I wanted to help other people, and I saw teaching as a way to help people understand things that they didn't understand before — to help people to better themselves. I think if you don't start with the young children, they're not going to get anywhere in the world. The older we get, I think, the more set in our patterns we get. And I think it takes a special kind of person to interact and appreciate young children of any age group. Not everyone can do that. I had an opportunity to work as a computer analyst at twice the salary that I'm making, and not only because I would just be sitting at a computer all day long talking to no one but a computer, but also, mainly, because of the students — I prefer to teach. And I didn't see working in business as a way of helping people . . . helping mankind, helping young children.

"The children are so appreciative of what you do for them. All children, especially in the inner city — need special attention. Just being able to respond to them in any way, shape, or form, letting them know that you care about them, means an awful lot to them. I have students who come back ten or fifteen years later who tell me how thankful they are that I made them stay in a math class and made it meaningful to them even though at that time they didn't want to take any math. They hadn't seen that they needed math for whatever job.

"And I do things with the kids outside of school; I take them places; I care about them. I get them to come to me with their problems; I think they need that because they don't get that kind of counseling and they don't have parents who, if they see there is that kind of need, would take them for counseling. I think they need someone to talk to, someone to take an interest in them and in turn, they respond and it makes you feel good. You feel like you are important. And I like those little pats on the back — thank you for this or that. Our kids never, never, never leave without saying thank you. People don't know that about inner city kids and I think that's too bad. I've taken kids to Disney World, to Montreal, to New York City . . . we're going this Easter to Washington. And for students who can't afford to go, what we have always done is some sort of money-making thing. They don't have to feel that they can't go because they can't afford it."

(Tell me about why you like working in the inner city.)

"I did my student teaching in a very affluent area of a suburb of this city. I was offered a job teaching there and offered a job teaching in the city. I took this one mainly because I didn't . . . what do I want to say? When I was student teaching, I thought the kids who were interested were under a lot of pressure from home, but they were able to keep up with me. The kids were dressing up to me or beyond me. The clothes that I was buying to be my teaching clothes . . . were their everyday school clothes. If they didn't understand something, they never thought to come to me for extra help because they went to a tutor. And I tutored some of the kids; they paid me to tutor them. But while I could relate to the students and could certainly do some of the same activities that I do now, I just felt that I wanted to be somewhere where they needed me. Most of the students I graduated from college with opted to go into the suburbs. I just said — if they all do that, who's going to be left to teach these kids? Whether you want to believe it or not, these are the kids who need it."

(Do you ever fear being in a school like this?)

"Never. I was here in 1969-70-71; we had riots and the kids were walking up and down the halls with bats and canes and beating each other over the heads. I was on the first floor at that time, and one student threw another student out the window right in front of my window — [I] saw him falling. It was awful, truly awful . . . but I never had fear for myself because through it all, the kids would come up and say to you somebody is going to come into your room and do something or other, you know, 'stay to the side,' do whatever . . . or if they saw somebody coming at you, they would throw you out of the way . . . I think they're very protective of you when they feel that someone is trying to help them. And none of any of the riot violence was ever directed towards a teacher . . . ever . . .

". . . I can't tell you the number of parents I've talked to who don't know if their child went to school that day, don't know if they have a test the next day, don't know if they've done any homework in the last month. I had a parent conference with a mother a couple of years ago, and the mother came to the conference with a suitcase and put it down and said to the principal, 'I can't do anything with this child; here are her things, if you think you can do something with her — good luck.' At that point, I cried. I mean, I cried for the child and for the parent, because it has to be awful for the parent to think — here's a child who at that time was fifteen years old — and the parent must realize, if they can't do anything with a child at fifteen, then something must have been wrong with the parenting. But then, how could I do anything for a child whose parents have already given up on her? So I felt bad for her too. That's really sad. And I think that there's just so much of that, that they come to school needing other things, other than education. Society expects education to provide for everything now. And I don't think education was ever meant to do that.

"I think the solution to getting better people into education is — money. It's sad. It's sad that we have to say that it is money; it's not sad that we are asking for something that is comparable for our education background. I think the sad thing is that society doesn't see that we should be getting the same amount of money. I have a student who graduated from here seven years ago, who went to work at Ford on the assembly line; and after five years of working on the assembly line, she's making twice what I'm making and never went anywhere after high school. I'm happy for her! But I certainly don't think that I'm happy for me. I can understand wanting to pay a scientist a lot of money, because he's making the machinery for tomorrow and the defense systems for tomorrow, but we are making, shaping, molding those same scientists of tomorrow and the politicians of tomorrow . . . and nobody cares what we're doing."

(Would you become a teacher again?)

"Absolutely. You know — it's not a pretty world we live in, and I think that anything we can do to make it better helps. And I think that most individuals have to realize that we can't think about ourselves only. You're not the only person in the world. You really do have to be concerned about the person who lives next door, or down the street, or right in the house with you. You really do . . . and be truly interested, and let them know. I think a lot of times people really feel strongly for someone, but they don't know how to tell them that. And I don't think it necessarily has to be verbally, but I think a lot of the time they don't let people know that they really care . . . and I think that is unfortunate."

Section 2:

THE SCHOOLS

There are two school systems in the United States … the suburban and rural districts that have money, and the city districts that do not.

Tape #227

The school: all the windows on the doors had been replaced with metal. But inside there was a concerted effort to keep the school halls clean and looking well kept. Yet, it was still gloomy-1950s looking. The teacher's lounge lavatory had a metal latch to keep the door closed and the toilet tank had no top. There was an old curtain in the window, a very old curtain. I couldn't help but think in one of the most beautiful northern California cities — this was where a professional worked?

Ms. C. was now a counselor who was filling in that week for an assistant principal.* Our talk was constantly interrupted by students' needs and other teachers. It was odd to this Midwesterner to hear her speak in Spanish to many of the students. She had worked in this inner city middle school for years. She was now forty, married with two children of her own in private schools. Would she let her own children attend the school she worked in if they lived in the district? No.

Poor area, poor schools. Equal education? Tell it to the suburbs.

"I enjoyed teaching because it's a fun element to work with kids. Any kid likes to play, and it was a way to help kids to get along with each other, a nice medium for helping kids to deal with other races and other people. I enjoy counseling because I think it gives me a little bit more access to be able to *concretely* help kids deal with problems that they're having, either

---

*This is one of just a few interviews not dealing with working teachers.

me personally or having access to the community services that can help them. They're trained way too fast physically and sexually for their emotional stability. They've gotten into a place where many of these kids assume adult roles at home; they are left on their own. As a result, they are left alone with younger siblings, and they are quite accustomed to giving the orders and being obeyed; and when they come here (school), they don't feel that they should have to go back to being the child. And that creates, I think, a lot of problems.

"It is difficult; I know kids who take care of their parents — who are disturbed, emotionally disturbed — and they come here and you tell them to sit down in class and it's — 'Who are you?!' You know, 'I fought with my mother to make sure she eats every day' . . . so you have a lot of that here; many of them lead very adult type lives. And yet deep down underneath, when you scratch the surface and you really get to the core . . . they'll cry like any twelve year old and their emotions are really raw; they try so hard to hold it together. And when they fall apart, they know when they fall apart, they have nothing else to rely on.

"One of the things that can happen is that they fall apart and don't cope or they're very strong and they come out of it. I've seen kids I had twenty years ago and was floored at the togetherness that they had, because it was scattered all over the place at age thirteen. A lot of them fall apart and become a dredge on the system; a lot of them turn to drugs . . . although drugs not so much anymore. More of these kids, if they're into drugs, it's into selling them, not into taking them. Although drugs are very, very prominent in the projects . . . it's a real problem. But rarely do our kids get caught with them — very rarely. We have sixth through eighth graders . . . discipline problems?

"There's fighting, possession of weapons — probably the two biggest. Some threats on teachers . . . I [don't] think in the last few years that we've actually had an assault on a teacher, mostly verbal threats. One teacher was sufficiently intimidated that she felt she needed to transfer. I think you deal with a lot more violent type problems here, where in the suburbs, where I live, you're dealing much more with — drugs, because they can afford it; you get more truancy — they have the money to go and the cars — and sort of a form of apathy. Here, we don't have a lot of kids who do a lot of homework; we do have most of our kids performing at least two grades below grade level, but it's not so much apathy as it's outside contradictions in their lives that make them see education as unnecessary to their survival. Being sure there's bread on the table, being sure dad doesn't get drunk and kill mom, or having to pick up your three or four year old sister to make sure she gets home safely . . . that's all more important than having to do a math assignment for tomorrow. I think probably seventy percent of our kids are educationally disadvantaged — poverty level kids. I would say the average income here for most families probably falls between ten and fifteen thousand."

(How would you defend this city's school system?)

"Well, it depends on which school you're talking about. If you're talking about some of our schools that have a more middle class population, I think you can point to this, this, and this, and sing its praises. But if you're talking about a more inner city school which has more poverty kids from single families, then you're going to find that the system doesn't work nearly as well. Here, we have an incredibly large non-English speaking population. There's no parent support because none of the parents speak English.

"I think the schools are [making] a sufficient effort to make sure things don't blow up, kids aren't hurt, teachers are not attacked, you know, etc. And on the whole — we do a fairly good job at it. Discipline needs to have been started from the time they were born. And the other problem we have here, and are seeing all over now, with so many working mothers, kids are left alone, for extreme lengths of time, unsupervised for hours on end. Sometimes for nights — a kid will go home and mother works nights and he'll only see her in the morning. And self-discipline is something I think that either comes innately in your being or has been very slowly and carefully developed in you; and for a lot of these kids, that has never occurred. They've always been given to someone else to deal with because mom doesn't have time. A lot of time they're given to a seventy-five year old grandmother and she's tired. She's doing the best she can, but you know, she's tired. So I think more self-discipline and more parental support has to occur here.

"It's always the school's fault that the kid is in trouble, at least as far as they're concerned. If he can't sit still, if he doesn't have his books, if he hit Johnny in the face, if he pulled Susie's hair — it's still our fault. We don't get support from parents. We're getting the first generation of extremely young mothers who are now having children that are of this age, and now their daughters are becoming mothers. By the time they're twenty-eight, they're burnt out. And they don't know what to do with this teenager, because they didn't know what to do with [her] to begin with. Most of them are single, trying to support them; they don't have the energy level; they're tired. And as far as they're concerned, they don't want to hear from you and they don't want to hear from him. You get some of that and you get some who truly care but have no skills or know what to do. You get a parent in here and you tell her that he's hitting the kids and he's hitting the teacher and she says, 'Well, he hits me.' Well, you're dead right there; he's established a pattern that is acceptable."

(Would you send your kids to this school?)

"To this school? No. My kids go to parochial schools."

(What would be your number one reason you wouldn't send your kids here?)

"Fear of violence. The reason I send them to the private school is that, number one, at least to my knowledge, the kids who behave in a violent manner no longer attend that school. And number two, education is number one. You're studying and the things that go on for that is paramount and is started when you are very young. And discipline is so strong. My son, who is an average student and has to work very hard, with all the distractions here, he would find it very hard to learn his stuff. It's not like when you're trying to do something while people are screaming obscenities at each other, throwing erasers across the room — and not that this happens all the time here, but it does happen a lot. When you're out in the yard here at lunch time, it's survival of the fittest. It's not something I want my kid to be exposed to. Survival of the fittest meaning — lots of push and shove. It's just meanness and bulliness."

Tape #220

Mr. H. had taught in the inner city for twenty years in a large city in Northern California. He was forty-seven, divorced with three children of his own. For hobbies, he painted, scuba-dived, backpacked, and woodcarved.

As I walked through his school to his science lab where he taught, I couldn't help but notice the age of everything. The ceilings were chipping and plaster was falling everywhere. It was painted pretty much institutional green with patches of color here and there. It was dark and kind of gloomy, but in a seedy way — kind of proud. The kids seemed to be everywhere after the bell rang, including outside. I heard one girl cussing out a boy fiercely as we walked by. Mr. H. turned to her, glared and told her not to talk that way; he got little reaction.

He told me that the district had just spent six million on fixing up the school and redesigning some of the rooms . . . I couldn't see where . . . neither could he. But we sat in his lab, I on a stool and he on a lab table, and he told me what he liked and disliked about teaching in a very ethnically mixed inner city California high school. Outside the sun was shining in its typical California way.

"I enjoy teaching; I've never considered getting out. And since I have a degree in chemistry, I had some choice. I work here in an inner city high school. The advantages are that you meet very interesting students who come from a variety of backgrounds and make it very stimulating. The major disadvantage of working at this school in particular is the hall environment and the outside-of-classroom environment. It bothers me to have students running around the halls or outside of the school and being disruptive. Although it has improved here dramatically lately, over the past twenty years that has been a powerful irritant.

"I think kids here might even be doing better, though, than kids who go to the suburban schools. A lot of the students are very focused here because they've come from environments that have been deprived or they haven't had opportunities. They focus very seriously on education in this environment and this environment allows them to be ignored — there's no particular group in this school that they're going to have to gravitate towards to be popular or to be social. With so many people from so many different areas here, you are completely on your own. If they choose to get something out of it, they have the advantage because of the fact that other students don't. Consequently, the classes of serious students can be smaller here, while some of the other students who are not into learning are actually tolerated and just stay out of the way. I'd say about fifteen percent of the students here are giving it serious effort, working hard. They are very serious; very high achievers. I would say there are probably fifty-sixty percent that aren't very highly motivated and twenty percent of those have enough of ability to probably do whatever they chose to do but just don't care. And we probably have ten-fifteen percent in there who just can't do it even if they would really try hard. I'd say thirty percent leave this school with the skills I'd consider they should have.

"I always envision that because of all our minorities we have all these problems. And then I talk to teachers at meetings and I'm surprised that they have the same problems I do. And the first thing you run across is that there basically isn't any difference between minority kids and any other kids. It always amazes me when I go to an all white middle class school, and they have the same problems I have . . . and sometimes worse. Your prejudice kind of comes out; you think, 'Well, I've got problems but these are minority kids,' and it's just not true. I don't really think there are major differences between this school and a suburban high school. I think we have some visual identifiable differences that people look at — like black students standing out in front of the school. They don't see, in other schools, the white students out in front of their schools or around their schools — it's that difference that they see, 'Hey, look at those twenty black, Latino, etc., kids.' But you go to a suburban school and there may be these teenagers drifting around, but they're not different so they're not so highly visible. They don't intimidate anybody. I've always gotten along with my minority students very well; I don't really pay any attention to who or what they are. They're all raving individualists, as much as any other group of kids.

"But I think for most people who would walk in here, it would take them a long time to get past the visual difference of the students and realize that they're no different than any other kids . . . their names are just harder to pronounce. But it's hard to overcome the visual and obvious."

Tape #27

"You know at some point in time,
these murderers, these robbers, these rapists have been in
the public schools."

Ms. D. had an office; she was teaching only one class now and coun-
seling the rest of the day. She had chosen to keep that one class; I was
impressed. Her office had no windows to the outside and was dark blue in
color. There was an opening, barred, that went out to the main lobby. It
was dingy and dismal though she had plastered posters here and there.
Our meeting was interrupted by two students and one teacher who wanted
to straighten out whether Steve really had two lunch periods. "I don't
have two lunch periods, Steve, why should you?" She's taught math for
nineteen years at the middle school level and was now counseling at the
high school level.

We were interrupted one last time by a phone call about college sport
scholarships and one about a student who was "busted." "Send him down
during the fourth period." She was forty . . . she looked forty.

Oh yeah — this was inner city; the man giving me directions referred
to Ms. D's school as "the fortress." It was surrounded by barbed
wire . . .

"Today we have society's problems. Public education's dealing with everybody; we're dealing with the very bright to the very slow to the crazies — you may want to say — to the normal. We can have a fight here and it can be between two kids and it can be blown out of proportion in the neighborhood. We get neighborhood problems all the time here. We deal with the schizos. You know, at some point in time, these murderers, these robbers, these rapists have been in the public schools.

"And so basically that's probably it — because it's society . . . *we're* society. If we were more into a utopian society, schools would function more effectively. But it's gotten better over the past twenty years.

"Problems here today? Out of 1800 . . . 1750 students in this school, on an average day we have at least 300 absences. Mom has to pick up the truck and lets me stay home with the kids. Mother and dad don't have groceries — someone has to go get them. Mother and dad never had an education, why should my kid? But it's basically because of where the school's situated; five projects, only one of which is bussed in. The needs of the kids are not the same needs as in a rural area. We're more concerned here now with food, a coat, and a place to live. They have a one-parent family life for some of them on one side. Ninety percent are dealing with no money.

"I started out with the seniors this year as freshmen three years ago. Out of 655 then, I know I have 300. I had the highest [dropout rate] in the school.

"About twenty-five to thirty percent will go on to some school after this, whether it be a college or a two year program or beauty school or a ballet school or whatever. Ten to fifteen percent will go into the military. Probably about thirty-five to forty percent will . . . get a job. And the rest will remain on welfare, what the ones who dropped out are doing now. Well, I can't say that's completely true. Some are juniors, or sophomores — they've been put back because they haven't had the grades. But I guess basically that a good quarter of the class is out doing nothing.

"Skills, lacking in basic skills is the main reason for dropping out . . . and nobody at home to push them. Our reading level in this high school probably averages fifth grade. It's just that there are a million things at home, and if they are little and mom wanted them at home, they stayed home. Which means they'll have higher absentees than the Middle West schools or the Asian schools. Education is not important to most of these people.

"How do I succeed? I was a friend. I have two former students — they're my 'sons.' One's going to Ohio State and playing football and one's at the University of Cincinnati playing football. Both of them came from one-parent families. Both of them had Ds, Fs ninth grade year, tenth grade year they worked on football all the time. I happened to keep the stats for the football team. That's not a paid job; it's a job I enjoy doing. My volunteer work. So I went and said 'Hi' to them. 'Great game.' 'Oh, how'd you find out?' 'Well, I keep the stats.' 'Oh.' They still write. I get telephone calls and letters from both. Oh yeah, their grades improved. Well, we scraped a two point, but when you start out with a .08 . . . I think both can be very successful. Somebody showed them interest. Mom didn't have time. Mom was working, sometimes working on the street. Mom wasn't interested in what they were doing. Mom never came to a football game unless it was parent night. But I was there, and they still call me *mom* today.

"If you pick out several things that you need to go to, that you want to go to — you may be very interested in music, and go to the music concerts here, and the kids see you. They [feel I'm] interested in [them]. I may have not even known the kid was in choir, or the band or whatever, but I've now become interested in them as a person, not as the person who sits in the fifth row in the third seat and falls asleep in class. I think teachers have to show an interest. I think they have to be on the phone talking to people. They have to become involved in school. We were runners-up last year in boy's basketball. I saw two of eleven player's parents up until the tournament. They never bothered to come in. The girls were state champs last year; three parents came.

"Why should we be at those things? Think of the kids' attitudes if their parents don't show interest. And kids' attitudes are important. It probably goes back to my first year of teaching, when I learned real quick that 'a white fuckin' bitch' was going to be my name for a long time."

(I don't think I could survive in a school like this.)

"You'd be surprised."

Tape #153

We sat in her farmhouse-looking suburban living room. There was a hooked rug on the floor, a cello in front of the fireplace, a metronome on top of the piano that had to be unplugged so I could plug in my tape recorder. It was snowing lightly outside and the cat sat looking out the large picture window in front of the cozy living room. Ms. B. wore a tartan plaid skirt that hung stylishly long. She was fifty, had three children (one in college), and a lawyer husband. Her hair was graying but well kept. Her hobbies were swimming, reading, and sewing.

For nine years, on either side of a long period of raising her children, she had taught at the grade school level in several different suburban school districts. This year, in October, she had taken over an inner city second grade class. As she will explain, she felt like she needed a challenge; she felt like she could accomplish something . . . some people would smile, but I respected her for her attempt. Success in life has never seemed to me to be a matter of what we do so much as what we sincerely attempt to do, regardless of the result.

When I left later that January night, creeping slowly down her slippery iced driveway, I considered the world a slightly better place, no more close to a solution for its problems, but better.

"One learns to walk decades."

Chaim Potok

My Name is Asher Lev

"Why did I become a teacher? Oh, I guess the reasons are altruistic. I really do believe that each person should try to help mankind. When the school where I was teaching phased me out due to a student enrollment decline, I thought maybe teaching in the inner city might be a good challenge for mid-life crisis. And it definitely is. It was a conscious decision to teach in the inner city. I really did think, 'Now that would be interesting.' Because before that I had taught very affluent, very bright children, and that was very interesting. And it was rewarding in a way to see their minds grow. But they'd had everything. Any field trip we'd want to take, most of them had already been. And they'd been to the Bahamas or places like that.

"I really did, then, think it would be a pretty interesting thing, but I went in — pretty idealistic. I had no real ideas what their home backgrounds were like. And that they were only in my class for six hours a day and that there are eighteen more hours in the day. Many things surprised me. Their attention span, truly, is not even one minute long. I was used to the teacher saying, 'Sit in your seats, we're going to do work, we're going to read,' or whatever — they all sat in their seats. But if I say, 'I'd like to see all of your eyes' and I start to write something on the board, they're either out of their seats or they're poking somebody — 'He hit me first, Teacher; I ain't got no pencil.'

"It's just sort of mind-boggling, just how much they need to learn. There are one or two who are bright and you think they can achieve something. And I keep trying to say, 'You are all somebody special; you can do something; I don't want any of you not to graduate.' I try to keep stressing the same things that I tell my own children. I don't know if it's effective, but I just want them to hear it enough. And one little girl today said, 'I keep trying to remember that you told me that I wasn't dumb and I could do it,' and before she'd always copied and said, 'I can't do it.' Now at least she [reminds herself of what I said]. Oh, I love these little children, but I get so frustrated with them. My own kids said tonight at dinner, 'Oh good, somebody's coming and you don't have to tell us all about your kids today.' (Laughter) But I don't want to just let it consume me.

"There's one little boy, it's an all-black class, and at first he didn't smile at all. He doesn't read even on a first grade level. But every time I'd ask questions, say on the vocabulary lesson — 'Who knows the word this means — everybody *wandering* around and getting loud' — Rodney always gets it. He always knows the word no matter what we're talking about. I tell him how smart he is. Then one day in reading class, we were working and asking questions and one of the other kids said, 'I'm not even going to try because Rodney is so smart.' And before they didn't even think of Rodney, but they bought into it and now he really tries. Anyway, he wanted to do well. And I said, 'I can guarantee that if you read for fifteen minutes every night, your reading will improve. I can guarantee that.' He said, 'Ain't nobody want to hear me read. I ain't taking my book home.' And I mean, it just breaks your heart. So you just can't go home and cry and think what am I going to do; there are those other eighteen hours . . . .

"We took them on a field trip at Christmas time. Their apartments are subdivided from lush apartments from years ago. Now three or four families live in each one. Anyway, we took them home from this field trip. And my husband left me in the car, door locked. He took them each in and he said you just couldn't believe the noise coming from each house. How can they find a quiet place to study?

"I've only been [at this school] for three and one-half months; I'm the fifth teacher that's had this class. And I've had something like — five days I would call good. Some of that was caused by staffing problems and one teacher got sick, but the one before me — she was a white teacher too — she was only there for six days . . . she just couldn't take it.

"I think they're learning something. And I'm learning a lot too. A lot of them don't really know how to read. They do need to learn to listen . . . and to read, and their numbers — counting without using their fingers. And to write sentences — that's a big order. I try these things that I think are great ideas, but everything is so new and doesn't seem to get learned. So I don't know if I'm accomplishing much. A few people are feeling better about themselves. They think they can do things. I had them make little flash-cards for their math, but nobody cares at home like with middle class white children whose mothers would make sure they knew their numbers. They keep them in their desks and a few of them do work on them. A lot of them have Ds . . . if you're not on grade level, you have a D. Nobody has an F except in behavior. There are probably about ten out of twenty-one Ds in reading and in math. Twenty-one, now that's a nice class size; you'd think it would be ideal. You'd think . . . but we never have total quiet class time for more than five minutes.

"And there are definitely cultural differences between inner city and suburban. Last year I subbed at a magnet school which draws from both the neighborhood and, well, the middle class and there were some simi-larities. But now — well, I might as well be teaching on the moon! I'd like to think that over half of my kids will graduate from high school . . . and more boys than girls. You know . . . girls and babies . . . they think that my husband is my *boyfriend* (laughs). And a lot of them have babies in the house. One mother came in and said she couldn't help her daughter with her math problems. And she said, 'the father of my baby' tried to help. But the boys might finish. I guess they have more of a chance, but the girls . . . well, I don't know.

"What motivates them? I would like to think that it would be intrinsic, but it isn't. I'm all for doing it because it's the right thing to do. Take their papers that I return, though. See, nobody wants to see these papers. Nobody cares. Even the ones I put a sticker on and write all sorts of good things — they never take their papers home. 'Nobody wants to see these papers,' they say . . . so they just scrunch them up and throw them away. They do like to see their papers up on the board. I don't like the idea of giving them food. I have tried to use field trips with my daughter and her boyfriend, taking those who have done all their work and have not been discipline problems with their names up on the board for one month. I'm hoping that will motivate others. And then those who do their homework also get to paint with the lady who volunteers. We did take the kids into town at Christmas time to see the lights, and most of them had never been into town."

(Have you had much communication with their parents?)

"No, two out of the twenty-one came to the conferences. And on the week of visitation, only one mother visited. I talked to these three and they

— (long pause) — seem like they're supportive. But the one mother who seemed intelligent said her little boy was held back last year . . . she said because he didn't have glasses. But I checked and his teacher last year wanted to have him tested because he had all this aggressive behavior, beating on the other children, etc. And [his mother] wouldn't allow it. We noticed when we went to town that he was very, very interested in everything around, and he had a very good vocabulary, but he could not restrain from hitting the other children. So even when mothers seem to want to help, . . . they don't. They must not trust the system or something. I guess the kids have some respect for me as a teacher; some of them do. And now that I have shown a little bit more authority, they do."

(Do you think that public education works?)

"It probably does in some places. (Laughter) You like to think it does. I haven't been where I am long enough, but it seems like most of the teachers are hardened . . . and don't have real high expectations."

Tape # 267

"Every suburban teacher should be required at some point to
be in an inner city school situation . . . so they don't
complain about how bad they have it."

Ms. E. had taught one year in an inner city situation and one year in ultra suburbia. It was interesting to hear her tell the differences as she had only taught for two years and they were such contrasts to her.

She was twenty-four, married, and her hobbies were crocheting and softball. I spoke to her in her large fifth grade classroom — out in the suburbs.

"When I first started teaching, I was downtown in a city school, and I was literally scared to go to the school because I had to park two blocks away from the school. And we're talking downtown — I'm on Scott Street and there was a bar across the street. There would still be dwindlers in the morning when we got there and I was scared. When I got to the building, I found out that they never locked the building so anybody on the street could walk into the building. I would leave immediately when the kids did each day, and I didn't like that; I had things to do. But I just wouldn't stay there because of fear.

"I had only ten to twelve kids the whole year. I was Chapter One. I taught everything, but my students were really low kids. I was a brand new teacher, and I was scared to death these kids weren't going to learn anything. Never did I get support at the beginning. I finally made friends with another teacher who also taught Chapter One. We worked closely together. But I never had anyone come in and say, 'Well, do you need anything? How's everything going?' And that's a shame! There you're put into a brand new position, first year teacher, you're scared to death, and you don't have people coming in asking you — you know, do you need this? Or anything . . . or, 'did you have a bad day?' Well, sure, you're supposed to have bad days. But every time I'd have a bad day I would feel so guilty about it because I thought this wasn't supposed to happen. So for several months I was misleading myself, feeling pretty bad. I almost considered getting out of teaching because I just felt so miserable. You know the kids are supposed to catch on, but because of the ability group that I had, they were so low — it would take a lot of repeating and nobody told me that. It was just — throw her in there.

"A large problem in city education is lack of funding for materials. I literally had no health curriculum. I made it myself. They gave me a 1957 health book! It was 1985, and I refused to use it. So what I did was I went to the bookstore and I ordered a couple of things on my own — I was only given a fifty dollar purchase order — that's terrible! Here again, a brand new teacher and I didn't know what to order or anything like that. There's got to be more money out there than what the administration says to get just general supplies. I ran out of paper that year and had to borrow from other teachers.

Another problem was the discipline. Just in the two weeks I had a seventh grade class, I had a group that just gave up on the first day of school because half of them had failed the year before. They knew the stuff and they just took it upon themselves that they weren't going to do anything. And I didn't know what to do so I talked to the principal right away, and he came in one day and just stood at the door and for — it was a good ten minutes — they didn't even settle down. And he was standing at the door. And they were big kids, too; they were bigger than I was. But that's a problem with the big public schools. Here [in the suburbs], I don't see that much.

"There's a real difference between suburban and city schools. There's the type of kids you have. We still have some problem kids here, but it's not as major problems. When I heard the teachers here talk about the problem kids, I thought — boy, I wish you were at the downtown schools, because I had all of them, I mean — every kid was a problem kid. I think every suburban teacher should be required at some point to be in an inner city school situation so they don't complain about how bad they have it. See what it is really like, because I think that that's part of the real world of teaching. I learned a lot from it. And materials! I was shocked when I walked into this room and saw what the other teacher just left for me. She left her desk full of things for me and her file cabinets were full of things. And paper? Paper is just in the lounge for you to use! You can just go and get some paper! You don't have your little box just sitting in your room! You can use the copier. I was never allowed — 'Don't you touch my copier in the office.' You just didn't do that as a teacher there. Here you can use the copy machine, which I'm still not used to. I'm very reluctant to do that because of the past. I ask for things that I need here and I get it. That's surprising. I see a huge difference money-wise here."

(Do you notice any difference in the parents?)

"Oh, man, a tremendous difference! When I first came here, I couldn't believe that there were visiting parents who come in and ask you what they can do for you. At the beginning of the year somebody told me that if you need a parent to do anything just write it down . . . I still haven't used a parent yet. I'm not used to that. I would like to and next year I probably will after I get myself more organized. Parents call all the time. I had a parent call just the other afternoon. She was just wanting to know if her son had stopped this behavior that we had talked about before; and it was wonderful! Just keeping in touch. Now I have a lot of that, especially with my homeroom. I have a lot of parental involvement, just concern about their child, how they're doing and things like that. It isn't concern like — what are you teaching my child? It's the concern that just wants to know if [their children] are ok.

"And downtown where I taught, during open house I think I had two parents show up. And when I had tried to get in touch with the parents, I never got a response. If I sent permission slips home and asked for them back, it would be several permission slips before I got them back — the parents just weren't involved at all! PTA meetings — you were lucky to get twenty parents at PTA meetings. Here, the gym's full! It's just unbelievable! And with that community involvement, it makes your job easier. You know somebody is out there backing you up. Downtown, I just felt like I had no outside support at all.

"I would prefer this job to that one! But I can't go back and say I wish I'd never taught there because I learned so much in just how to deal with the problem kids I had, how to deal with the situation, scrounging for chalk and things like that. I think you need that . . . .

Tape #160

> ". . . I had a county municipal judge
> whose daughter didn't make [honor society].
> He wanted to subpoena the ballots."

Ms. A. and her teacher husband lived in one of the most exclusive, ritzy areas of their large Midwestern city . . . and when I walked into their home to interview her, I remembered thinking, "If they can afford this, then good for them." I began to like her immediately and was not disappointed by my hour and a half with her. She was forty and had taught high school English for eighteen years. She was currently at a very yuppie high school where she was very happy.

Her hobbies were reading, quilting, and herb gardening. She had short, reddish hair, was a bit plump and wore very preppy clothes. But she was cute, both in appearance and in an inner something. She was the kind of teacher who did the profession proud. But then, she had an easy district in many ways.

"I think maybe teaching should be a full-year job. I'd hate it, but it might make people see us as having a real job instead of like seasonal workers like ball players and migrant pickers. And I hope they improve standards and let kids see more what this is all about. I had a male student teacher who on the second day burst into tears and said, 'I didn't know it was work! I don't want to work.' I guess he thought he just went in there and stood behind that desk and talked and sent them on their way.

"I first taught at a blue collar type school in an industrial area that increasingly was losing industry and was one of the jumping-off places for Appalachian whites who were migrating to Detroit. The pluses there were that teachers had a lot of clout from the standpoint that you had a lot more education than almost anybody. And the value put on education from the home was pretty strong because the parents didn't have any. And they said to their kids that if they get their education and stick it out, they'll be better off than dad and I are. And another thing was, that even in those days when I was only making one hundred dollars a week . . . back in 1969 . . . by comparison I was affluent. I was a yuppie before we knew what they were. And there was a very strong administration with very few discipline problems. It wasn't too hard to walk in there as a first year teacher and teach.

"Then I went to a very, very suburban, upwardly mobile type school district where I am now. I realized that I was at the bottom of the pay scale for our county. And I was scheduled to go in as a negotiator for our association, and I didn't want to do it. I didn't envision myself as a crusader who wanted to go in and fight these people for money. I mean, I wanted the money, but I didn't know if I was able to tackle this. Plus, they wanted me to take the department chair, and I really didn't want to do it because for only about an extra three hundred dollars you had to do all the scheduling and deal with all these diverse personalities. Well, I had met the principal where I am now in a committee the year before, and he'd told me if I ever wanted a job to see him. I also knew they had just got an enormous pay raise in this district and I found out what it was. Well, I looked at that pay scale and I looked at the department chairmanship and I looked at that negotiation things, and I thought — geez! The handwriting is kind of on the wall here. They picked up on me right away. They called me at seven o'clock in the morning and said, 'Where were you last night; we called and wanted to offer you a job.' And I thought how wonderful! I was going to be making eighteen percent more and they offered me good classes. So I said ok.

"But the pluses were not parental support. Oh! that was [a large problem] when I moved there . . . and it still is. I used to be the honor society advisor and I finally said last year, 'I'm not going to do this anymore.' I didn't want the grief anymore. I had more parents call. The kids would say, 'I didn't make it — oh — gulp.' And that was that. And then I would wait for the bombs to explode. And the parents would call and take me to task. And it wouldn't be so bad if this were confined to a two day period, but this would go on from December to April. I would have to justify and defend, and all I did was tabulate the votes of the other teachers in the school. I'd keep saying, 'Why are you yelling at me; all I do is count votes. It's not my fault.' Finally, I had a county municipal judge whose daughter didn't make it. He wanted to subpoena the balloting, and I refused to turn it over. I was going to come home and burn it. And I'd say, 'Oh gee! I guess they got lost or stolen from the car.' He was going to subpoena those things to see who had voted his daughter out of honor society. And the kid really didn't belong in it! To me, that's this district at its worst . . . over honor society membership!

"Now, my district at its best is small class sizes and definitely college-bound students. For me, too, it's complete academic curriculum freedom.

Nobody asks me why I teach what I do; they just say go at it. We gripe
constantly about the lack of discipline out there, and yet I can't tell you the
last run-in I've had in my classroom for years. But in the building itself,
it could be better. And money is there; I've never asked for something that
I didn't get. I've been able to go to all the national conferences — paid by
the district. And the pay scale is very, very good. It's one of the best in the
state. And now I've gotten used to the little brats, I kind of like them."

(How about the parents?)

"Oh, a good example of that recently is a junior advanced placement
students's father called me the first quarter and said, 'It doesn't look like
he's going to get an A.' And I said, 'No, it doesn't, not for this quarter, but
that really doesn't mean a thing because he could bring it up by the end of
the semester and average out to an A.' And I explained about the difference from going from tenth grade AP to my class, etc., etc. So I told the
father that I really wouldn't worry about it too much. And he said to me,
'Well, I just want you to know that the target for Robert is an A.' I just
chose to give no response to that and said something like — we hope he'll
get it. So he called me about three weeks into the second quarter and said,
'How does it look?' So I said it was hard to assess that early in the quarter
and explained that we were working on a building process and the final
assessment is yet to come. So I said it wasn't realistic to say what he had
yet. And he said again, 'Well, the target for Robert is an A.' And I said,
'You know the last time you said that I let it go by, but this time I'm not.
The target for Robert for me — is to learn something. Ok? And if he gets
an A while he's learning something, that's marvelous. But if he gets Bs
and he's still learning something, he's just fine and it's not going to keep
him out of an Ivy-League school. And not to worry.'"

(Did the father have a reply?)

"Well, he might have, but I said, 'I really have to go,' and did. I'm
getting really brazen about that. I guess I'm lucky that a lot of those AP
kids really do know why they're in there. No one forces them to take
advanced placement; and they really do want to work and learn, for the
most part. And they know my reputation for grades . . . I think I must be
awful about grades. You know sometimes I think, if my own child were in
my class, would I be happy with my grading? And I might not. (Laughter)
But I've never kept anybody out of a good school; in fact, I think I've

helped a lot of kids get into good schools. So I'm not going to worry about it too much."

(What's the benefit of having advanced programs in school?)

"I had a girl come back from college who had been granted eighteen hours of English credit at a prestigious university. This was due to AP courses. I think all of this is good for them, maybe not for everybody, but for them. I've never had anyone so bad they walked in front of a bus. I mean, they may mope around a little bit about grades and they may feel pressure, but they cope. One of the nicest things that happened to me in the last couple of years — for the past two years I've gotten letters from colleges — MIT and Stanford — letters saying they had required essays from their incoming freshman saying who as an adult had influenced them. And I don't know why, but two kids had chosen to say that I had been instrumental in expanding their world view — I mean, wow! That's pretty heady stuff. I'm going to get those bronzed. I'm going to be buried with those letters. My wedding ring, a baby shoe and those two letters I think are the three things I'd like to take with me when I go . . . (Laughter) It sums up a nice life. To think that those kids are getting into those schools and having that kind of success and think that I had some sort of part of that . . . it must be all right."

Tape #278

Ms. W. was a little overweight and a little country. She had very short hair and glasses. She now taught business education in a rural high school in the Midwest. She had taught for twenty years. Among her duties this year were running the school newspaper, the school yearbook, and advising the senior class. It seemed like rural teachers were expected even more to do extracurricular activities.

Ms. W. was single and forty-two.

"Twenty-five years ago, teaching was probably one of the few professions open to a woman, especially when you're from a small rural community like I am. It really was teaching or nursing, and I had no desire at all to be a nurse. And I had a teacher that I admired greatly so it's really the only thing I ever wanted to do. I don't have any regrets about teaching . . . no, not at all. Sometimes I feel that if I were a young person just starting out now, I might look at other fields a little harder, but I have no regrets."

(What would you say sort of characterizes a rural school district?)

"Non-mobility . . . you don't have a lot of people moving in and out of the community. It's a very stable situation. I came from a very conservative area and this is a basically very conservative area too. We have discipline problems but in comparison to what we hear from other areas, they're really not very much. When you don't have to be spending half of your days disciplining, when you can work with your kids on a different sort of level, I think that's a good situation. Here, school is the focus of the community, more so I would think than in a city school system. There's not much else to do here. (Laughter) Church and school is about it.

"I don't think the suburban or city schools are any better . . . I think the potential is there to have a broader horizon than we do out here in the country. I think academically — here, we've done very well. Our kids succeed when they go on to college. Probably we don't send as large a percentage, but those who do choose to go on do well.

"I think basically the parents of this rural area are pretty supportive. They're pretty supportive of what's going on here. As long as the basketball team's doing well, they're very supportive! (Laughter) Our school is getting a new addition and the sort of central focus of the addition is a new gymnasium, and our basketball team went to state this year — so you can see the focus of the town there. "I think they're willing to try things. If the kids get in trouble, they want to find out what's going on . . . but they're pretty supportive of the school. I don't get into contact with many parents, not on a discipline area one on one, but going to ball games and things like that, I have a lot of contact. It's more of a social contact than teacher-parent contact. I don't live in this community, but they know me, who I am. I don't mind that. I haven't had very many negative contacts with parents. I can't think of too many.

"But I think our conservatism in some ways is a negative, a fear of broadening horizons, I think. We have a very conservative church which is a major power in this middle part of the district. Some of the homes here don't have TV's so you have to be aware that some of your students don't watch TV — ever. The church[es are] very conservative and they sort of stick together. If you would get them on your side, I think in this area you'd win. We've had some calls about some of the books and stuff like that; I'm not really sure which area of the community it came from. But I think we're aware of that segment of the community that is here and we're more aware that we have to be a little bit careful. So there might be things the school does or does not do because of them. There's been nothing major — no book burnings or anything . . . but I would say a majority of our kids are churchgoers. I would say we have about thirty to thirty-five percent that probably don't.

"And another negative of this district is that we are rather spread out. It's difficult sometimes to do things with the students. You always have to be aware that you have to get the kids home and sometimes people have to come fifteen miles to come and get them and then fifteen miles to get back home again. Now, they'll do it for athletics (laugh) but for some of the other activities . . . you have to be aware of that. I am senior class advisor; I have the yearbook and the newspaper. It's all after school. We meet a couple of hours a week. I only use seniors and juniors so I don't personally have to haul younger kids back and forth. The kids that don't drive or who don't have a car [need rides]. We're not supposed to leave until they're all gone. I spend a lot of hours on all that. I probably put in seven hours a week. I get paid for it . . . but not enough. (Laughter)"

(Do you think it's good or bad that the students here are in such a one-sided culture — all white, all about the same economic background?)

"I grew up in the same sort of environment . . . and I'm still in that environment. I think it's probably negative in a sense that we don't get the exposure to the other, and when they do go out, they have these stereotypes that they get from watching TV and that sort of thing. They should be exposed a little bit more. They probably have different conceptions because of their lack of exposure. They have different prejudices from somebody who grew up in the city, but they have prejudices, too, towards different ethnic groups.

"I think the problems in education nationwide would probably be a little different. I think the major problem is the perception that the schools aren't doing their jobs. But yet the schools have been given so much more to do than the three Rs of fifty . . . sixty or a hundred years ago. It's like comparing apples and oranges; you can't compare the two, and that's what these back-to-basics people are doing. They're comparing the two things. Especially down in the elementary level . . . I didn't have science until the seventh grade and now they start it in — what? — the second or third grade, clear down in there. And it's probably important; the Russians beat us with Sputnik and we probably needed to get it down lower. AIDS education, sex education, morals education — all this other kind of stuff that they are supposed to be getting into their curriculum, and something has to go because the school day is only six or seven hours long. I think we have to do all these other things; it has to come from someplace. Some-body is not doing it, and society finally decided that we need this, so where else to do it but the schools? Whether it's good or bad . . . I really don't know."

TIRED TEACHERS

Every teacher is a tired teacher . . . every good teacher, that is.

For several years I kept track of how many extra hours, outside of the paid school day, I put into working on teaching. One year I spent 565 hours on school work. That averages out to about seventy-five extra seven and one half hour days of work — none of which I was paid for. So much for three months off during the summer.

Yet teachers work with that summers-off mentality till it hurts. We keep thinking: "If I can only make it until June." There's no pacing whatsoever like there is on a regular fifty week job. This leads to tired teachers; this leads to burnout. The amount of hours that teachers put in non-stop for nine months makes those "summers off" mandatory, even if most of us are working through them anyway.

What else makes for a tired teacher? I was tired when I took off to do this odyssey; that was part of the reason I took off. Like one teacher said to me in an interview, "I was tired of working for people who were less intelligent than I was." I was tired of just getting to the most important part of a lesson and being interrupted by the PA system to tell the janitor he was needed. I was tired of all the interruptions when I was working. No control, terrible bosses, no respect, a change in the attitudes of both the students and the society that produced them — all of this added to the horrible conditions and hours, wear out good teachers and turn them into . . . ?

In what other profession is it possible that you can spend your whole day working out of a briefcase and off a small cart —no desk, no office, no phone, no secretary, no overtime or bonuses . . . and regimented bathroom breaks?

Tape #60

> "I was in Viet Nam and Korea too and of course, you're
> looking backwards and that kind of dims the memories, but
> in a sense teaching's a lot more draining."

*Mr. S. was an ex-Navy man of twenty years experience. He had gone
into teaching after that, thinking it would be an easy way to make some
money. Thirteen years later, he's here to tell you that it is not.*

*He was typical ex-military in many ways . . . but I liked him. He struck
me as a gentleman, in the best sense of the word. There was a sincerity to
him that must have come from teaching high school math for the last
thirteen years. He had even found some handouts for me and information
he had collected on time consumption in this classroom and the extra
hours he'd spent. It was sweet and interesting. He seemed very thoughtful
and just a little nervous. He was fifty-seven, married with two grown
children, and thinking about retiring at the end of the year. Why?*

He was tired.

"I entered teaching by accident. We didn't want to leave this area after
I retired from the Navy and I was doing some substitute teaching that first
year. I'd always felt like I'd wanted to try teaching. So the department
chairman here told me they were establishing a computer science course
in this school and asked me if I'd consider teaching it, and I said yes. So
I worked for a couple of years teaching that and teaching some math
courses too. And then the next thing I knew, I had been here for four years
and I was actually beginning to enjoy teaching. What did I like about it?
Mainly the one on one, the satisfaction one can get with the kid who's
having trouble, but is performing more or less on level, but you work with
him and then all of a sudden they say, 'Oh, I see!' Or at the end of the year
they say, 'You know when I walked into this class, I thought you were an
asshole, but I see what you're getting at now.' Of course, you can't take
that down to the checkout counter at Giant Foods, but that's why generally
I've stuck around for a while. Still, it's becoming harder and harder to
create that . . . with the students."

(How would you contrast teaching to being in the Navy?)

"It drains you a lot more. In a sense . . . I was in Viet Nam and Korea
too and of course, you're looking backwards and that kind of dims the
memories, but in a sense it's a lot more draining than those experiences.

You have a staccato of interruptions all day long and a staccato of deadlines all day long. At 8:15 — bingo, you've got to be ready to go. At 9:10, bingo — you've got to wrap it up. And at 9:15, bingo, you've got to be ready to go again. And you don't wrap it up because there're always students at the end of class, and they want help and there are other students who come in early and they want to know if they can leave early because they have to decorate so and so's locker because it's her birthday and — you gradually by the end of the day reach a level of tension . . . now I don't care how relaxed you are or how you try to make things go — it's a beehive. And that plus the other administrative things that go on all the time. You can be hit by 130 things in any given day. I happen to have a list of interruptions here; I've been going through a lot of stuff I've got here because I have to decide if I'm going to stay in teaching or not next year. It's a very busy job; you don't let down for a minute; it's going from extreme to extreme all of the time.

"Well, like Julie, the teacher that was just in here. She said to me this morning, she doesn't even know why she came in today because she's still raging over last Friday. She didn't have all of the quizzes graded from Thursday and she told her class she wouldn't hand any of them back until she could hand them all back to be fair, and one kid came in and called her a — *bitch*. It's that kind of thing. We used to think it, yes . . . but we never said it. But the freedom to verbalize it and the — acceptance that it seems to get — and nothing's going to happen to that kid — he's going to be here today. And if he gets suspended, the teacher is obliged to give him whatever time and effort it takes to help him catch up when he comes back. So essentially the teacher is the one who winds up getting punished. She gets called a bitch and then she has to help the kid who did it.

"Before I started teaching, I thought, 'Hmmm — that's great. I'll teach from say 8:00 and maybe get off at mid-afternoon. Well, that's great, I'm retired now and I could use some extra income, and I've taught tennis' — No way! Teachers have at least one to three hours homework every night. A half-an-hour quiz in the class can take two hours to grade at home. I was surprised at the amount of time I ended up putting in. Here's a list of things that go into teaching besides the regular that people think of . . . And if you're not prepared and ready to go, particularly in this day and age with discipline being what it is, even if you don't have their attention, if you don't have something to present to keep them working — you're dead! I mean, they'll just run all over you in the classroom. Look at all this you have to do: LD [learning disabled] reports, evaluations for parents, college recommendations, scholarship recommendations, failure alert forms, book collections — some of this sounds nitpicking, but it all adds up.

"And then the students quite often are absent from class for one thing or another. And here's a list for this: I mean grocery shopping for a gourmet foods class would make them absent from algebra, but this was all right because it was an academic class . . . Peer counseling, for example . . . I have a girl who is taken out of my fourth period class to talk to another student who has been trained in peer counseling. There's a program that sort of works but not nearly as well as most people think it does. Besides, this student needs to be in algebra; that's part of her problem! She's failing and she feels bad about it. And then we have kids taken out for pep rallies and minimum competency tests — if those tests are so damned important, why can't they bring the kids in after school? Field trips — the cosmetology class went to New York — now come on! The newspaper staff went to New York, the student council went to Philadelphia for a day, the zoology class went to the zoo to study animal behavior . . . hell, they could do that out here in the hallway! (Laughter) I'm trying not to turn this into a gripe session, but these are all things that impinge on teaching . . . so I found these lists for you the other day when I knew you were going to be around.

"And look! This is my desk . . . and I'm lucky, I have a locking drawer. Look at that over there — that's a teacher's desk! Now a teacher is an executive, right? A manager. A manager is somebody who influences human behavior — academic stuff. The span of any manager, and any business or business school will tell you this when they talk about their people — the span is six to nine people under one manager. The teachers have 150 and they have a desk, that falling-down thing, to work with. And no secretary. No telephone. And if I do find time to call a parent and they're not there but I'll be glad to take a message and have them call you back . . . when do I say to call me back? During half an hour at lunch, which I get about twenty minutes of. Now one teacher last year had this for a desk — this, what is this, a sort of card table? — we were so proud of this (smile). If they would just give teachers basic facilities, telling you you are really worth a little more even though we can't pay you any more, particularly giving us a decent desk. And particularly for women teachers who have purses, because purses are always getting stolen around here. Now I'm lucky, I do have my own classroom, unlike so many — it's one of those Quonset huts outside that you may have passed as you drove in. Some teachers have three desks and four different classrooms so I guess I'm lucky, although I have to walk through the rain and whatever with all my papers all the time. Some push a trailer all over the building — their lives are in their briefcases. You never know where you left anything if you all of a sudden realized that you didn't have what you needed. Or you have to spend productive time trying to remember what it is that you have to take with you when you go from A14 to E101. It's impossible. It's particularly galling in a so-called rich county like this . . .

(What makes you consider leaving at the end of the year?)

"In a phrase — it's lack of personal time. I can't choose; I don't feel like I really have any control over my life, not that I want control over the school or the students or anything else — I just want control over what I'm doing *for* the students. I don't have it. I don't have enough of it. But I'd miss the youthful enthusiasm of the students. This nervous energy depletion at the end of the day is not all negative. I'd miss the approval of the students. They really have done something to help themselves and they therefore think you had something to do with it."

Tape #130

Was Ms. B. just another worn-out public school teacher? She had taught for twenty years at the fifth grade level in a Southern city school district. She had seen the segregated and the integrated schools. She was forty-two and single. She was also a former local association president. She looked intelligent . . . but tired.

(Have you ever thought of being anything besides a teacher?)

"Not until recently . . . I was the association president for a while on two years of paid leave of absence, and I guess I saw the other side of the world. Plus, I've become very frustrated of late with a lot of things that even four or five years ago I thought could be changed; but I've come to see that in my career as a teacher — they're not going to be changed. I'm concerned about the image of public education. I'm concerned with parents who pull kids out to put them into so-called private schools. I don't know what they're after. School is not number one with parents, and with all the talk of educational reform, I've seen nothing in the minds of parents to make it number one. I've seen parenting skills go downhill over the years . . . the child gets everything he wants and — the school work is secondary. I get real tired of hearing, 'We want homework, we want homework.' And then every morning a child comes in and says, 'I had to play soccer last night,' 'I had to go shopping,' 'I had to do this, I had to do that.' School's just not number one. There are too many other things competing.

"There are a lot of problems in education, and of course money has to be taken care of, but there are other problems besides the money. I mean, I need help in the classroom. I don't know if I'm just getting older or what, but there is just *too much work*. I can handle the discipline. It's just more is required of us. I need an aide. And I don't want an aide to sit down and teach. I want an aide to help me. Now, in this state, first through third grade teachers have aides. Well, now I've never thought much about having an aide, but I see these first through third grade teachers. Now, I will just be getting something out of my box that has to be done and the aide has already gotten it out of that teacher's box, filled it in completely, and brought it back to the office. And there's so much Mickey Mouse stuff. Attendance is not dumb . . . but it still takes time. And I'll invariably make a mistake when the busses have been late three days in a row and mark a child absent and forget to go back and mark them tardy. I have to take a lunch count every morning. Who wants ravioli, who wants spaghetti, and who wants salad? I have to list two or three times a year the busses that the children ride, their addresses and so forth. I still have to take up money for this and that and see that it gets to the office. When children are absent, we get a call over the intercom that so and so wants homework for her child — have it ready in thirty minutes. Today I had two bad situations that took my time away from the children. One was a child who can do very little — he's under medication. He's under two doctors' care. I get a note from the mother wanting all this stuff. The other extreme — a child had not been home since Friday night. And getting in touch with the proper people . . . . Now, some of these things I would still want to do as the teacher . . . but it's still time-consuming.

"You know, I want to teach. I don't want anybody really to grade my papers unless it's an objective type. Ok, running materials off. That takes so much time. And all the new textbooks that come up have the guides with them that have to be copied. Having been the association president, I know what it's like to have a secretary . . . and I'm involved in a program right now called Leadership. It deals with twenty-five people from the city and I'm the only teacher. Everybody else is either a lawyer or architect or what-have-you. There have been several meetings during the day. And they just — go when they want. Me?! (Laughter) We're supposed to be learning about the city, and this month we're doing the education of the city, so I had to go visit a school. And the only one that I could go to was the one that was open from 2:30 till 3:00. Everyone else was going at like ten in the morning, or eleven. For human services month we had to work at either the night shelter, which is for homeless people, a soup kitchen, or Meals on Wheels. Meals on Wheels met during the day, the soup kitchen met during the day, so I had to work at the night shelter. (Laughter) We don't have normal lives as teachers.

"And there are interruptions in the teaching day, constant interruptions, not only intercom interruptions but pulling children out here, pulling children out there. Those types of things are always frustrating. I know kids have to go to resource classes. There's no getting around that. But I for one wouldn't care if I never saw another assembly program, let alone put on one, which is facing me in February. I have to put on one with four other classes, which means every afternoon will be taken up with that. I don't want to be put in a totally structured traditional classroom, but I like a traditional classroom. I don't want to be in a school where nothing happens. By the same token, there's too much happening right now. We have to expose children to this, and we have to expose them to that. And — the puppets are coming Wednesday. It's all just driving me crazy. For Christmas — our musical and PE teachers put on a program so they took children out of every class to rehearse. They had to rehearse two or three times a week. I just feel like there's been more of this in the last couple of years . . . .

"You can't put your finger on it, what has changed. Are we less able to cope with it? But I do have children who go to a learning disabilities class, a reading lab, a math lab, and a multiple retaining program because we do have promotions standards. And speech classes, and gifted . . . children are just going in and out. Now all this is well and good, but when I'm supposed to be teaching everybody something? There might be two hours during the day when we're all there. Now take this — in this state every child is expected to have thirty minutes of computers a week. When am I going to do that? I can't get social studies done; I can't get reading done. When am I going to teach computers? In the past we had it in the classroom. I had it one day a week. Then those kids who finished their work could use the computer. Now, I know that's not right; the other kids need to use it too. But I'm also responsible for their learning math and science. And now, every child has to be on the computer for thirty minutes a week, and you know, we don't have but four or five computers in the whole school! (Laughter) Our state is notorious for that; they mandate you do something but they don't give you the money to do it. We have 400 kids to split those five computers up amongst. And they just stay in the library.

"It would require hiring more teachers to take care of all these problems . . . if they want us to do all of these new things. Of course, if you lowered class size, and I mean to between from one to fifteen, you might not need all these resource classes. You could handle that.

(Do you think that public education works?)

"Yeah . . . yeah . . . I mean, I *have* to believe that. I couldn't stay if I didn't think that what I was doing had some meaning 'cause every now and then I run into a student who says something that makes it all worthwhile, you know.

Tape #217

I appreciate your taking the time to be interviewed."
"Well, I allow myself one free evening a week. This was it."

I interviewed Ms. M. at 8:00 p.m. in her living room; she told me this was her one night that week that she wouldn't grade papers. After thirteen years of teaching, she had moved from junior high to senior high English and with four preparations and six classes, she was spending sixty-five hours a week on work. As she said, she had no social life, and she felt like she was neglecting her own two children. It had become necessary to see a professional psychologist to deal with all the stress. Ms. M. was divorced and raising her children alone. She taught at a small rural high school directly outside a large Midwestern city. She was thin with short dark hair.

(Would you go into teaching again?)

"If you had asked me last year, I would have said I loved teaching. This year — I don't like it. I have six classes a day — fifty minute classes. I have four new English preps . . . every single day, and it's too much. My standards are such that I can't live up to my standards. It's causing me a lot of trouble. It was my choice to go into the high school. I knew it was going to be difficult, but I didn't think they would give me this many classes. I'm working sixty-five hour work weeks. If you weren't here, I would be on the computer working on worksheets, tests, quizzes — anything. And our curriculum is such that it is fairly fluid. We have certain skills that we want to get across, but how we teach those skills really is up to the teacher. We have a literature book and we have a grammar book, but I never stick to one book so I'm always gathering materials, which means I have to copy a lot . . . and it's a lot of work. Like the NCTE (National

Council of Teachers of English) has been saying for fifteen years — no more than one hundred kids for English classes and four classes and with that — you could teach English.

"But the way things are structured now . . . at least in my situation and most that I know of, it's impossible to do what you're supposed to. My first choice for improvements in my situation is to limit the number of preps that I'm responsible for, but it couldn't be done easily in my school because it's a small school. You have only so many bodies to fill those slots . . . if we got one more teacher, he wouldn't have his own classroom. I didn't have my own classroom when I started. But they added on classrooms for the junior high to come up and they just happened to build one extra classroom — which I got. The first three months of school were horrible; I was English on a cart. And as the weeks went by, I added more and more books and materials, and you could tell my arms were getting bigger from pushing this cart around the halls! Every single period change, I had to change. And it was so awful — being the kind of teacher that I am with so many different kinds of materials. And my office was the teachers' workroom; I had a shelf in the teachers' workroom. I had all my stuff piled up . . . and sometimes I'd get to my class and I wouldn't have what I needed. It was horrible. I now have my own room and they'd have to dynamite me out of it."

(Have you ever considered getting out of teaching?)

"Definitely — this is one of those years. One other time — I was tired of the whole thing after I'd been teaching . . . only about four years. I didn't consider the building principal to be a good principal. And I'm seriously thinking about it this year again. Over spring break I'm doing my resumé, and I'm talking to some people now to see what's out there in the business world. I have no idea . . . never having been in the business world. And I never particularly wanted to be in business. But I need a good job to make — well, I'm making fairly good money now because we are a well paid district, and to start a job now I'll probably have to take a pay cut . . . but . . . I'm giving myself this coming school year to interview and get off my butt.

"My major reason for wanting to get out? The increasing feeling that I can't do the job the way it's supposed to be done because of the structure of the school system . . . of public education. It's blocked out in neat little blocks and I don't think you can educate people in neat little blocks. And teachers have too much to do, too much paperwork that's not even related to the classroom. For people who really want to do the job right . . . it becomes harder and harder to do every year. No, money isn't the largest part. If I were concerned with money, I would have gotten out long ago. It's more frustration with the work and what I can and can't do."

(Give me a typical day for you.)

"Well, today's not typical because I'm sitting here talking to you. But yesterday — school is over at 2:20. I stay till 4:00. I'm grading papers, checking homework. I am running off tests. I have to make up all my own tests and quizzes. I don't use standardized ones. So I'm typing them out; now I come home and do those on the word processor. And I'm looking through books and trying to decide what I'm going to teach next and how I'm going to treat it and what would be good for the kids — just trying to gather materials and organize steps, you know, on how I'm going to do this. I come home and I run and then I cook dinner and then I prepare for the next day by reading — say the act for *Julius Caesar* that we're going to be talking about — again for the umpteenth time so I can get everything out of that I can get out of it. I'll read the next chapter in the *Pigman* book, be looking through how to teach headline writing for my journalism course — whatever we're on. I want to get all this in my mind and organized for the next day — maybe an hour's time. It depends — an hour to an hour and a half. Then I usually have papers to grade. I have sixty-seven book reports in there to grade. I have twenty-two mysteries to grade. And I have about forty chapters of a book that they wrote from a different person's point of view to look at. So I spend about an hour grading papers at home though sometimes if I wait too long . . . I go to bed. I try to be at school about seven and I need my sleep so I go to bed by ten. I get to talk to my children for a few minutes . . . during dinner. Really, I have neglected the children because I have worked so hard. This won't go on . . . I mean, this can't go on.

"My big goal was to make it to March . . . which it is. Now, my big goal is to make it to April. I'm learning to live one day at a time — just like the alcoholics. Because it seems like I'm just spending all my time on school and not doing much else. I don't have much of a social life. At the beginning of the year I was spending twelve to fourteen hours on the weekends at that dining room table doing the lesson plans for the next week — four new preps, five days a week. And there's nothing there for me; it all comes from me. I had to plan it all. It's been worse than being a first year teacher because . . . my expectations are a lot higher because I know what I'm capable of and I know what the kids are capable of and

I know what we should be covering and we're not! I think I needed to switch to the high school, even though it's hell. It really is! I'm seeing a psychologist now, and it's mostly because of my job. I'm unhappy with the amount of time I'm spending on my job. I try to make myself back off but I can't. I back off for a little while and then you creep back into it again. I'm burning out — definitely, definitely. I know that I'm undergoing a lot of stress; I don't sleep as well at night. I'm grouchier with my own kids than I should be because I'm not grouchy with my kids at school. I'm discontented . . . I'm not happy. I've neglected my social life and it hasn't been the best experience. I knew it would be hard, but it's been a lot tougher than I expected it to be. And I spent a lot of the summer preparing — I read two literature books this summer. I also went to school. I've been taking a course a semester for the last three of four years . . . and in summer. Last summer I also wrote curriculum — all by myself for three weeks on the two extra courses I'm teaching this year. I didn't get it finished. And at the beginning of school I couldn't sleep at night. I had to go over my lesson plans every night in four different courses. It was like sensory overload. I started chewing calcium tablets before I went to bed so I could get some sleep. So it's been a real tough year.

"Education today has been given an impossible job. It's supposed to be all things to all people. Not only are we supposed to teach them the academic subjects but we're supposed to feed them, we're supposed to counsel them; we're supposed to counsel children of split families and keep them in a state in which they can learn. With some of the things going on in some families, there is absolutely no doubt in my mind that some of these kids can't possibly be thinking about what is going on at school. They can't! We're nurse, we're psychologist . . . we're everything. We're supposed to be everything . . . except we're not supposed to teach them morals and values. So we're given an impossible job and I think we're trying to do it. That's one thing in public education's favor . . . we have not given up. The system continues to try to be all things to all people. But that's also its biggest problem, because I don't think it can be . . . or at least we haven't found the way to do it yet."

(Would you go into teaching again?)

"If you had asked me that last year, I would have said yes. But this year? — no. It's too hard to do right. It's impossible to do right. That's the way I feel about it right now. The thing is that I have to tell myself that you can't do it right one hundred percent of the time so give yourself a break and that's what I don't do well so it's driving me crazy. A person who would go into teaching and like it has to be the kind of person who can be satisfied with hearing, 'You know, I never understood that before' . . . or 'I never liked reading until I read this.' You have to be able to be satisfied by those little kinds of things. Maybe that will get me through till the end of the year. Today, I had a little girl come up and tell me, 'Did you hear about Steve and Traci — they broke up.' It's not as rewarding as, 'You made me love reading' — but at least I was included. You have to be included in their world if you want them to listen to you. At least I was included. And when you talk about good teachers, there are some people who maybe aren't that good in the classroom but are good out of the classroom. They're doing other things for the kids like coaching, advising newspapers, whatever. That extra little bit that kids are learning a lot from, although it's not academic."

"It's an important job; it's an extremely important job, and we aren't given the skills or the time to do it right. We've boxed ourselves in too much in public education, but I don't have any solutions. I thought when I started teaching, I would . . . but I don't have them . . . I don't know; I don't have any answers. I just work on myself and my classroom . . . and what I can do. It's not enough . . . but . . . that's all I can do."

Section 4:

LEFTOVER LIBERALS

It was amazing to me how similar the conservative and liberal teachers were on stands in education. I couldn't help notice that they both saw the greatest problems as the changes in society and class size and administrators . . . just as I did. But by and large teachers came off sounding much more liberal than conservative. Why was that? Could it be that when you see the problems facing society, and when you're forced to deal with the offspring of those problems, your social consciousness is so raised that you know you must have changes?

Like several teachers said, where do you really see our priorities as a country, as a society? Do you really want to spend billions on defense and millions on education so you can preserve from outside attack a country that is falling apart on the inside? If society would put into pupil expenditures the money that they put into prisoner expenditures, maybe we'd have a lot less prisoners. Like going to college, teaching turns you into a much more liberal person. You are faced with the stark reality of the have-nots: economically, socially, intellectually.

Tape #23

> "Why did you go into teaching?"
> "There are no more cowboys."

Mr. S. was a retained radical. He was thirty-four (one year younger than I) and we had immediate rapport. "I've been looking forward to this interview all week!" He had wild, curly hair, a mustache and dressed without the tie. He admitted he was a radical of the 60s . . . and proud of it. I loved him.

We talked in perhaps the worst room I did any interview . . . a dungeon. It was the furnace room and a place where he could smoke. He taught social studies; he coached football; he had no children of his own yet though he was married.

If liberalism is correctly defined as wanting change, wanting progress, perhaps the liberal teachers were the real hope for improvement in public education. The conservative teachers may have seen the same problems, but they yearned for a return to the past. The liberal teachers were trying to adjust for the inevitable future.

"I've been looking forward to this interview all week. I really think teachers love to talk about education, and I don't have enough outlets. My wife doesn't care; my friends don't care. And I know I just bore other people with talking about teaching.

"I've wanted to be a teacher for so long . . . after I realized that I wasn't big enough to be a professional football player, and after I realized that there are no more cowboys. So that was just the thing that I wanted to do. I've wanted to teach since I was in grade school. It's just always appealed to me and I don't know why. My parents beat it into me . . . all of us kids . . . that school is the most important thing you're doing until you get out . . . graduate from college.

"I don't know about you but I really come home from school exhausted. I don't want to think. You know, maybe that's one of the reasons I don't have kids yet. It's like, I've got to come home and I've got to do it all over again, sort of. I mean it's not the same thing . . . but I already have 150 kids I have to worry about from day to day. And I don't turn off my thinking processes on kids because the day is over. You think about them constantly. You wake up in the middle of the night in a cold sweat . . . what am I going to do about Charles?

"What do I do with an unmotivated student? I try to get them on my side. If they won't work for themselves, [I] try to get them to work for me. So I guess I don't care [how] I get them to do it, because they'll learn if they work for me or not. And with kids that are their age, if parents aren't providing the motivation for them — and I really think that's where it needs to come from — then maybe they'll do it for me. They'll do it for me; then they'll learn. A parent at home can help — talk to them about school. Give them an hour every day when they have to sit home and do homework. Maybe sit down there with them, but then again if it's a single family home, we're over-expecting with parents. I don't know. I also think it's important for parents to do stuff with kids. Take them to zoos; take them to parks; take them on vacations. Expand them — give them more experiences. Talk to them about it. Talk things out with them. Kids don't know what's important and not important. It's up to adults to tell them what's important, to point things out to them. I'm sure that we see the world differently than a ten year old or five year old or twenty year old. And I think that's a part of being grown up and educated — of giving you a way to see the world and deal with the world and to function in the world. Teachers are role models. I mean, that's what we're really doing. Teachers are giving them a second-hand experience on what the world is like: what does it look like? What are people like? The same way with history — it's a lot more than names, dates, and places. What did it *mean* to live in thirteen colonies? What did it mean to be a Spanish explorer? What was your life like?

"I never looked at a career as a way to make money. I looked at a career as a helping thing. I've got to be interested in it because it's hard enough to get my butt out of bed in the morning. And yeah . . . it really is part of our generation. To me, being brought up in the 60s and 70s was very exciting. I was proud of being concerned about people. I was proud about being different. When I graduated from college . . . you're going to laugh at this — my goal was to teach for five years and to save up my money and I was going to go up to the frontier of Alaska and build myself a log cabin. I was going to be a mountain man. For you know, personal growth — personal development, making myself better. . . . But why did so many of us become yuppies — practicality. It's real easy to lose your ideals in the real world because you've got bills to pay. You've got your wife and your kids and your family to take care of. But a lot of teachers are idealistic when they start. I think you better start that way, because you aren't going to get more idealistic as you get older.

"For me, being radical — that's important to me . . . well, I've probably gone from radical to liberal. I still wear my hair long; I still dress sloppy. I still go to an occasional rock concert. Kids probably do look at me as being a bit bizarre, and I promote that. I think that's ok. I want kids to think that they're a little bit different class than the usual run of the mill class. As long as you cover the curriculum and stuff — you do that by saying and doing silly things. And I do say silly things, off the wall things as just an attention getter, a part of my personality. I like playing that; I like being different. You have to stay within the realm of your personality or you come across to the kids as phony as a two dollar bill. You can't do what's successful for somebody else. And if I were a very proper, very straight-laced person, I think I could teach just as well and be just as effective. You can expect me to cover curriculum, but don't tell me *how* to do it. That's my job. I can't cover material as fast as other people. Like American history — I want to create moods . . . I want kids to be able to have a movie in their heads and put themselves in — like 16th century Europe, and see what it's like. What did it mean to live in Europe in the 16th century? It's nice to know the dates and the facts and all that stuff, but I want [the kids] to be able to picture it. I want [them] to be able to feel what it's like. That's what history is — it's feeling what it's like. I always find my tests to be much less than what I did in class because I can only test the facts.

"What would my perfect school be like? Well, I'd hire me as a teacher . . . but not as a principal. It would be a building that would be a real pleasing building to be in. It would be colorful, stimulating, modern. It would have air conditioning. I would have a basic curriculum, but also we would do things; we would go places — take them to a sewage treatment plant; take them to a dam. Take them to a day in downtown Cleveland. Take them to a steel mill. Kids at this age are to me still 'concrete operational.' They've still got to *see* it; they've still got to *do* it. Learning about tundra is one thing, but when I was walking on tundra in Alaska . . . . That's what I try to do in my classroom; I try to create what it's like. I tell them stories about things . . . but that's still only second-hand. Ok, now you're going on a Lewis and Clark expedition, and you talk about it. Now you're on a Lewis and Clark expedition; write a journal on it. What are you seeing? What are you afraid of? What are you thinking about? Kids have a little difficulty doing that. You know, you're not just asking questions now. You've got to think a little bit. Picture it; see it.

"I don't know if I've lost a whole lot of idealism from the first year of teaching to now. I'm harder on kids than I used to be. I don't know, maybe that's losing idealism. I'm more demanding, but I don't think I care any less. Kids will meet your expectations so I've raised my expectations. I see me retired at fifty-two . . . that's when I can.

"And public education *is* working. It's just if a kid can't learn in a regular classroom, you've got to create more options for kids. It really gets me when we sit down and have retention meetings at the end of the year. What are our options? Our options are failing him . . . passing him on . . . or *maybe* letting an overworked tutor work with him. That's not enough options. Kids fall through cracks."

Tape #170

From SDS in the late 60s to teaching junior high social studies and language arts in the 80s, Mr. P. was the activist teacher. I loved him, no

matter how abrasive he seemed at times. He was now forty and his hair
was thinning, but he still had a beard and that angular intensity in his face
that you don't seem to see as much as you did in the 60s. And he had done
it all — construction work, car racing, drug counseling, special ed.,
college teaching, professional comedy routines, clerking . . . . Now, he was
married with two grown children, and he taught in a lower middle class
junior high in the Southwest. It was his eighteenth year of teaching when
I talked to him in his local association office . . . yes, he was active in that,
too.

"Why I decided to teach . . . I don't know. I was working as a heroin
counselor and I was getting my first B.A. in liberal arts and I took an
education course and I guess I just fell into it. I got interested and just did
it. It's much more fulfilling and fun than the other things that I've done.
It's much more encompassing; it's a full-time job if you make it that; for
nine months you really bust your ass. It's a sixty hour job; sometimes I put
in about seventy to seventy-five hours a week. You need your summers
just for the break. But, I think why is being from the 60s — I was a child
of the 60s — SDS radical type thing. I thought there was a need for a more
caring posture and doing something one can do for the world . . . and it
doesn't have to be something you make a lot of money at. There should be
a lot of money, but there doesn't have to be. I taught for ten years and then
had to get out of it for a while because of the lack of money. I came to this
district because of the strong union it had and picked up about a 12,000
dollar raise. And that makes a hell of a lot of difference. I'm making
$40,000 and in other school districts I'd probably be making $32 or
$33,000, if that. Forty's not fair; forty still pisses me off, but compared to
other districts — this is the strongest district in the Southwest but mainly
because of the union."

(What do you think is the biggest problem in education?)

"Money. We don't have enough materials, supplies. We did a study in
this district a few years ago; it was a study to see what jobs were out there
on the professional level that are comparable to what a teacher does. You
know, a junior high teacher can do everything from cleaning up barf to
blowing up a basketball to pregnancy counseling to the bathroom pass to
somebody crying because they have to have Reeboks — all in three or
four seconds, I mean, all that crap can go on. So we tried to identify what
jobs were the closest to education since you don't have very many people
in business that are blowing up basketballs. What we found was that there

were two jobs that were basically the closest as far as the characteristics were concerned. One was the civil engineer and the other was a manager of a TV station. Both of those jobs averaged like 15,000 dollars a year more than teachers' jobs. Their median pay is what maximum teachers are getting."

(Do you envision teachers' salaries rising that much in your career?)

"You better believe it! Part of the problem here is that because benefits and salaries have risen so much since we had a strike in '78, the s—t's pretty well settled since then. Part of the problem here is — newer teachers come in and kind of take those changes for granted; they don't remember the classrooms with forty and sixty kids in them. They don't have that concept of kids sitting on the walls, things like that. I've seen that happen. It's kind of like they say — you were there in the old days . . . because the old days really sucked. The power of the contract allows for a lot of freedom as far as the teacher is concerned; we choose what we want to teach within some administrative guidelines, which are so loose that you can fit almost anything into it. Many teachers who are retiring now had gotten to the point where they're willing to accept that they had to have another job or their husband or wife had to work; it wasn't considered a profession; we didn't have the golf carts and the $80,000 a year. Now we're getting a new generation of teachers in. Many of the five or six year veterans are single or single parents with a demand for the money coming in from this job. I see that kind of a change going on. So I think more and more teachers in the next few years are going to get more and more angry and say — hey, we can't cut it on this kind of salary."

(What would you say to people who think teachers are professionals and shouldn't be involved in things like unions and associations?)

"Oh, they're full of s—! If you can't be involved with the changing of your profession, then what have you got? You can't do that as a single voice. Too many times I've seen at too many school board meetings, somebody coming up with a righteous cause — it can be a community member; it can be a teacher; it can be an administrator; it can be anybody in the world that comes up and says we have a real problem — no one denies that and the board tells him to buzz off. He's one person; he doesn't have that power group. Where I live there's a neighborhood group and when it comes into the board, the board listens. When it goes to the city, the city listens. It collects and has a lot of power. Also there's a certain sophistication involved with that. Now, I've only been involved in two unions as a teacher and the decisions in those always broke down to what would be best for the students. To look at that from the outside sometimes you get some crazy teacher in New York who says, 'I had to go home at four o'clock because I couldn't work with a kid after that because it's not in the contract' . . . but that's not what I see. I see — you can't be *told* to work past this hour; it gives you an option as a professional. Unions can get in the way sometimes. Politics always arise from them, but by and large they're run by the membership and the membership has the vote as to what the final consequence will be. They're a good reflection about what those people are. The community here was very supportive of the association when we struck in the 70s. They'd had enough of it too. You know, you look at your kid and they're in a classroom with forty other kids; you look at a teacher whom you not only know as a teacher but you drive down to the convenience store and they're stocking beer at night — those are things that the community is not necessarily proud of. Too many studies in this state, as conservative as we are, have shown that this state is willing to vote for a one cent sales tax to pay for education. And that was all done at a time when unemployment was in double figures and every- thing else was being cut down — but when it comes to education, when it comes to paying teachers, no, we want to support that. So when we struck here, there was a very supportive group of people; one of our school board members was on the line.

"You know, kids today are much more responsible students than in my day. A lot of those junior high kids go home and there's nobody there; I'm so glad my mother was home when I was a kid because I would have burnt the house down! These kids have a lot of responsibilities; they've got cable TV, MTV — the whole bit; and on top of all that, they're still getting their work in; they still appreciate things. We're discussing things now in junior high I didn't get until I was in college. The level of sophistication and the needs for those students [are] there now and they understand what's going on. What are test scores? Test scores don't have anything to do with education. Test scores waste educational time. I waste from four to ten days a year in the classroom on tests and they don't mean anything to anybody. All they do is pay the company that makes the test. Then [the teacher] has to prove that a certain amount of people took the test and they scored on certain levels. This state mandates that. If this state mandated that each teacher would have 200 dollars worth of supplies in each classroom, they wouldn't need test scores. I don't teach those tests. But the same age group students in other people's classes are taught — if not the test, then how to take the test, and usually my students fare better. There are no reasons for test scores. The state is going back to some sort of archaic belief in mandating these tests. It's some sort of proof to them; this child scored this point on this test so it puts him on number two level or whatever that b———— is. It has nothing to do with learning. There's no carryover. If I'm given a telephone operator job and you employ me, aren't you going to give me a computer that will tell me all the phone numbers people are going to call to ask me about? When we give these kids a test, all the sources for the information they've been taught to find is withdrawn from them, and they're supposed to bring into this some sort of memory bank. I'm walking around with the fact that the peregrine hawk is the fastest animal in the world; it goes 256 miles an hour. Why the hell do I need to know that? Just because I happen to know that if I see that on a test, *that's* going to knock my standing up? And what am I going to do with that when it comes down to the nitty gritty, if I have a conflict management situation that I have to deal with or if I have a job situation that I have to deal with or if I have an emotional reaction in the classroom — what does that peregrine hawk mean? And what does it mean to the kid? It doesn't mean anything."

(How would you like to evaluate students?)

"I would rather not. I spent probably six days out of the nine weeks just putting the grades in the grade book and averaging out grades, not even grading the papers themselves. And then you've got to send notices home, all this stuff — I don't have time. That evaluation process — what is that? A student writes a paper on whether or not we should have euthanasia — what is that? How am I going to evaluate those feelings and put that into a grade? It doesn't make any sense . . . ."

(Anything you think should be done to have a student get the diploma?)

"Yeah, I think the parents ought to come down."

(I beg your pardon?)

"I think the parents ought to come down nine times a year to the school, every parent — not one of the two parents, but every parent ought to come down at least once a week, at least once a week to be in the school. That forces the parent to be involved in education; that's where the carryover is and that's what we're not getting. The PTSA (Parent, Teacher, Student Association) — sixty to seventy percent of the membership in our association is students. That tells you one thing — who runs the school. We're in an area with a lot of narcotics, a lot of problems. I said the kids are more mature; most of them are not into it and it's available at their home; I mean, we're talking really dangerous narcotics. We have two or three really great, highly motivated people who are coming down to talk about Alateen, and I doubt whether more than five or six parents will show up at the meeting. You send home flyers and you do all the different things but parents don't show. We'll have probably about five students. Of the ten parents, they'll probably be parents who are there all the time and their kids are doing fine . . . and that tells you something.

". . . I have no trouble with administrators; as long as there's straight communication there's been no problem. I have had real rubs with what some administrators have done, but I learned a long time ago, in a good junior high, the kids run the school anyway. There's a reaction to it. You have maybe forty-five teachers and seven hundred students and maybe two building administrators — maybe a total of fifty adults and those kids run the school and what they do makes a lot of difference in what happens . . ."

"I like junior high kids — fantastic! I like the change, the behavior; about the second or third week of school we were talking about capital punishment; one of the students had an uncle or whatever that was on death row in some state. And we got into a real strong discussion about that. And I had them write a paper on whether there should be or there shouldn't be. And the one that was the most adamant about whether there should, I had him stand on a chair and I put like a play rope over the light and put it around his neck and had him read his paper, and about a third of the way through there was a real feeling that maybe capital punishment wasn't as cut and dry as he thought. And the next day I brought in a couple of stuffed animals that I had that ran on batteries, and those students generated as much energy into that as they did into capital punishment. You have the intellectual and the need to learn and all that going on and still the most elementary emotions that need to be tapped and continued."

(Have you ever had a fear that you might influence them too much?)

"Uh — no. I allow my opinions in. You have to make sure they understand that stuff. And I find myself being overzealous about the opposite side to mine. When the ERA was out and being voted on, I would be over-zealous about the anti-ERA part; I just wanted to make sure that they saw that part. That's part of the responsibility that's there. I change my mind on those issues too. I've gone back and forth about one hundred times on narcotics laws; I still can't figure out what's the best for society. A lot of times I won't agree with somebody in what they deal with in their journals and I'll write down, 'I totally disagree with what you say,' but at the same time, they get the points, get the A; that's not the point. In junior high you know everything. (Laughter) You know. I was like that once too."

(Do you think public education really works?)

"Yes."

(Would you go into teaching again?)

"I'd f— up; I'd do it again. I would — even though the money is a major issue. Teachers are professionals; they're sophisticated people with the champagne tastes and the beer budget and those are real problems. If we were paid more, we'd have teachers that weren't burnt out. Right now it's an average of seven years and they're off; they're gone. It used to be twenty-two years. Fifteen years ago the average teacher stayed in the profession twenty-two years. That cut to fourteen about eight years ago and now it's down to seven. I talked to my son who's a freshman in college who's going into business, and I said, 'How does $20,000 a year sound to you?' and he laughed. We're going to be losing teachers like crazy in the next ten years . . . you're darned right paying more would get in more and better teachers. Women and minorities are not going into education; there are other possibilities. What is it? Half the people in law schools are women now; one-third in med school are women. Twenty years ago that was a dream . . . thirty years ago that was impossible . . . . We're at a point here in this state where soon half of the kids in public education will be speaking Spanish and where are those minority teachers coming from? We used to have twenty-two percent minority students in the colleges of education; now it's seven percent of people. That's terrible. We need those bilingual teachers.

"Two years ago we had a math teacher at the school I teach at — nice guy, Mexican-American, bilingual, the whole bit. IBM picked him up and he's making $60,000 now, as soon as he got his master's . . . He's working the twelve months and all that kind of stuff, but he came back and he said, 'It's a piece of cake.' He goes home from work and that's it. He's not on the phone dealing with the kids; he's not dealing with the police; he's not trying to focus on some suicidal bullshit or even grading papers; he's just doing his thing. He has all his supplies there.

"When I did my study on other professions, not one business talked about lack of supplies. I'd say, 'Well, what happens if you run out of these forms?' 'We get some more.' 'Get some more' 'Yeah, get some more.' (Laughter) When their copier breaks down, they call the company and they take the old one, and replace it with a new one or they fix it right there. They say, 'What do you do?' I say, 'When we're out, we're out. You go look for paper that's got one side written on; you flip it over and you go for it again!' (Laughter) 'Oh . . . well, doesn't that mess up the copier?' 'Well, that's why the copier's out . . . .' (Laughter) The copiers down at the district office work just fine; they're the new ones. The one at our school is twelve years old . . . the one we had before it was fifteen. Lack of priorities."

Tape #236

"The people at AT&T that I worked with during the summer refer to my teaching as my missionary work . . . ."

Ms. R. was an articulate young black woman who looked a great deal like Whoopi Goldberg. She was sincerely dedicated to teaching, but she planned to leave in three more years after having put in fifteen years at teaching high school math. She figured then that she'd have something to point out when she went to heaven and St. Peter asked her what she'd done for the world while alive. She impressed me immensely.

She wore attractive clothing and had a wild, free hairstyle. She was thirty-five and single and seemed to be following a master plan she'd concocted for herself. She had worked summer jobs in industry and at city hall.

"Most kids in this school don't do that well in math; the majority of our classes are remedial math and only a small portion of it is academic. A lot of them are doing poorly in math because of their backgrounds; they don't have anybody to help them at home. If they don't get it in the classroom or from the tutoring systems that we have here at school; there's no support. My father is the one who intrigued me about math because he was a construction worker; he was a foreman and he had to lay out blueprints. So when I was small, he used to share it with me."

(What keeps you in teaching instead of going into industry and business?)

"I feel that if no one takes an interest at this point, we're going to have a population that is going to be not only illiterate in English but illiterate in math. We're living in a technological society, and we're just hoping that if we can get through to a few of them, then they can take it back to their cousins and their brothers, and we're just hoping that there'll be a snowball effect. They need to see that it is important and that we should be attending school and we should learn as much as we can.

"I didn't really consider the money aspect of teaching because I don't put that much value on money; I put more value on people. I like working with people. I've worked in the city government and that's very un-people. I worked in industry and that's awful! Teaching is relating to people and I like relating to people. If I had to put a value between people and money, I'd go for people every time. I think that when you're in a profit mode industry, people are insignificant and the profit is important, and after a point, you get the check and it's nice but you know what you have to continue to do to get that same level of money, and then you lose perspective about yourself and the people around you because you're chasing after profits and dollars. You don't have that human factor. I like being, you know, human. (Laughter)

"But the kids here are more concerned with money, and what they're going to have to realize is that they're going to have to get the education to get the money. There're legal and illegal ways of getting money, and I think they're more influenced about the money than thinking about the values of how they're going to get it. And they need to realize that education is the way to get it legally, because all they see are illegal ways, glorified, so you need to put the, how should I say it — moral factor back into school. I live in this area and I see a lot of drugs and prostitution, and you as a teacher have to say, ok, that's all well and good if you want quick money, but if you want to live a long time, you've got to have an education to get what you want. I don't think drugs here are prevalent, but it's there, and they need to see that education will provide. I think a lot of it can be done by the schools by bringing role models other than teachers into it. If we bring other professionals into the schools and let them tell their stories on how they got where they got and let the kids know that there are possibilities — that there is hope in education. Education's not a dead road where you just get a diploma and that's it. A lot of professions out there that make good money don't require a college education. Our kids need to know that. There are trades that you can learn and make more money than a professional."

(What makes you the sort of person who wants to teach and cares about people?)

"I think — experience. I think — background . . . knowing options . . . being able to go into industry or into teaching . . . having that freedom that I have. I also have a degree in finance and computers and business and I can do what I want when I want it and I like having that freedom. But at the same time, I'd feel the guilt of not going back, and reaching back and saying, we can do it too. And I think the only way I can do that is to be in the classroom."

(Does it bother you with your master's in math to be teaching remedial courses?)

"Yeah — it's boring. I admit, it's boring. But at the same time if you can turn somebody on to math who's been turned off, then it's worth it. I come to school excited and I think that my excitement transfers over to the students. I think that most of them are — just here. They come here because they have to. Only a few are excited to come to school. Many just want to get past the classes that they have to pass to graduate; that's their attitude. I've taught at a suburban school too and there the kids are often forced to learn too; parental pressure was very intense. In an urban school like this, it's more exciting for me because in a suburban school, they're expected to be an achiever. Here they're not expected to be an achiever but once they are, it's a great accomplishment. In an urban school so few have potential that you can see where you've made a difference. I get satisfaction from the seniors on whose lives I know I've made an impact, maybe *the* impact."

(If I were a real yuppie type who made fifty or sixty thousand a year, how could you explain to me what you get out of teaching?)

"I had to do that. I worked for AT&T this summer and I ran into a lot of yuppies. I told them that I wouldn't be where I was if people hadn't cared . . . and I think that we need to bring caring back at all levels. As long as we ignore the problem, the problem grows. And we don't want it to grow to where we can't handle it. You know if we get to the point where we don't care enough and they don't care enough, then what kind of future are we going to experience? That future's going to make our lives so miserable that no matter how much money we make, it's not going to do us any good — putting bars on our houses, afraid to go to grocery stores with extra cash — we carry credit cards instead of cash now. That's going to be a little bit more intense unless we start caring. I asked them, what do you want? A welfare state? We got it. If they don't find proper jobs, that's what we'll have because the reality is they're going to have families. Sex is going to go on. You want a welfare state, you got it! . . . unless you start really caring."

(Did these yuppies think different about you because you were a teacher?)

"Oh yeah — *missionary* was the word that they called me. *Missionary* . . . that's their definition of a teacher. A modern missionary . . . and all of my friends think I'm just a high class babysitter. Sometimes I agree, because sometimes I do feel that way. But on the other hand, I feel that I am teaching."

(Do you think you'll stay in teaching?)

"I put my limit to fifteen years so I've got three more to go. And then I'll go into industry and become a yuppie. (Laughter) I'll get my eighty percent retirement then from teaching and I can start from zip on a new retirement plan. I guess it's like being in the Peace Corps, I've done my duty so if I go to the Pearly Gates and St. Peter is there and he says, 'Did you ever help mankind?' — I'll say, 'Yeah, I have fifteen years in teaching.' (Laughter) I won't feel guilty; I've put my time in. I think that people who stay longer, unless they have a really exciting schedule . . . . I think they're doing it just to be doing it but the excitement is gone, that we all need diversity and change in our lives. To just do the same humdrum stuff for thirty years — I don't wish that on anybody, especially myself."

Tape #221

I noticed that the principal gave me a very dirty look when the secretary told her I had come to interview Ms. B. I thought it odd, but I had learned that almost anything can happen when trying to find the interviewee. Then Ms. B. met me in the office and was everything you could wish for in graciousness and intelligent conversation. I found out, though, about the dirty look. The school association had just sued the principal for firing a teacher in front of his class the week before . . . and Ms. B. was the building representative. Score another one for educational politics.

Ms. B. was thirty-six and had taught for nine years, a few of those on an Indian reservation. Now she was in special education in a grade school that had all inner city ethnics, in a northern California city. She was thin, intense, and friendly. She was a leftover liberal . . . just like me.

"It's almost like the people you knew in the 60s are the bilingual teachers today . . ."

Amen.

"I went into teaching because when I was in high school my brother was born with Down's Syndrome and that got me interested in special ed . . . I think I'd always known that I wanted to be a teacher. But going into special education was really because of my brother being born retarded. I taught special ed. for five years then and I quit; I couldn't take it anymore. I moved out of the city I was teaching in and came to California. I really had burned out on teaching so I quit. There was the stress and we had been working on a full year basis . . . it was kind of a moral decision because of being able to control little children's behavior so much. I was questioning whether it was right or wrong. I needed to quit at that time. This was outside of Chicago. But I had always been on a September to June year and I could never get off of it. I don't like working the whole year; I think people need more free time for themselves and I wanted to travel, and working in a corporation does not allow me to do that. And I never felt in a corporation that I was doing anything good, changing people's lives. And that too was a reason why I came back, because you have to feel like you're doing something worthwhile, and being an accountant was not letting me fulfill that need. So I came back to teaching. Actually I kind of fell back into teaching because I was hiking in the Canyon and found out about the job at the Indian reservation. I wanted to be in the Canyon; I needed to get out of the city so I went and stayed there for a year. It was wonderful!

"It was so isolated; to get there you'd have to drive maybe 120 miles down a dirt road, park your car at the top and hike in eight miles — totally isolated. The people speak their own language. And it was the most incredibly beautiful place in the world. It's a place that is like a dream. I had kindergarten and special ed. The kindergarten class was delightful; I had nine children. They had gone through Head Start in English and they spoke English. They were just a delight. They were very quick, very sweet. We did a lot of things. We would hike and go swimming. It was like a perfect situation to be in. The older kids I think learned more about hating white people. They were all Rastafarians; they were really heavy into smoking pot, not being mainstreamed European white culture. And most of the kids dropped out by about seventh grade. The school in the Canyon only went to the sixth grade, and then they went out to a large Arizona city or some Mormon homes in Utah and went to Indian schools . . . and most of the people on the reservation never left it. They had no skills or coping mechanisms to be in the outside world. They quit school then because they weren't with their families; their families were all down in the Canyon. And they had lived so long without television; they don't have TV or radio down there — it was wonderful!

"The difference between those kids and what I have now is just the difference of being completely away from white society. And [the Indians] had no motivation to do anything else. The only kind of jobs that they could get down there were packing. I don't know if my kids now have more of a drive to succeed, but they are more aware of other things going on, mostly because of television. And in a city like this there are so many different types of people. We have such a big population of Asians and Central and South Americans, refugees from war-torn countries — they have a lot more exposure to other things. I think that this city is a wonderful city for that — where different cultures get together. And the bilingual teachers that I have met have been really concerned with people acculturating and also keeping their own culture. It's almost like the people you knew in the 60s are the bilingual teachers today, who are fighting for people's rights, and it really is a question of human rights. Everyone that I've met is really pro human rights.

"I'm always defending bilingual education. I always explain that bilingual education does not mean that those students are not learning English. They are just learning their language and the concepts that they should be learning in first through third grade in their native language and having English as the second language. As the grades go up, they're no longer speaking just Spanish but they're using more English, and in the meantime they have not lost the concepts. The goal is the same: they want the child to be a good fluent English speaker but also to be able to be proud of their own culture and learn the concepts that children in English are learning. But they're being taught that in their own language. I think a lot of my kids were put into kindergartens and first grades, and no one else had ever spoke English to them before so they were far behind, and they got report cards that reflected that this child is not learning. And, you know, even looking back and seeing the psychologist's reports, they don't question that they have two languages. Maybe they're speaking in English but that doesn't mean that they're thinking and reading and writing [in English].

So these kids have fallen behind because of that. I've tried to pull two or three kids out and say these kids are not special ed.; we've hurt them by keeping them in these classes. I got fought all the way. No one supported that except a few bilingual people . . . not the special ed. people. I had fights about it. I had to bring in psychologists who were bilingual and have the kids tested. But all the way to the top I fought it. They're still in the special ed. program even though I don't feel they belong here. What will happen is I will just route them from special ed. once they leave here and go to a middle school."

(Do you think the kids who leave here are successful?)

"From my class? No, I think they have a hard time because they've been labeled special ed. I think their biggest problem is their self-esteem; they don't think that they can do it; they think that they're lousy. Every day I hear 'I hate myself.' 'I'm going to kill myself.' I have four kids who are in heavy therapy. I have one who almost started the school on fire. I have kids who are sexually abused, physically abused. You know, they don't have much to start out with. They don't have many breaks. They've been given all the bad breaks to start out with. What can we do for them? Give them self-esteem. Tell them that they're good. Let them know that they're good. Hug them, kiss them; get them therapy outside of school. Get the parents involved in the therapy. Let them learn about their own culture, that it's ok to have two languages. Most of the kids who have two languages refuse to speak their Spanish. And you really have to say over and over again, 'But you're so smart! You speak two languages! I can only speak one! You're much smarter than I am.' You say it over and over and over again. We spend our whole hour first thing in the morning talking about behavior and how to cope and what it means to be an individual. I think in my program specifically that even if the kids haven't learned to read, I do hear comments that they are acting better; they're coming to school, which is a change. Before they would have maybe thirty or forty days missed out of the program from last year and this year they haven't. I see that as something positive."

(Have you ever felt that you'd like to teach in a nice, little suburban school?)

"No . . . I do at the end of the day when I'm beating my head against the wall, but I like this city because of its diversity. I like multicultural areas . . . .

"But most people that I know don't have any idea of what's going on in public education. Nor do they care. Most of the people I know wouldn't send their kids to public schools. They are very much standing in line, getting their kids in private schools. I think that's bad. Education should be equal. To attract those people back? Yes, make the school better; give the teachers twice the salary; have teachers that are good teachers. They can make the classroom sizes smaller; they can have equipment. We go through half the year — we didn't get crayons until December. We could have books; I mean, there is no money for education. Here in California, which is the second richest state, they're number forty for money spent per child. It's mainly economics; it comes down to money. You have a Republican governor and there's no money being spent on education. I would agree that there would be better education in suburban areas where they have more money. Parent groups in many of those areas have fund raising to get more money for their schools.

"And this facility stinks. It's one hundred degrees in here in the afternoon; there is no ventilation. When it rains, everything is wet. And they tore down a beautiful school because of earthquaking to put this up. It's just horrible. The kids have to walk outside to go to the bathroom, to go down to lunch. I open the door and you get a bucket of water on your head. And the student traffic comes through here to get to other classrooms and interrupts what we're doing all the time. This whole area was without walls last year so you'd have Chinese and Spanish languages all going through the air at the same time. Now last year, I was downstairs in a beautiful classroom but I'm being punished. It was an administrative decision to put special ed. here even though everyone on the staff said this would be the worst room for me because of that constant student traffic that has to cut through here to get to the bilingual classrooms. Special ed. does need a certain amount of privacy to not have their attention taken away . . .

Even you would know that and you would think the principal would know that too — that you don't put special ed. in a room that is being constantly interrupted by changing classes. (Laughter)

"But the biggest problem in education in general is not enough funding. And I think everyone should be more aware of what's going on in education. Here we are in California, in an area that's all the Silicon Valley; we should have a computer in every room and the training for everyone to use it. They should just have available what's here, and for the richest country in the world? These kids shouldn't have to eat slop in the mornings and the afternoon. They should be concerned about the holistic child — what they eat, what exercise they get, if they're happy. Because, before these kids are going to start learning, they're going to have to be well fed; they're going to have to be a little bit relaxed so they can start focusing on their learning.

I tell people that what is good about public education is the children. You can see changes when you're affecting their lives. And that's real rewarding. And I think that most of the teachers that I know are very caring and work their asses off to do things. And on the whole, they're very wonderful people. And the kids and the teachers really are what make the difference. I have kids who see things in their lives, things that no kid should ever see. I have a kid whose father is in jail for murder, and I think a lot of the kids have learning problems because of drug dependent mothers. Most of the grade school kids that I have here know what alcohol is, know what drugs are; they know the terms; they know what it is. We even have the pre-schoolers lining up the chalk during lunch in little lines and pretending they're snorting it. In my class I'd say seventy percent use drugs or alcohol. These are fourth and fifth graders. But we are doing something about it; we have a real strong drug program on. I think it does some good. For instance, today we talked about the effects of nicotine, and to know what it physically does to your body. I think when kids are aware of that, then they start thinking about it. I remember when we were growing up, there was no campaign about not smoking so I got started. But then my sister who was ten years younger came through school, and I remember her always doing things like taking my mother's cigarettes and throwing them away or hiding them because she was made aware at school that this could kill you. And children today don't want their parents to smoke, and it teaches the children not to smoke.

"But there are negatives. I was once involved in trying to contain two boys larger than I was and I got pretty hurt. I had a black and blue mark on my back from one end to the other. These were just boys who cannot control their own behavior; this was in my room. In the last two years, of kids in my grade school class, I've had two kids accused of rape. I had one of the students accused of rape just last week. I had the principal come in to me at five till eight when we start at eight and say to me, 'Bob raped someone in your room during recess.' And then she turned around and looked at me and said, 'Have a nice day.' Can't you just die?! They called the police and it was investigated. The kid's a trouble maker; his father's the one in prison. He masturbates in class when he thinks no one is watching. I know what he's doing but the other kids aren't aware of it.

What do you do? 'Bob, you're not on task.' (Laughter) If you can't laugh . . . ."

(Do you think public education works?)

"Yes."

(Would you teach again?)

"Yes. I came back to teaching; I like teaching. I would like to get paid more and I would like to have more respect from the administration, but I know if we had a different administrator that things would be better here. There's no question in my mind about that. I stay here because I feel like I'm doing something worthwhile; you know — I am a child of the 60s. I want things to change. And if they're going to change, then I'm going to have to go out and change them. The only way that we're going to have equal rights and less wars are by teaching children some morals and teaching them that they're ok. I may leave and come back to it. I'm not sure I want to stay in the same area. I like taking breaks . . . but I'll come back.

"Today, one of my kids said, 'Gee, when you smile, it's so nice, and we really like you.' Just for them to know — I think that's one of the nicest things."

Section 5:

STUDENTS TO TEACHERS

When I first started teaching, I thought I'd teach for thirty years straight through at the same high school and then get out when I was fifty-three and open a book store . . . actually at twenty-three, I wasn't thinking I'd live that long, but that was what I planned to do if I did. In those days I tended to give my loyalties easily. But in talking to students who were preparing to be teachers and first and second year teachers and then finally those ready to retire, it all hit home how cynically I'd changed from the new teachers and yet how incapable I was of stoic shoulder-shrugging like the retiring teachers.

Probably some of the new teachers have it right — things are not right! Probably some of the retiring teachers have it right — what can you do? Oh, to be old enough or young enough to not be schizophrenic . . . .

I didn't learn anything in education courses in college, and certainly nothing about teaching. How can colleges train teachers? Look at what they think should be a teacher — publishers! And yet, young people with lots of idealism and arm loads of desire to do something in the world are still going into education colleges and are still not learning anything. It was amazing to me that none of these teachers-to-be really considered money at all in making the decision to be a teacher. I sincerely doubt that raising salaries, especially the little bit we can realistically expect to raise teacher salaries, will attract any better people into the profession. Those who are going to be good teachers did not consider money when making that decision to begin with. I do think that some kind of teacher-intern idea would be good, starting teachers out like the medical profession starts doctors out — paying them enough and teaching them enough on the job. You best learn to teach from teaching . . .

Tape #106

Ms. B. had muted idealism. She had graduated from a fairly prestigious Eastern university with a degree in English, and she had returned to her large hometown in the Midwest to get certified to teach high school English. As a grad student, she was twenty-two and had about one more year of classes to go before she could be certified. She hadn't student taught yet, but she had done some classroom work as an observer at a public school. She rarely looked at me as she talked, and I was amused by her too short (very contemporary) hairstyle. But what she said gave evidence to a lot of thought and a great deal of sincerity. Though she dressed and looked like a high school student of the time, she talked like someone who, with a modicum of experience, might harden into a good teacher.

Ms. B. had muted idealism . . . perhaps the right compromise to reality at that point in her teaching career, the very beginning.

"Well, there are a lot of reasons to teach. I come from a background of teaching. My mother was a teacher and I kind of grew up with that. I thought it was neat, teaching people how to do new things. And it was special. What my mother did for those children was really special because she gave them something that they didn't have and that they didn't get from anyone else. That's one reason. Another reason is that quest for a career or whatever. I was looking for something that would help me continue to learn, pay the bills, and satisfy something in me that needed to give to other people. And finally, I'm good at it. I'm good at communicating that way. I'm good at getting other people to think about things. And you have to go with what you're good at.

"I absolutely cannot imagine going into business or something like that, just to make a lot of money. I mean that's the only motive, as far as I can see, that people have, you know. I mean maybe you care about whether P&G makes a better soap or whatever, but I can't believe that you can really think that that's important."

(Was money an issue for choosing this career?)

"No, it wasn't. A guy approached me about a job starting at 22,000 dollars the other day. But you can't change yourself. It was to be a promotion manager for this large piano production company. But I just don't see the point of raising the sales records for pianos.

"In a way I think that probably students will see me too much on their level. I had a discussion with a friend who teaches, about whether or not I should change my hairstyle and how I dress. And she said she didn't think I should. I questioned things like that, but I don't want to change who I am. It was interesting. When I taught a lesson at the school where I was observing, I had one response from a student who wrote and said, 'Well, I really felt lousy that day so I didn't really pay that much attention to you.' But she said, 'I loved your haircut.' So yeah, I think there's a problem with them seeing me too much as one of them. And I'm really going to have to guard against that. I'm going to have to guard against things like — like I can't get used to being called Miss _____. I mean really. And cussing, oh my god, I have a very foul mouth. I have to really change that. And letting them cuss, you know, that kind of stuff. But I didn't respect most of my high school teachers, some [of them]. You know, it's — it was their apathy, in a lot of ways, their apathy toward me. And sometimes it was just their general incompetence. My chemistry teacher was just incapable of explaining anything. And you would go in after school, for help or whatever, and he still couldn't explain it. He couldn't. He wasn't a good teacher. He didn't deserve my respect. And you know, that's what I want. That's what I want, is their respect, more than I want them to like me.

"And I think it's important for teachers to understand who the student is, and I think that it's important for teachers to understand that, even though they know who the student is, it may make no difference in what they're able to do. And I think it's important for teachers to understand that even though they know who the student is, they may not get to attend to all of the [things] . . . that you can't do as much as you might want and that you have to accept your limitations in terms of your effect on someone else's mind."

(Would you say that you had muted idealism?)

"Is that what you'd say? Is that the term? I don't know. Yeah, I guess. I don't know. I think I'm a little more — I think *real* muted idealism. Almost non-idealism. Part of it has to do with things that I've thought through as a person, a large part of it. Part of it has to do with things I've seen in teaching. Part of it has to do with things I see in society, that we can't seem to get along. I'm starting out jaded, really, instead of ending up that way."

(Maybe you'll come out idealistic.)

"That would be nice."

Tape 106B

Toward the end of this school year Ms. B. was given the chance to teach full time for the last twelve weeks of the school year, even though she hadn't student taught yet and wasn't certified. A long-term sub for a pregnancy leave teacher was driven out by five low level classes. Ms. B. took over and succeeded. I thought it might be interesting to see how she felt about teaching after she had done it for a sample period.

(Was there anything that you found different after having taught for twelve weeks?)

"Well, I expected administration to be more helpful than it was."

(On your original tape you said that a principal should be a "maintainer and a PR person.")

Well, this principal certainly was a PR person. But as a maintainer I thought he did a lousy job. I had better luck with the assistant principal. I had lower level classes mostly. And they were ninth and tenth graders and the ninth graders especially were very, very squirrelly and there were discipline problems, that kind of thing, and the assistant principal followed up with those. And he was good about that, about following up and helping me with the kids and that kind of stuff. But as far as the education part of it — I was given no guidance at all. I think the thing that I found most surprising was how much I was left alone. I was not observed until I had been there six or seven weeks; no one oriented me to the school; no one told me what to do. I was handed a key and a stack of books and just kind of left there. The principal didn't even speak to me — I mean, I was introduced briefly to him when I was hired, but he didn't speak to me until I had been there three or four weeks and even then he didn't observe me. I was hired with twelve weeks left in the school year and I was non-certified personnel at that time. And I had never taught before; my experience in the schools had been limited. I certainly wouldn't have trusted me!

"One of my biggest complaints about the job and I'm afraid one of my biggest complaints about teaching in general is going to be the isolation. I think it's true that the other teachers were just so busy that they didn't have time. You're trapped in your room — well, not trapped, that's a bad way to put it — but you're in your room and you have kids there from A to Z basically and you have about fifty-two minutes off during the day and that's all the time you have to prepare your materials for the next day. You could spend fifty-two minutes waiting in line for the copy machine!

"And I ended up not having even really that fifty-two minutes. There was a problem with my classes. There were certain kids who were incapable of being in a group setting and functioning. I did not want these kids to be thrown out of class, and so I went to the counselors but there really was no other class to move them into. So what the counselors decided to do was to move them into my conference mods. I had three kids who ended up doing that. Two of them were moved into my conference mods and one of them into my duty mods — now, I was on hall duty; the counselors decided all of this and I more or less agreed to it — well, friends tell me because I'm stupid! But it was because I really didn't want to see these kids get thrown out of class. And two of them definitely were worth the trouble. But what it meant was that I had basically seven classes every day. And in my conference mods I had a ninth grader and a tenth grader so sometimes I would have to teach two lessons in there. So I had kids in my room all day long."

(Do you think they were kind of taking advantage of you because you were young or just a substitute for twelve weeks?)

"I don't know. I would like to think not, but yes, I'm sort of drawn to that conclusion. Except for that — I allowed it . . . "

(Do you think a ten year veteran would have said yes to giving up their conference mod?)

". . . no. I don't think that most of the people who have been around a long time in that school would do much to acquiesce to the higher ups."

(What about the amount of work you put into it?)

"The amount of work I put into it was phenomenal. I was basically, like I said, handed a copy of the books and the curriculum and no help. I just really had to do a lot of homework, and especially at this level, you not only have to think about the material itself, but you have to think about how to get it to them. You have to translate everything onto a level where they can understand these concepts. So I think the workload is incredible. It's much much more than a forty hour a week job. And my kids had lots and lots of small assignments so there was grading all the time.

"But I have no regrets. I didn't take the job offer I had in business . . . even though the pay would have been much more. I have no regrets. I'm really convinced that this — teaching — is in the right area, that it's meaningful. I'm convinced about that. And that was confirmed for me in teaching, even with the kids being unmotivated, even with the support I didn't get from the administration, even with the isolation, it was confirmed for me that that was a good area for me to be in. I still can't imagine going into a business position and going for no other reason other than to collect a paycheck."

(Do you feel that this twelve weeks of teaching made you want to be a teacher more or made you want to be a teacher less?)

"Well, that depends on the day that you talked to me. No, I would say it made me want to be a teacher more, but I'm more disheartened about things. You know, I was fairly realistic going in."

(Non-idealistic I believe was your term . . .)

"Well, I may have made that transition from non-idealistic to quite a bit cynical. It's difficult to teach kids who are not motivated. And you are never going to motivate them completely, which means that every day you go in and you listen to — 'This is so boring,' etc., etc. And I think that that just wears you down."

(Do you think that you've accomplished much with the kids that you had?)

"Well, I suppose if you think of *much* in a relative way. I accomplished a little bit with each of them. And I think a little bit is enough with those kids. But I think that you just have to accept that you're not going to change their lives with the hours that you spend with them."

Section 6:

FIRST AND SECOND YEAR TEACHERS

Tape #143

Ms. C. was twenty-three and in her second year of teaching at the fifth grade level. She had a sweet smile and a lot to say about the evaluation process being tried at that time in her state, a perfect example of educational bureaucracy. Why are teachers getting out or not doing the work as ordered? No other career has had so many attempts to regiment it lately. People don't seem to realize a good teacher is an artist . . . and you can't regiment artistry.

"If I were working in say a bank, instead of teaching, I'd be working with adults. They're not as flexible as children are. You can change routine with children more easily than you can with adults, and they're all right; they'll go with you. Where if you go into a bank and you say, 'Hey, let's try this,' they're going to say, 'I'm sorry, that's not the way we do it. We do it this way.'

(Do you feel as a teacher you have more control over what you do during the day?)

"Right now I do not. I'm on probation. I'm on effective teacher training so I have no control at all. I have three, at least, observations a year by a team of my principal, a master teacher, and a member of the central administration. They come in and they rate you on about fifty different points. They stay for about an hour and they're supposed to draw up a plan of action for you to work on certain things. And then they come back the next time and see if you've improved those, and then they pick another small section for you to work on. It just started last year. They're trying to put it in the schools so that all teachers are on it every year, the same evaluation. Last year I was about the only person in my school on it and this year there are about fifteen on it. Last year nobody said anything; this year there are a lot of people angry.

"One thing they're angry at is that they can't always guarantee that the supervisor you get from central administration is always the supervisor in the field that you're teaching in. So you've got someone coming in that may or may not know what you're doing. Another thing is that there's no flexibility in this point system. You have to have everything in it; you can't deviate at all or you're graded down. It limits you as to your flexibility and your changing things around. You have to have a very set lesson. Veteran teachers are trying to get it stopped. They don't think it's a fair evaluation of what kind of teacher you are; they're saying that different methods work for different students. Maybe you have a class that needs something very structured, for which this system works fine. But if you have students like I do, where some are really very upper class students and some are from low income families where there is no money, you have to resort to other things than 'you have to do it because you're going to need it when you get to college.' But I still have to stick to their system.

"I don't give it five years. It works the teacher to the point where — I go to work at eight o'clock in the morning and I work until five and I take work home. You have to have boards up constantly, immediate feedback on paperwork . . . everything has to be almost perfect. It takes you four days to prepare for one observation for an hour. And technically they're expecting you to teach six hours like this so you can imagine preparing to teach a whole day. You'd have to start three years before you got out of college (laughter) just for preparing to teach a year! I think the ideas are fine, but it doesn't work this way. Everything has been proven by re-search, but what works in a research setting doesn't necessarily work in the classroom.

"If you get along with the master teacher involved, it helps. Mine was just across the hall. And part of it is personality. Before this all started, I had gone to her and said, you know — 'What do I do, what do I do, what do I do?' And she had helped me so I felt calm with her. And I can take criticism from her because before she mentions it to me she tries it in her classroom. So I feel like it's ok. But the problems come with the principals and administrators who have been out of the classroom for years, and, unfortunately, usually the master teacher's observations are pushed aside nine times out of ten. Because mine — my master teacher — has come back several times and said, 'I told them that wouldn't work and I want you to know that off the record but' — it's almost like a majority rules situation.

"I didn't feel too threatened by all this because I got very high ratings across the board; and because they have a schedule they have to stick to, I never got a plan, ever. So I figured if it came down to it, I could raise a big ruckus — I never got told anything so how can [they] take my job away? And the more people I talk to who are on it, very few plans are being written. We have to do things on time; administrators don't. It did make my first year of teaching miserable, though. There's lots of pressure. And the fact that I don't have a certificate . . . when you graduated, starting in 1985 down here, you did not get a state certificate. You were issued a temporary certificate. You have to teach two years and pass this thing to get a state certificate which means that technically I could work for six years, four years of college and two years of teaching, and then be told — 'Sorry. That's it. You blew it. Trash it.' I think you need to do something freshman and sophomore years of college. Have students who are interested in education go into a classroom earlier. Who wants to trash four years of time? Even if you find that you're not really thrilled with it, you feel obligated to continue with it. And with a tenured teacher — well, you'd have to slap a child across the face and have fifteen witnesses before they could get rid of you no matter the evaluation.

"Other things that made my first year of teaching negative? Well, you were expected to know everything about your subject matter. And I was trained kindergarten through sixth grade. So there was no way I could walk in on the first day and be completely competent to teach everything. I mean, it took a lot of extra work on my part just to keep up with the class. I was like one week ahead of them in every subject. And I was surprised at how much basic math you forget when you're in college. I mean, who finds common denominators and factors? You have to just about relearn everything. I was also shocked at the amount of pull that parents have. You know — 'I want my child in the gifted program.' 'Well, your child is making B's.' 'Well, I'm sorry, but I want my child in the gifted program.' The next thing you know, the child is being moved. I guess I didn't realize how much pressure parents could pull. There are other more stupid examples like — 'My child didn't get on safety patrol.' And I'm like, 'Well, I'm sorry. It was a girl's turn last month and a boy's this. And you know I have twenty-four other students.' And they got all bent out of shape. The next thing I know, I'm putting the girl on safety patrol to get her mother off my back.

"And then there are meetings that you have to go to. 'We've got a meeting; we've got a meeting.' It's your planning period: 'we have a meeting.' That and no time — no time for anything. I'd say almost every hour that I'm not sleeping or eating I'm working on school work. My husband's having fits. He's been known to do bulletin boards at night. It's either that or never see me; you have to work together on the bulletin boards. If they keep the evaluations the same, it will always be this busy . . . either that or I'll quit. I've considered it. Because of the amount of work and the pressure. And I feel that with the amount of work and the years of education I have, I'm not getting anything in return. I'm getting things from the children, but not — you know, when you go out and people say you do *what,* you're a teacher? You do what? I had a friend of my husband talking about some — poor person — who was cashing his paycheck and he said the amount and I just kind of looked at him and said, 'I make less than that.' He didn't even know. I don't know; you're kind of put down.

"It's not the work, though; it's the pressure. I love what I do; I love the kids. But I have more work. I have so much paper-pushing work. I spend more of my time doing paperwork than I do actually teaching. Not in the class — but in all the time I put into it. If the situation stays the same for the next couple of years, I'll either get out or I'll just quit caring and doing all that. I'd be like a lot of other teachers I watch — all burnt out. In fact, my principal had me take a sick day because he told me I was getting burnt out. And I'm a second year teacher.

"I see a lot of burnt out teachers, but still ninety-five percent are good. Burnt out doesn't necessarily mean a bad teacher. They're just putting those almighty checks on the papers instead of looking at every one. They're pushing paper, just pushing paper. But I'd say they're good teachers one on one or in the classroom. There, they're honestly going to the limit for the children. It's the paperwork and the planning. A lot of the good teachers know what they're going to do when they go in there, but whether they've written it down with an objective and all that . . . that's what I have to do. But I think a really good teacher can do without all that written work and be just as good as someone who writes it all down. So I'm saying, they've quit with paperwork.

"But *we're* trying to hold it all together. I don't care what the child needs; you get it for him. If a child comes to school with no food, you see that he gets lunch. You hold together the parts that are falling apart. We have a 'brush your teeth' program. We have lunches and breakfasts offered. I know of teachers who themselves have bought crackers from the lunchroom or from the lounge to give to children. I also know of teachers who have bought clothes. If they don't have a warm coat for winter, they bring one in or they actually *buy* them. So I think we fill in a lot of the empty space. It puts a lot of strain on teachers; it takes away from your teaching time."

(If you were back in your college career and you knew then what you know now about teaching, would you still become a teacher?)

"Yes, I'd just trash the memos."

Tape #272

"I like to teach, but I hate to babysit."

Ms. G. was exceedingly thin and admitted that teaching for her first year had been much more of a strain than she had imagined. She repeated several times that she didn't know if she had the emotional stamina to put up with it every day. But she was teaching all low level classes and all English when she really wanted to be a history teacher. She was teaching grades nine and eleven in a fairly rural high school. What good school district would give a first year teacher all low level classes . . . what good school district would give any teacher all low level classes?

The year before she had worked as a campus minister at the university from which she had graduated. She was twenty-four and single.

I felt Ms. G. was in the most realistic situation of the new teachers I interviewed and was the most honest. The first year of teaching is hell; education colleges hardly prepare you; administrators rarely help you . . . and most don't know how.

"[One] thing about teaching which unpleasantly surprised me was that it was so exhausting. I was physically sore all over for like the first two or three weeks. It was hard to student teach but then you knew there was an end to it. I was like — I have nine months of this? It's tiring and I resent bringing my work home and all of my other friends who are professionals like pharmacists and things — they don't bring their work home. And I've been tutoring pregnant girls mainly because I need the money — they were offering ten dollars an hour and that's more than I make teaching.

(Laughter) I think I'm making $14,400 for the 6/7th's pay. It would be $16,000 if it were full time. That sounds like a lot to me . . . and then I make $1,200 coaching, which is a joke. My friend the pharmacist started at $33,000 the first year . . . .

And I was unpleasantly surprised by the students' real apathy. I guess being the good little student, I should not project myself onto everybody else, but I can't believe the kids care that little. If they pass — if it's a 69.9 and it's passing — that's ok and they don't care about doing anything better. This idea of just getting by which I've heard from so many of my students — I thought, this attitude is just ingrained in them and I thought when they go to work they'll do the same thing. One day when I was real mad at them I told them this was why an auto plant in the next town was closing — these people had the same attitude and had the highest absenteeism of any car plant in the nation! They just wanted to get by. It's just no pride in their work. Not much seems to work on them; I've kind of run to the end of my ideas. I've used lyrics from rock songs and I've had them work in groups and work with each other's writing and reading plays aloud. Sometimes each of those will work once but it won't change the whole thing, you know? I'll have a good day and the next day will be horrible even though I did something really good that day. Now, I'm like — let's just get through this year! Then I'll think of something great and wonderful."

Section 7:

READY TO RETIRE

Tape #103

Ms. L. had been successful in elementary education for almost forty years when I talked to her; after a few minutes of conversation it was easy to see why. She was retiring at the end of the year, but she spoke in her peppy way about starting out at $2,200 a year (while her husband started at $2,600 because he was a man) and about the changes she'd seen throughout her career. She was sixty, widowed, and heading for retirement with grace and personality. It was easy to see that she was comfortable with herself.

(How have you survived forty years of teaching?)

"With a great deal of tears. laughter, a few children along the way who have made it worthwhile, a very patient, forebearing husband, wonderful friends, and after twenty-five years saying, 'Well, I've gone this far, I might as well go the rest of the way.'

(How did you get into teaching?)

"Well, at my time of life when I was a young woman, there were no real options for women. Secretarial work, work in the dime store, work in the grocery store, teach, be a nurse. That was it, unless you wanted to go into the theater, which was frowned on in my family. And aside from that, there really wasn't much of a choice for women other than getting married and having children, having a home. I was not interested at that point in time in being married. And my father probably was the biggest factor in my decision. He said, 'I want you to find a profession that no matter what happens to you in your life, you'll have as good a preparation to support yourself as possible.' He was a wise enough man to make sure that I understood what he meant. And it's paid off, because it has been a success. And I have been able to support myself, so — very adequately. I love it.

"But there seems to be less dedication on the part of young teachers. It's more of a job. Commitment is gone. Eight o'clock here; three o'clock gone. And there's less dedication to the teaching profession as a whole, for instance, teachers' unions. It's been very difficult for us more veteran teachers to say to them, 'Hey, look, we struggled through all of this and you're reaping the benefits, so how dare you not pay your dues and how dare you not make a commitment to our teaching profession, and declare and swear that you are one.' And I'm pretty successful with that, because I just say if you worked the hours I did when I first began teaching . . . if you had to go to the school board and the superintendent and say what you have to offer them . . . and if they smile at you for a moment and said here is the salary, you have no bargaining, you had to accept whatever they offered and be glad you got it. And they were very, very, very — what's the word I want which means *patronizing*. Not *patronizing*. Paternal, that's the word I want. *Paternal*. And, 'Well, your husband works, why should you expect . . . .' I did the same type of job, but I didn't get as much money."

(They decided salaries depending upon the person they were hiring?)

"Yes, indeed. And the number of years of experience that you had in teaching.

"And I see a great change in the children. I see a lack of responsibility on the part of the parents. And whether that is due to the fact that we have a generation of people right now who are having to work, both parents having to work, or whether it's just a — perhaps a feeling that — 'I don't want to alienate my children' — I don't know what it is. I can't put my finger on it, but there is something there that the children are very much more sophisticated than children of twenty years ago.

"There is a difference in the respect of teachers. As I said, the kids are more sophisticated. Their parents allow them to speak more as adults and are expected to, I think. Their language, the whole demeanor of our sixth graders is more like the teenagers of, say fifteen or twenty years ago. My first class of teaching was in the first grade. And my first graders that I had then were nothing like the class I had six or seven years ago. I would not have even recognized the same type of child. I would have expected to see that way of behavior and that attitude of perhaps — second or third graders. Their total realm, their way of behavior is totally different, much more grown up. They know a lot about drugs. They know a lot about sex that I didn't know even when I was a teenager.

"I believe that in our country in general in the last maybe fifteen years or ten years the general populace has less respect for education in general. That's a problem. Because those of us who've been at it a long time, worked hard at it, tried to make it a good experience for children, have never shirked one thing, and yet we get lumped with those that don't. I resent that. That's a problem, to me.

"Teaching has never been accepted. Even back in the old days, teaching was not looked upon with a great deal of respect. In our history, as you well know, the first teachers were masters. And then unmarried young women with very little education. And people who respected the idea of learning, they wanted their children to learn. But the teacher came and went with the wind. And the populace in general were never willing to put out the money that it would take to have a quality person. If a business wants quality people, they go out and they look for quality people and they pay them commensurate with their quality. I feel like I'm a quality teacher. And for the first time in my life, now that I'm ready to retire, I'm earning what I'm worth. And now I'm ready to quit.

"My first salary was $2,200 a year in 1948. My husband's first job, because he was a man, was $2,600. It was a fortune to us then. Of course we couldn't figure out why we didn't have enough money. You know, we were stupid enough to think that we could get along on it. And he finally decided that he had to have another job. There were a lot of times he worked two jobs.

(If I had asked you five years into your teaching career what you thought the problems of education were, would you have had different answers then?)

"Back then I would, yes. Back when I first began, teaching was very exciting to me. Children came to school, they were calm, well ordered, well disciplined. You didn't have the problems — maybe one or two, but not a whole room full of problems. You didn't have a lot of emotional problems. But you had almost a lethargy. Children who were — 'okay, I have to go to school, mommy says I have to come to school, I need to be here.' And they worked at it, but there wasn't the excitement. And that was one of the things that bothered me, because I felt like teaching is fun and I always stirred my kids up about it every time. And we got into a lot of trouble. Because — yeah, I was supposed to be — well, quiet! Quiet classroom. And it just didn't fit with my idea of the whole idea of education. So that was the problem then. I was trying to stir things up, where everybody else was trying to keep it quiet. The time in which I grew up and the time which I first began teaching was a very placid time. It was right after the second world war and people were content. Their husbands and boyfriends had come home; they had gotten married; they'd bought a little house; everybody was settling down into a kind of a nice, comfortable, lethargic atmosphere. There was a slight rate of inflation that kind of scared people, but it eased off. And the children were very calm, because the families were calm. They had had enough excitement for four and a half years, enough worries, and they were glad enough to be static. And the children reflected that. So I think that was the problem then, I guess, if you could call it a problem. Today . . . it seems to be the reverse . . ."

(From forty years to now, have you been given more and more things to do as a teacher?)

"Yes. Yes. I would not have had to dust my room. I would not have had to wash my own blackboard. I would not have had to spend my own resources. I would not have had to do lunchroom duty. I would have had time to call my own when it was time to eat lunch. I would have had at least one time during the day to be free of the children. I mean, they get tired of me. I had a great deal more control over my curriculum when I first began teaching than I have now. I had the option of selecting from a set group of series what I wanted to use. It was within certain parameters, of course. But each teacher was allowed to select whatever reading series they chose to use, whichever they felt comfortable with. They were all related. Now back in those days the reading books had more or less the same general vocabulary. So it was easy to shift over, say, from one publisher to another. There were three publishers who were pretty much the same as far as their vocabulary, that you could shift from one book into another. I felt it was more effective to have the teachers have that choice because each teacher's style is different. No two people teach the same thing in the same way. I had read everything in the teacher's manual; then I did my own thing within the directives of whatever was going on in that particular skill development. The stories were far more interesting than they are now. The vocabulary was much more difficult. There was a great deal less stress on picking apart a story than there was on — what about this story, what did it make you think of. There was more a thinking type of thing going on. The development of the stories were such that you got the kids' interest, got them excited about it, and then they wanted to read it. I don't find that what I'm having to use right now is particularly suitable or exciting or interesting."

(Do you have much choice in what you use now?)

"No, I think teachers have lost a lot of control because of testing of kids. I think that there's been a genuine effort to upgrade, of course. But again, education slipped so slowly into this state that it's in right now that I don't think anybody [knew it was coming]. You suddenly woke up one day and you looked around and there it was. It snuck up on us. I guess that's the best word I can use. And it's different. It's just different."

(Competency testing for teachers?)

"Ok. Ok. I will be very frank with you. I can pass their competency testing for teachers, and I have done it. But that does not make me a good teacher. I know people who can pass that test with flying colors, and they couldn't teach a fly to walk up a wall. You're either a teacher or you're not. I believe that teachers are really born. I don't believe you learn how to teach when you go to college. You either know or you don't know. One of the aides at our school has to be, without a doubt, the best natural teacher I've ever seen and she's only a high school graduate. She has a sixth sense about children. She's a marvelous teacher."

(Does public education work?)

"Yes."

(Would you teach again?)

"No."

(What would you do?)

"I'd go against my mother's wishes and go into the theater. I dreadfully wanted to go into the theater and act . . . I might be famous!" (Laughter)

Tape #149

"Who wants a job where you have to mop up vomit on
your lunch hour?!"

*Ms. Q. was the quintessential grade school teacher. She had taught for
thirty years and was just doing it half time this year before permanent
retirement. She worked in the inner city of a Southern city and she was
filled with warmth and love. At fifty-one, after thirty years of teaching she
could still say, "We need enough money to make sure no child fails."*

*But she also had noted a future problem of education that few people
seem aware of; in the past women swarmed into teaching as one of the few
acceptable professions for women, and so the teaching profession often
got the cream of that crop. But that just isn't so now. Cream of the crop
women are going into medicine, law, and engineering now, and making
men's money.*

"When I started teaching thirty years ago, I really had no choice. If I
were living now, I'd never do it. There're so many good things happening
now for women to go into. I would have liked to go into something else in
the midst of my teaching career, but teaching is so specialized that the
other things that I would have wanted to do would have involved a lot of
going back to school. And I was really too good at what I was doing at the
time to change, but I really wanted to. I loved what I did; I love what I do
now. But I would have loved to have done something else.

"Teachers are leaving today and I think that if you're intelligent, and
you're doing a good job at it, and you have no more control than we have
. . . then it would be easy to leave. For instance, still in the schools, you
have to get permission from your principal to leave the building. I think
also that teachers should participate more in the decision making. I think
there is a great wealth of information there and although teachers are
busier than the devil, once you got them together, there would be a great
wealth of information there to use; teachers on the whole are pretty smart
people. Why don't administrators do that? Because most teachers are
women . . . number one. Schools are controlled by a man, usually an older
man. We need to get more dynamic younger women into education to
change that old blood. The only problem with that is I don't think we're
going to get those women in. Let me give you an example.

"When I went to college, there was a class of maybe two, three, four
hundred women. And they said at the first assembly — everyone who was

president of your class . . . raise your hand. And hands from just everybody everywhere went up in the air. Then they said, everyone who was the president of their honor society raise their hand; and hands everywhere went up. And it went on like this — all the intellectual and leadership things were there. You know, this is it. The last student teacher I had, I had to teach her how to speak grammatically correct English before she could talk to my class. What goes into teaching now is not the top of the class; women can go into other colleges now.

"I think a lot of it is salary. The starting salaries are so low and then they just don't progress. And then you don't have any say-so about what you do. You don't have any say-so about would it be possible to buy more books to read. Or could I carpet my room because it stops the noise? You have no say-so about your surroundings, the physical areas. You have no say-so about what you teach, as far as textbooks go. There are some creative things that you can do in the classroom; don't get me wrong, but then — who wants a job where you have to mop up vomit on your lunch hours?! Who wants that kind of job! Do you want to clean up vomit and then go back in and eat your lunch? So, all right, there are things like that that make it unappealing. If you don't get the money up there, what's going to get the bright and young to think about it? My generation of women went into teaching because there weren't that may other options for us. So education got some of the brightest and the best, but if more money isn't put into it . . . it's going to go downhill. Absolutely.

"Also, we're going to have to make some changes for the community. Oh, there's a change between what people think of teachers now and what they used to think of them. I can give you a concrete example. The first year I taught school was up in the mountains and the people were, by and large, very, very poor. But when Christmas came, I had a Christmas present from every child. Now one of them was a jar of homegrown green beans. One of them was something that a roach crawled out of — but I had a present from every child. And it was a present given with love, roach or not. It was a present given with sincerity. At that time I had a *box* full of things to carry home and a box full of notes to write. The last year I taught school, I could have carried everything home in less than a grocery bag. Our children here have a lot more money, but I could have carried the whole lot home in a grocery bag and could have replaced any one of them for a dollar ninety-eight. That shows something.

"When I first started teaching, I would go to parties — and I didn't look a thing like this (smile) — and people would walk up to me and ask me,

'Now what do you do?' And I would say, 'I teach school,' tickled to death. About fifteen years ago, I began to go to nice places and not tell anyone what I do. Because of the public's perception of teachers — 'not very bright, couldn't get another job, didn't have very much initiative' — and you know, I'm *none* of those."

(With those perceptions of teachers, would you go into teaching now?)

"Honey, I'd be the cutest thing in high heeled shoes with an executive job. I would not be wearing old leather shoes and be equipped with a smock.

"But you know, I don't think it's the basic child-teacher relationship, but the child-parent. I had a little girl hug me today and she was sick; she should have stayed home. And I told her — tomorrow would be better. And I think the major reason for all that is we've got too many working mothers and not enough people taking care of their kids. I mean I've got parents who are of course single, parents who are divorced, if they were ever married, and she's got a car that has to have the payments paid and there are things that have to be worked on on it and then there are these children who have to be taken care of after work, and her job isn't in that great shape anyhow, and then there's a husband over there who isn't paying the child support, and the kids need a certain kind of shoes to wear and there are ages when it's very important for the child to have a certain kind of food to eat — so you see . . . they can't win. They have no time for their kids.

"What do I think is the largest problem in public education? Defective children. Before I came here, I was talking to a little kindergarten boy whose mother is divorced again and living with her third fella. There's also a little sister and their step-daddy abused them. They are right now in their third apartment this year. Before they moved to where they are now, the child was told that there were murders happening outside and then the child was left alone at night while the mother went off to work. And this little boy — he acts like he is enraged . . . enraged. And every now and then he needs to be calmed, and I'm old so I know how to do that. He needs to be hugged. Unfortunately, he has a younger teacher now and she doesn't know that you can stop and love them instead of — putting them out in the hall. She doesn't realize that that child is just in need of attention. I'm old and I can see that.

"The problem in the future is that there aren't going to be enough people who want to teach. We're just going to go out there and register them. There's a crowd of people my age who are getting out. The next three years all of my friends are going to be out, and we're going to have a *good* time! (Laughter) No more mopping! And they'll fill our spots. But with people who are qualified? No.

"There are people in there doing their job . . . that are loving them every day. There are people in there who are teaching every day, who are going a world beyond the call of duty for a lot less money than they deserve. There are people in there who are loving and caring and giving and accepting."

(If I were much younger and I were just coming into teaching and I knew you'd taught for thirty years, what would you say to me?)

"I'd say — John! Are you sure? (Laughter) That's exactly what I'd say. I don't think that the best and the brightest are going into teaching anymore. They don't want to. And you know if you go to work in industry and I go into teaching, although your job won't be near as interesting as mine, status-wise and payment-wise it's better . . . and you don't have to mop at lunch either!"

Tape #2

Ms. H. was speaking at the end of thirty years of teaching. She had, a few weeks before her interview, just taught her last class, been feted by her department and district, and watched the last teenager walk out of her room. "I have always said that when teaching became more of a chore than a joy, I would get out of it." Still, as department chairman in the English department of a fairly large suburban high school, there were obligations to fulfill yet throughout the summer: book orders, curriculum corrections, and just cleaning out a room and a closet filled with the accumulations of thirty years of teaching. In the last fifteen years or so, she had taught mainly honors and advanced students, though she had also done her turns at summer school work. When she spoke, her voice was loud and clear, rasping nasally pronouncements. She leaned forward to talk and when she had a point to make, her voice got even louder. She sat under a lamp in someone's living room, her neatly coiffed but fading red hair glowing faintly.

She spoke of the attempt at changes in education and how ironically these great new innovations were usually just the "old hat" of the past. She intimated there were no solutions to public education's problems, at least no one solution.

"You know, there are no simple solutions in education because you need to have a specific problem to have a simple solution. Possibly the biggest thing that I can see is getting away from the concept that there is a panacea, that there is one handy-dandy solution for the problem. I think we have become very simplistic in education and we seem to believe in a miracle drug or that something is going to emerge, some technique that is going to catch all students and transform education. And I don't believe that. This has been one of our problems all the way along. And in the years I've been in education, shall we say, the particular panacea has changed. Very abruptly we have seen first of all the modern math. Sight reading when I was a kid was supposed to solve everything. Therefore I had to learn phonics to be sure I learned to read. Mastery learning is a new one that has come up. Competency testing is supposed to do something. But there *isn't* just one simple solution. It depends on what the problem is, and we have to apply a number of *different* solutions to solve anything. And if you say 'what is the one thing,' I can't say the one thing because I don't believe there is one solution. There need to be a variety of teachers to educate a variety of students. And that's why when you talk about master teachers, one has to smile a bit because you have to have all kinds of master teachers. I have known people to teach one way and have splendid success and maybe someone else to be —much more authoritative and use a lecture method and yet be so interesting and so fascinating that that can be successful. One person's style is not necessarily the other's and sometimes you have to modify your style and try different things if you're not getting to everybody.

"We've come around in circles since I started teaching. When I started, we were on a kick of see how fast the individual can progress at their own pace. I don't go for that because I don't believe that socially that's a good idea. And they were mainly interested in the academics. Then we went through a period where we were into the whole child development. We weren't going to rush the little kids. There was a time when you could learn. There was a reading readiness state, I think. And there was a period where you could handle math. Now I don't believe there is one period where you are ready to read. I had one of my own kids teach himself to read at three and another I had trouble getting him to read at seven. To say that there's one particular time, that's just not true. It will depend on the child. But we were very, very relaxed about things. Then when I started teaching, it was right after Sputnik and we were already getting hysterical because Russia was going to beat us out in space, and we got very, very academically inclined again, first in the science and the math and then the humanities came along. And in the 60s, the late 60s, early 70s, we began to figure this was all too much and we were going to be much more laid back as far as the school was concerned. We had pressure to ease up on the academics and to consider other things. We are seemingly back to basics movement now. Or at least we hear it a lot . . . we're not sure exactly what basics are. But anyway, it's been going around in a rather amusing circle and what is always so amusing is that we are always a little behind what is the advanced thinking of the time. So when you're usually innovating . . . we are frequently innovating something that was considered to be old hat twenty years ago. Normally these innovations are coming from — on high . . . and we're never too sure where the 'on high' is actually. Usually it's from curriculum hands or the school board or even parents groups . . . Some innovations are talked about in the school rooms, but usually [the teachers] are not the ones given a free hand to do it."

Section 8:

TEACHERS WHO QUIT

It's odd but the major reason people mentioned to me for getting out of education wasn't the pay — that was always the "accepted" second reason — as in, "Oh, yeah, there wasn't much money in it." It seems to me that administrators and not being treated as professionals came in as the number one reason to get out and get into the "adult world." I must admit that administrators do usually treat teachers as if they're dealing with just some more kids. Unfortunately, they're also seen that way by so much of society in general.

There is also a lot to be said for burnout as a reason for getting out of teaching; it's real; it's there. And lack of control adds to the burnout problem. Also, women teachers still often leave to raise families.

Tape #89

Mr. M. had been a former student of mine — my first year of teaching. I was somewhat saddened when he quit teaching after five years . . . but not surprised. I went to his new house, where he was feeding a two week old first child, to find out why he quit and what he thought about his experiences as a high school English teacher for five years in a very suburban district. He was still young-looking to me, his curly hair just a bit more conservatively cut than his student and teaching days of blatant hairiness. He also seemed thinner. For the last two years Mr. M. had been working as a technical writer in the business world. He was twenty-nine.

(Why did you decide to be a teacher when you did go into teaching English?)

"Well, I was inspired by this high school English teacher . . . (Laughter) No, I wanted to be a journalist. And I became very disillusioned with journalism, but I knew I wanted to stay in humanities or a related field. And I really hadn't thought about teaching much at all up to that point. But I guess that it was once I started taking linguistic courses, I knew that just being a literature teacher didn't really thrill me. But I liked the grammar and composition and linguistics . . . that's when I decided that I might be able to do something. This was all sophomore year in college. So when I came into the building as a new teacher and said I wanted all the grammar and comp. courses, they couldn't give them to me fast enough. I think I knew more about the techniques of teaching writing, etc., than they did. They were basically literature teachers who wrote well."

(What else attracted you besides the humanities idea?)

"Well, the salary . . . (Laughter) I think I was excited about the idea of working with kids. I had worked in some summer camps and things like that. I thought that would be really something. I liked the high school age kids. I think . . . at that point . . . I felt like teaching was regarded as sort of an average career to go into . . . all the altruistic people go into teaching or nursing, yeah . . . the flower children like you. But I think at that point it had lost some of the altruism as far as people's view of it. It was sort of like an average career to choose."

(What was the stuff behind your getting out of the career?)

"Reality. I can give you categories or anecdotes . . . Administrivia chased me away a lot. I just couldn't stand administrators and all the crap that went on. When I was thinking about leaving, if I went to one of the administrators . . . it's just the fact that there's nothing there . . . no image, nothing . . . nothing . . . no leadership from the administrators. It's the old — you heard when you screwed up and you didn't hear anything when you did well.

"One of the counselors thought she was doing everybody a huge favor one day. She was doing me a big favor, I guess, but not the way she wanted to. She was trying to give an in-service [workshop] during one of the faculty meetings about teachers and self-image and those sorts of things. And the way she did it was she had some overheads that had the average ACT scores for people in different professions. And doctors were like 29 composite and lawyers 26 . . . and engineers 23 or 24 . . . and teachers were 17. And I said, that . . . that's an average. You mean that's the average intellect I'm dealing with with professional colleagues.

"And then I looked around at some of the people that were teaching . . . and yeah! it was. I mean, there are some real bozos out there. That was just one situation that made me think that maybe I wanted to start trying to do something else. And at my high school I thought that fifty percent were good teachers . . . maybe a little less. I'd go lower nationwide. I mean, there were some really outstanding teachers at the school I taught at. There were some really, really outstanding people, some people I admire and who are still my friends. But there were some people that I really wondered why they were there. No, I know why — because they collected their paycheck every two weeks and they only had five more years to go.

"There's another anecdote for you. When I went to grad school, I came back to do some subbing. I was hard up for cash. Well, I walked into my old school and saw a guy I had known who was about twenty-five years along in his career. I said, how are you doing? And he said, 'Only got five more years, only got five.' And that was the way he began his mornings. And it shows in everything he does. That person shouldn't be teaching. That's like, a doctor would be accused of gross negligence for doing what he does. A lawyer too — they'd be disbarred. And I had this guy as a teacher when I was in high school. At that time he was competent. He was interested. I don't think he ever really understood the kids.

"What happens to a competent teacher to turn them into that? Lack of stimulation. It's a lack of intellectual stimulation on a professional level. They've got their basic knowledge set; they learn the curriculum they're required to teach and they just replay the tape recorder. And there *is* no motivation for them to be challenged. What difference does it make if — well, you get the master's degree, you move up a pittance on the pay scale. I think that after a while, that teachers learn not to care about challenging themselves, challenging their students. What difference does it make as long as they do what they're supposed to do. They're not going to get fired. I think tenure is most of it . . . but also they learn not to care because they're not supported. They go out on a limb for a student and they really have good intentions to help, and the parents come in and the administrators bow down and bend over backwards to parents. I can't even count how many times administrators backed down in instances that I knew were true or that I saw right with my own eyes, often with counselors playing advocate for students, counselors and special ability teachers, LD teachers and people like that.

"And money. When I left education after five years, went back to grad school and then went to work full time in a different profession in which

I had no experience other than my English-writing background, non-technical knowledge, they gave me four thousand dollars a year more starting out with no experience than I was making as a successful fifth year teacher, a supposedly qualified, competent professional with experience. That's not the 'A number one' reason why I left or why I'm still doing what I do, but in the place I work now, they tell you when you really do ok. And not only do they tell you, they reward you when you do ok, both monetarily and prestige and whatever those things are that float your boat. And they try and find them. I mean, education doesn't have the money to give nor have they figured out a way to get it to give, but not only do they not do that, they don't even do the stuff that's free. They don't compliment people. They also don't publicize themselves very well.

"I also feel more treated as an adult, by people who are — bosses — especially. Now, I never felt as treated as less than an adult by my colleagues in teaching, but I did by my administrators, counselors and parents, parents probably more than any of the others. In business, yeah — that's not the case. They may treat you like an adult they don't like, but they put you on a level as a peer. I felt like my principal talked to me, like about the newspaper room, telling me something *will* be done — like you would tell an eight year old to clean up his room and take his bath. And you know, from that point on the whole first year I taught, when the newspaper room stuff happened, I don't think I ever heard from the man again. And I guess I just don't miss the hassles. If you want file folders, pens, papers in education, it's like that stuff's gold. I mean — a pad of paper for this child's mind. You know!

"If you're going to put money into education, of course put it into teacher's salaries, but also put it into continuing education. I can't even believe that out here in the business world, they'll pay a thousand dollars for me to go to a class for two days to learn something which I may or may not ever use again. And when the NCTE [National Council of English Teachers] was in our city, we couldn't even get a personal day to go to it. Not that they were going to even pay for anything; they wouldn't let us off to go to it. It's ironic that education doesn't support education.

"I would go back to teaching, but the bottom line — number one is teacher salaries. You know I sat down and figured it out once . . . I wish I had the figures here with me. You know how people always say, 'Well, hell, you're a teacher — you only work nine months,' etc. I figured it out to days. Teachers don't work that much less than the rest of the world. It's like a month's worth of days different, but not like what we get paid compared to other people — listen to that *we* . . . . Anyway, it's not three-fourths or sixty percent or whatever. And if I went back into teaching at the level I left at, I'd be dropping back into the poverty level. I couldn't have any of this for my family. I couldn't support a family. You know, my wife would have to work just about full time. On a practical level, money is the major reason for not going *back* to teaching. On a professional level, I need some guarantee that I would be treated as a professional by administrators and by parents. See — it was all well and good when you were a coach — Coach M. was a lot more respected than Mr. M. Now isn't that funny? You know I hadn't really thought of it that way, but some of the same parents that would pump the hand and slap you on the back after you just won the sectional title would call you up and rip your face off if you gave their kid a C. If they start paying for good people in education, they'll get the good people; if they start treating them like good people, they'll keep the good people."

(What would you tell someone who wanted to go into education today?)

"What did you tell me? One word — *don't.* (Laughter) And I didn't listen."

Tape #252

Ms. P. was, she admitted, the type who couldn't sit still. I interviewed her in her living room after she had given her youngest son to her husband to sit with in another room. She had taught for eleven years, high school PE and then had left teaching almost five years ago to raise her two children, the oldest now almost five. But even now she can't stay away from teaching of some sort on at least a part-time basis — and she continues to coach high school tennis teams. At thirty-seven, and five years out of it, she admits that leaving teaching was the hardest decision of her life.

"Deciding to leave teaching to raise my kids . . . I would say that was the roughest decision that I have ever made. I had taught for eleven years. I would say that I probably had a year to decide — about five years ago — and I would say I probably thought about that decision every single day. I would discuss it with anybody. I talked to people who had kids, to people who didn't. I was tearful in the middle of the night. I mean — I think that basically I knew. I went to graduate school that June and I put it off for a whole year. But I think in June of that year, I knew that I couldn't go back full time. We had to put the baby with a sitter every day that summer because my husband taught summer school. It was just very, very difficult. And I said I'm not going to do this every single day for five plus years. I can't do that to myself. And it really didn't have anything to do with teaching. It didn't matter what profession; I just couldn't see me doing that to my kid. It was my decision to have them. I mean we thought seven years before we had kids. And that was part of it — do I want to leave my job. One day my husband said, 'Make up your mind and just write the letter — just do it,' he said. And I guess I just knew in my heart that that was what I had to do. My final reason was that I just didn't want to leave my kids . . . I would kill today for a part-time teaching job.

"I have four part-time jobs right now and every one of them is teaching-oriented. But it means one hour here, two hours there . . . and it's not consistent. It drives me crazy; my car's my office. And it's just very frustrating. I'm now working with from kindergartners to adults, though. That's one thing I have gained through my five years off. I have a really good perspective now on what I think teaching is about because of the ages. I teach private tennis lessons; I teach gymnastics K-5 at a clinic; I teach aerobics at a recreation department — and I still coach tennis. All of this is after school or evenings and Saturdays and Sunday mornings. And my husband teaches one night a week so we have to merge our schedules somehow and it's all driving us crazy. The energy level dwindles down eventually.

"I don't do it because I need the money; I do it for a lot of reasons. I do like having the extra money, but I do it to get out of the house — it's healthy for me to get out. I don't want to be channeled in the subdivision with all the ladies that babysit all the kids. I do it because I plan on going back into teaching as soon as my kids are back in school — if my energy level permits. And I have to do something for me. Nobody can understand that until you go through this. Until you go through this day after day. And I'm not saying my husband isn't a good father because he is, but he's not a Mr. Mom . . . and the kids need that. I say that I'll go back to teaching when my kids are older . . . I say that now, but I've got four more years left and I don't know if I'll have the energy level to do what they're expecting now — meaning six classes and extra activities after school and all the written evaluations."

(How much do you feel like you've sacrificed a career for a family?)

"A lot. I personally feel a lot. Because in the phys. ed. profession I personally feel I could not go back. They'd expect me to coach three varsity sports . . . which is what I was hired for. There is no way I could put in that time. And they're not going to hire me back because I'd have a master's degree, plus hours, plus eleven years of teaching. They can get a college kid of twenty-two to do all that work . . . at half my salary, close to half. Now my options are open if I did part-time work — maybe because I don't need benefits (because of my husband's) they might hire me. I'd have to sell that kind of an angle. Or maybe because I might have fifteen years of experience in an after school program they want. Or maybe we might find a district that wants a good teacher; it's possible! I mean, I could do all kinds of athletic administration because I've coached every sport under the sun."

Tape #271

Ms. J. had only taught for four weeks . . . about three years ago. She was now twenty-nine and the mother of three children, the oldest in kindergarten. She had subbed for a few years and then gone back to get fully certified and her master's in education. She was certified for high school science and had been a biology major as an undergraduate student. We hear so much about how science teachers are needed. Her story makes you wonder . . . . I interviewed her in the immaculate living room of her suburban home.

"It was definite, like late spring, beginning of summer, 1980, that they had reviewed my application and I was accepted in the school system. I had made it very clear to them that I only wanted [to teach] at the high school level, but I would take any position at their academic high school because I really liked that school and it ran seven through twelve. So I went to a workshop there to get some sort of overview to a new health course I was accepted to teach; they were just opening up the position that year. In the meantime I turned down a job at a private school that was offering less money; it was an all-girls Catholic school. It was a high school level position teaching biology and chemistry, but I turned it down because I had that position given to me at the city academic school. It has a good reputation and the position at the girls' school was a few thousand less in pay. And so all summer long, I was preparing and studying to teach this health course.

"Three days before the opening of school the man downtown who I'd interviewed with called me and said that they didn't have enough funding for the position and the whole job was cancelled — three days! And I was really upset because we had started building this house based on my salary; if we hadn't started building this house I would have said, 'I'm not going to teach for you; I'll just have to find something else.' But I was so desperate and it was at the very end so I said — well, of course, and they told me over the phone then what school I would be at and I knew it was a junior high school; it was an inner city school and it would be difficult — very difficult. You know, you hear rumors, and quite often they're true. And it's just not what I wanted anyway. That's not why I went into teaching. Maybe that's not very nice to say, but I wanted to get fulfillment out of it and I wanted to use my science education. And I felt like I had something to offer to the high school level. I had done my undergraduate work in biology and chemistry and had put in one year of med school and another two years working on my master's in education. I really wasn't in it to babysit and to discipline kids. That's not why I went into teaching.

"But I decided to start even though I didn't want to at the beginning. And I hated it. I was absolutely miserable. I guess maybe four of the classes were seventh and two were eighth grade. And it was terrible. There were forty kids in some of the classes, and it was just — it was chaotic. I was a brand new teacher so obviously I did not have the experience. I knew that that was one of my problems in dealing with the kids; I don't have a lot of experience with black kids which was another detriment of mine. I realize that. And they were so violent; it was like I said — inner city and these were rough kids. Some of them looked like they belonged in twelfth grade they were so big. So the language and the roughness and the fact that there were so many kids running around in the room, I just — I went home and cried every night. I told my husband, I can't take this; he said, 'You've got to keep the job; we've got the mortgage,' and I said, 'I'm going to go crazy.' I was screaming at my own kids; it was crazy. They were in a daycare and that was terrible.

"I just had so many basic discipline problems . . . like I couldn't even get them to stay in their seats. You know — I got no support from the assistant principal or the principal; they basically would come down and they'd make some sort of a threat like — you'd better sit there and give this teacher some respect . . . and then they'd leave. And I just really got the distinct feeling that their view was — it was my problem; I had better learn how to deal with it. And I was just scared to death, you know. Every day I thought what else is going to happen. They wouldn't stay in their seats; they would fight with each other. I don't think there were any knives or anything but they would just punch each other and sit on the back ledge of the window and just hang out the window . . . just . . . I felt like I was just out of control. Like I said — it was partly because I didn't have the experience. I didn't even know what my options were. But the administration wouldn't help me. I'd go and talk to them and they would make me feel guilty like it was my fault that nothing was happening. They wouldn't even give me any suggestions. I'm trying to think what kind of tactics I did use. Well — seat work; I would maybe have them write a hundred of something — 'I will sit in my seat and do my work,' because kids that age hate that, especially those kids. And for a couple of them that would work. But they wouldn't let you send the kids down to the office. They wanted you to deal with it in the room.

"What could have helped me? Well, I don't know if the administration could have taken the kids out of my class because there were so many kids in that school, what could they do with them? I don't know. But if it were possible . . . if I had — I don't know — twenty-five kids or something, I think I could have done a lot better. There's no doubt about it. I just don't feel like the principal cared enough. If he'd have stepped in the room once in a while and maybe given me some advice based on his experience . . . .

"I do want to go back into teaching. I want to go into the high school and probably teach biology and chemistry. But if I apply, it will be around here now. But I want back into it — why? I just feel good about myself when I'm doing something like that. I really enjoy the standing in front of the kids and — it's hard to explain because there's so much involved in teaching — I enjoy the looks on their faces. I always picture myself in the biology room at the suburban school when I was doing my student teaching . . . and I was really on my own there, doing that week after week, and they would catch on to something and they would smile and say, 'Oh, that's really neat!' And I just think that's a lot of fun. I really enjoy when they learn something that they find really interesting and want to learn more and more . . . I just think that's really a lot of fun. And it makes me want to go home and delve a little bit deeper and learn a little more. I want to hit my college text and see if I can give them a little added insight . . . I just enjoy that. I don't enjoy the yelling at them or telling them to quiet down or that part of it at all, but I guess that's just part of teaching and just something you have to go with."

Tape #238

Ms. H. was a forty-two year old woman who had quit teaching three years ago to take an administrative position, in this case that of an assistant principal in charge of curriculum. She felt she could make more

of a difference at the administrative level. Before that she had taught for
seventeen years in the math department at the high school level. Her
current job was in a large Northern California city school which was
made up of almost entirely an ethnic population.

She spoke almost defensively to me . . . not seeming to trust me at any
time through the interview. She also seemed tired. She was widowed with
three grown children. Her hobby was sewing. And except for the obvious
attempt with the clothes she wore . . . she didn't look like an administrator.

"In teaching you're your own boss and I felt there were a lot of people
gains from one person to the other . . . rather than in business. I felt kind
of like a cog in the wheel of business. In teaching you have the capability
of being creative and selling your subject. And the people gains was a big
deal to me."

(What made you leave teaching three years ago for administration?)

"Actually it was the frustration of working to try and make curriculum
changes — about the only choice was to join them. I felt there were some
basic needs of kids that needed to be addressed. I felt as an administrator
I could manipulate the schedule to better meet the needs of students. It's
really a problem solving exercise; you're given x number of teachers and
the master schedule. Now how can you distribute these teachers with the
students to have the most effective model to put in your school site. And
that's appealing to me. Last summer I restaffed a lot of English; I changed
some people's assignments, based on what I knew about those people and
where their expertise was. I placed people where you can maximize their
potential. And not every teacher can teach every kind of kid so you need
to know the staff."

I have a lot of control over curriculum now. Not only here locally on
site — we've made some changes — but I serve on a number of committees on the district level, which are instrumental in making curriculum
changes. One example we did last year — we were talking about the
ability grouping. We had a high percentage of failures in [a] World
Civilizations [course] and so we decided to adjust the curriculum so
students would have World Civ. and Language Arts III, and the teacher
would teach both subjects and kind of use World Civ. as a vehicle for
discussion in the writing class. So we grouped about one hundred freshman with that kind of a core curriculum. And I just figured it out that our
World Civ. failure rate had dropped from thirty-three percent last year to

twenty-seven this year. So that's six percent more students that essentially passed that course, which, six times six — that's about thirty-six more kids. So it moved the pendulum in the right direction. You address a need and then you kind of chop away at the need.

"I miss teaching; I miss being in the classroom. You've always got a payoff working with the kids. I mean, when you're involved with the kids, it never seemed like a job. In administration it feels like a job when I walk in in the morning. But I never felt that way going into a classroom. Has it changed how I'm viewed by the teachers? I think I've always been viewed with respect by the teachers and the community, and I don't think that's changed . . . I don't envision this as any kind of power role, ok? I envision that I'll continue to have their respect. Lots of time in administration you have to make decisions that you know they're going to question, where if you're a teacher and you're just a part of the pack, it's just a different story. Basically, I don't see it that differently. Maybe because I stayed here on the same staff — these are people I'd worked with before. I think maybe I'm treated by the kids probably a little different — by the faculty? Different in the sense that they know that I'm in charge of the curriculum area . . . but not different from the personal point of view. I don't feel like I have to play a certain role. And yes, I've done evaluations of teachers for all three years.

". . . I'd say the major problem with public education is its inability to react to changes in a quick efficient way due to the bureaucracy that is built into the system. We tend to make changes now for studies that came out ten years ago or eight years ago instead of being able to react quickly to research that comes out. By the time the research comes out and we react to it, it's already changed. In the midst of the bureaucracy to be able to serve — like the immigrant population that comes into California — it's difficult. You can't change the system quickly enough that you can have newcomer's schools. The bureaucracy is so built into the system . . . and I don't know how to break it down. It's very frustrating."

(Would you become a teacher again?)

". . . probably . . . I don't know if I'd become an administrator again (Laughter) I don't know if I regret making this decision . . . see me in a couple more years time for your sequel . . . ."

Tape #86

"I guess I'm kind of biased, but I think there are many
more poor principals than poor teachers."

*I interviewed Mr. B. at a graduate school in a religious university. He
had taught grades one through eight for ten years in inner city public
schools and several smaller rural public districts. He had been out of
teaching for four years and wasn't certain that he might not go back into
that . . . or the ministry . . . or counseling . . . or as an administrator. He
was forty, dressed in a colorful shirt, dark and wore a huge mustache. It
was interesting to listen to how feeling burnt out forced him to leave the
profession.*

*At the end of the interview when the tape was off, he said that secular
humanism was probably the major cause of the public school system
decline. "When God left school, f_____ came in." He wasn't certain why
he didn't want to say all that on the tape. Then he asked if he could say a
prayer for my book. I figured people could pray for whatever they wanted,
but he meant right there and then. There I was, the most liberal, agnostic,
alternate lifestyle oriented person, watching a large man in a multi-
colored shirt bow his head and pray for me and my book . . . .*

(What made you decide to get out of teaching?)

"I had what they call teacher burnout . . . I never thought it would
happen to me. Well, it was really strange because most people you hear
about [have] this happen in the ghetto schools, but my experiences in the
inner city schools were wonderful. I experienced leadership in those
schools. It was a tight ship and we were a tight faculty. And I taught in the
number two lowest income rated school. And it was difficult but we had
a tight faculty, a tight staff, a tight principal . . . and I really enjoyed it
there. And I then wanted to try a magnet school because this magnet
school had offerings of the arts to the children where they could be pulled
out of the classroom. And a friend of mine thought it would be a good
school for me to get into. It would help me move up the ladder to get into
the supervision positions. You had to be interviewed for this particular
school so it was hand picked. Plus, it was nearer to my home. So I was
picked to be what they called a basic skills teacher.

"It was the most disappointing experience of my life. It was the straw
that broke the camel's back. I felt that I was lied to by the administration
in the beginning. They told us that the children that were picked for this

particular magnet school had to have a certain basic competency skill level and that these students were taken from their neighborhood school because they were at least average students and also they had an interest in the arts. It didn't turn out that way; it was a sham. What it was was a way to enhance integration. So you had a lot of children there who could not handle the freedom. And the administration was very, very weak. I didn't have books until well into November. I finally went down into the basement of the school and had to dig up my own stuff. I was teaching reading, science and math at this time. And there were seventh and eighth graders reading at a third and fourth grade level. And my math class was about a fourth grade level.

"Toward the middle of October I was experiencing a lot of stress. The noise levels in the halls — they were not really what you'd call really bad children, but everything was so scattered that everybody was so antsy and then being pulled out for all these programs, it was like a zoo. And I thought I was like maybe the only one that was experiencing this so I went to a teacher who had been there for a while and I said what can I do, how can I cope with this? And she said, 'Oh, I thought I was the only one that was feeling this way' . . . . (Laughter) So we called a faculty meeting . . ."

(The faculty called a meeting?)

"Yes, the faculty themselves . . . and asked our headmaster. Then we told her how we felt. It was only October and we were already at our breaking point. I had never had this experience before. I had always enjoyed my work. And the only thing she said was, 'Nobody asked you people to teach here.' And she walked out. Well, that did it. By December I had become so angry and so frustrated and felt so hopeless that I would wake up in the morning with a knot in my stomach. I knew it was going to be another day of no control, of kids throwing food in the cafeteria, of no discipline in school and feeling totally alone. I did something I had never done before. A child lipped off to me and I picked him up by his collar — he was like twelve or thirteen — and I slammed his head against the wall. And that's when I knew I was in trouble. I took off for a week to get my nerves straight. I did then manage to get my act together to be able to cope, but it was never the same. And my relationship with the principal who had been instrumental in hiring me . . . completely fell apart . . . . I guess I'm kind of biased, but I think there are many more poor principals than poor teachers . . . .

Tape #269

Mr. R had quit teaching two years before I interviewed him, simply left around October of the school year 1983-1984. He said he felt trapped in the job, and it seems that a lot of his reasons for leaving were personal. But education still played its seemingly negative role. "In teaching there was never any end product I could see; in what I'm doing now, sports reporting, I can see that story printed every week."

Mr. R. had taught for twelve full years, high school English and some history at a nice suburban high school. He was thirty-eight at the time of the interview, gaining weight, and going through a separation from his wife of thirteen years. He smoked constantly as he talked and gestured nervously with his hands.

But what he said about education still had the ring of authority.

(Why did you originally decide you wanted to teach?)

"That is a question that I would ask myself repeatedly over those twelve years. I'm not being facetious; there were many times when I would ask myself — why? What motivated me? But trying to remember why you made that decision years ago and then thinking on it years later can color your perspective on why you made that decision. I was comfortable in the classroom; I enjoyed being a student; I liked to write; I liked to read. Although later on, I decided that just liking to write was not necessarily the best basis for getting into teaching English. But that's what I was thinking at the time, as a twenty year old college student. And secondly, this was a time when I felt I wanted to work with people, to give of myself to help other people. I felt I could help other people through this area which was education. That was my general idea — it was an idealistic view, of course.

"I'll never forget a guy I taught with my first year saying to me one time: 'You know the problem is a lot of first year teachers run smack dab into reality.' Those were his exact words. And I had to agree with that. I ran smack dab into what the reality of what the teaching situation was like at that high school. At that time, that school was booming in enrollment; it was over-crowded; it was on split-schedules. We had classes of forty and more and not enough books — in the '70s, remember. And see, I came from one extreme to the other. I happened to student teach at what was considered a very ideal situation. The building was only two years old when I student taught. It was considered the new experimental, open high school concept . . . and I loved it. I saw it as being a very progressive high school and that just built up my teaching enthusiasm. I think my largest class there was seventeen kids. So you can imagine coming from that ideal situation to where I got my job where all of a sudden boom! I'm hit with five classes, and they're all huge, and in an overcrowded situation, scheduling difficulties, the tension, the strain, a pugnacious principal — [all] that had a large part in affecting my idealism."

(When did you first start thinking about getting out of teaching?)

"After my first year. (laughter) It was an ongoing process! (laughter) It's tough to pinpoint where it really [started]. I'll tell you what — you know it's funny how you can remember certain things. For some reason they just stick out. And I had many ups and downs in the years I was there. But I can remember — it was the August of '73, starting my second year. And I can remember going through some real cynicism that summer of '73. I had just gone through the first year — and actually I got pretty good evaluations for a first year teacher! It was good overall. But I can remember the seeds of wanting to quit were planted somewhere along the line the way that first year hit me. And I can remember in August of '73, sitting in one of those infamous first day back huge meetings — I just remember having this huge sense of apathy, not giving a damn, no enthusiasm whatsoever. It was the beginning of my second year of teaching, and I had this almost sense of doom and foreboding that this was going to be one horrible year. And it turned out to be that way. It was a terrible year. It was just a feeling [that] English teaching just wasn't what I thought it was. And it was all kinds of questions that I had about myself too. Also — there were such scheduling problems. Our principal and his henchmen, they locked you into those courses that you started with. And a lot of those courses — I mean, I never asked for those. There was no input from me about what I would like to teach. They threw me into things like — teaching a lot of grammar classes at varying ability levels. I was not prepared — see, that's the problem!

"For many people like ourselves, we were basically trained to deal with the basically motivated college prep level kids. I had no training — that first year, the thing that woke me up was — I had absolutely no training in dealing with all the different levels. I had a kid in a class who could barely write his name sitting next to a kid who was pretty good. I didn't have the skill or the experience or the training to deal with the kid of a different type of ability level. And the thing was, as a first year teacher, it was like you were thrown to the wolves; there was nobody to try and help me; it was like trial and error with me. Maybe this might work or that might work. There was no person to help me along, to help me deal with the different groups. I was ill prepared for that sort of thing. And I felt inadequate; I felt frustrated; I couldn't accomplish what I wanted to accomplish. I was not prepared for those real low ability type of kids, the discipline problems that those kids tend to be. And I think that's why that year I came out a little bitter and a little cynical; it was like — hey, I didn't expect all of this."

(Do you remember how you felt when you left?)

"Well, I left on October 9th . . . obviously it was a very painful decision. It was a very emotional and difficult time. Here I had two kids, a house, and I would have no job. It was scarier than hell financially. For all the problems I had to deal with here, I still was leaving the familiar and the known. On paper it was ideal, reasonably good high school, in walking distance . . . I had tenure. Why leave all that? And I'm sure some people thought I was crazy. But they weren't in my shoes; they hadn't had to contend with what I had to contend with, all those years and years of frustration. And it wasn't fair to the students; they deserved a teacher who was totally committed in that subject field, who could give them the most he could give them. I couldn't give them that. For a teacher to stay in the business, despite all the problems, he or she had to have an honest love for their subject. But I remember crying three times that last day right in front of the class. I never did that. It was a painful day, knowing this was it, this was my last class; I'll never be back. I cried three times.

"It's less secure out here without tenure. Tenure does make you feel very secure. But I can remember a teacher saying to me on the last day that I left, 'You are doing what a lot of people in this building would like to do right now . . .' "

Section 9:

ADMINISTRATORS

Ms. R. refused finally to be interviewed. She was all set until the night before when she was told that her building principal had been contacted to ok my interviewing her in her classroom during the school day. She was too afraid that he would "get her" for talking. The interview was hastily cancelled over the phone.

I can remember sitting at a meeting run by an assistant superintendent where the teachers in my building were asked to vote on whether they wanted to switch from quarters to semesters. At the end of the meeting he passed out a sheet that explained how this switch would be done in the following school year.

This is just one example of how administrators treat teachers. To me, the quickest and cheapest way — they'd be saving money to do this — to improve education is to get rid of the majority of the administrators at the central office and a lot at the building level. And believe it or not, I've never had a problem with any but one principal or assistant principal I've worked with on site. I don't think many of them were great educators, mind you, but they were nice guys, most of whom had my respect as people but typical for the most part of the kind of teacher who would go into administration. I always thought being evaluated by two ex-social studies teachers for eight years summed up what was wrong with public education.

Who goes into administration anyhow? If you care about kids, you stay in teaching. Teachers, for the most part, really are there because they care about their students. And I'd say the majority of their unions and associations represent this care. Principals and central administrators — they usually wanted larger salaries and in some (but all too many) sick cases, a sense of power. Consider this: central administrators wanted to be in a building where there weren't any kids at all. Board members? Status, ego, political ambitions, and a lot of naive do-gooders. And think about this: who has the final say on curricular matters in public education? You can answer either the members of the board of education or the state legislature. What education experience do these people have? I was in one rural district where they had board members who hadn't even earned a high school diploma . . . and they were deciding school policy. Oh, America!

School administrators were one of the three largest complaints teachers across the nation voiced about what was wrong with public education (along with class size and society itself). I couldn't agree with them more. Administrators — are teachers who quit.

Tape #73

I interviewed Mr. S. in his summer job office — swim club manager. A creaky window unit air conditioner was squeaking in the background and there was wetness everywhere (as is the norm at a swim club). We were constantly interrupted by phones and student workers and finally by his grade school aged son who wanted a tennis ball to play with. But through it all, Mr. S. remained calm and smiling, full of laughs and jokes. He had taught for fifteen years at the high school level, two at parochial schools, and was married with three kids of his own. He had short hair, glasses, and a homey face.

A personable teacher, often voted favorite teacher by senior classes, he saw the problems of education resting squarely on the backs of administrators. Like all creative teachers, he'd felt the effects of the narrowness of the administrative view — his latest principal had said no to his trademark soap-bar hall passes.

"I think the major thing wrong with education, outside of the salaries, is administration, from the building level all the way up to the superintendent's office. I've been in five school districts (two Catholic), and everywhere I've been it's more that people running the schools have been pushed into that position because they were not good at something else. They got there because of the Peter Principle; they have served their time and this is now the natural step whether they're good or not; they become the whatever — director or principal or super of whatever. They're not selected on the qualifications they have, and a lot of them are waiting for retirement and then don't want to rock the boat. I think that's my biggest complaint, that there are too many people who are there who are just not qualified to run the show. They'd never make it in the business world; they'd be fired in a minute.

"A worst case example? Way back in my early days of teaching I was a guidance counselor, and the principal and I worked together on the numbers that qualified for the title program of kids who were EMR — mentally handicapped kids — and he just pushed and pushed to get through those particular numbers. He was so concerned with the numbers needed to get the federal or state grant, [but] not at all worried about whether the kid was actually mentally retarded or had a handicap.

"There were also decisions by administrators that had to be made, but because they were close to retirement or didn't want to rock the boat, they did a nothing type thing. And I think a lot of administrators worry more about money than education; it gets worse out of the building level and on up the line. Examples like let's get rid of this top teacher because they're at the top of the pay scale and bring in a new one down the pay scale — early retirement too.

"Another example — I was up for the same counseling job this year that I didn't get last year, so I kept waiting for an interview like I'd had the year before. Finally I started asking around — what was going on? When would I be interviewed? And I was told by one assistant principal that they were waiting to see about the people out on leaves. Then, I found out that this counseling job was going to take up a lot more time in the summer — what they did was make all of the counselors' summer days half days so they could make them come in for more weeks in the summer. I couldn't afford to give up this summer job. And they're piling so much garbage on counselors and what they're supposed to do. I had been working with kids in what we call 'The Room,' a place where kids can talk and get some feedback, and I was just — literally wiped out. I had to get out of there for a while. So I went in finally and told our principal that I didn't want the position; just take my name out of the running. And he yelled and screamed at me and told me it had already been assigned to me and that I was ruining his whole social studies schedule by doing this to him. I told him — hey, I was waiting for an interview and it never came. He yelled that there weren't going to be any interviews; I already had the position. I asked him if the other teachers in the district who had applied and were also waiting for interviews knew about this? They were mad. 'I'll have to tell the superintendent that I've got another $30,000 in my budget if I have to give you classes; we've already computed the schedules for next year.' It was all that sort of garbage. But they redid the schedule — gave me five different classrooms to teach in and when I complained, they said, well, that's just the way it works out . . . . Then they offered the counseling job to this other guy, but they told him he'd have to give up coaching if he took it so he refused. A few weeks later they asked a counselor at our other high school if he would coach girls' basketball . . . that's fair, isn't it? It's like the lady here who'd done cheerleaders for years and they forced her out last year because the principal's wife didn't think she was doing a good job; this year they begged her to come back and do it because they couldn't find anybody who wanted to do it. She turned them down and was given a junior high English class to teach next year — she's a business teacher . . . that's fair, isn't it?

"Also in education I think the goals or the objectives change with every passing fad. Administrators say — we should go to competency testing, we should be master teachers, we should have ability groupings . . . we should not have ability groupings . . . we should get back to basics, we should have more electives. Education has changed so much, even just from district to district or year to year — they have different goals and different approaches that I think there's no steady course of where you're heading. I think this district has just been incredible as far as their planning on how many buildings, how many high schools, etc. I think what they've been doing is just running around in circles.

"Part of it has to do with the administrators. Your basic administrator is an ex-social studies teacher who may have been very good or mediocre or whatever and went to school and got a certificate by taking twenty-four hours. And you know how graduate school systems work. What do you learn? How do you become a good administrator from graduate school courses? Then all of a sudden they're in charge of curriculum and programs and big bucks and somebody up above them is telling them you can't spend this and you should do this and — sheesh!

"What's right with education? I think that the programs that we offer are good. I've been in Catholic schools and there's just no comparison as to what is offered in public schools. I teach psychology and a lot of people say they've never heard of psychology being taught at the high school level . . . they never knew that. And I think there're a lot of good things happening curriculum-wise. Also I think there are some good things happening with different teachers and their different approaches to education. Some are really improving or really changing or just becoming more creative in their styles or approach. I guess I don't exactly teach like everybody else. Unfortunately, I probably only take attendance in my first mod class because that's the one you have to turn in. It's kind of a waste of time for me to do some of these things that administrators want you to do. I photocopy my lesson plans from year to year and turn in a packet because nobody reads them anyway and nobody understands them if they did. But you see, a teacher has to be a motivator; a teacher has to be an entertainer, an actor at times in order to get the kids on a positive approach to learning; they have to be able to see their program. They have to be a good salesperson. That's a real key to it. The people who are the textbook-ish, straight down the line type teachers are the ones who are boring and turning kids off and who haven't tried a new approach or new idea, and I think that's where there's a lot of failure. Of course being the less normal type of teacher tends to make you less popular with administrators. Now in our district the master teacher is the in-type teacher. I think because I don't follow all the rules and don't give detentions . . . I can remember on one hand the detentions I've given . . . But I imagine the administrators are happy with the teachers who turn in their lesson plans, whose attendance is done just right. Me? — I use soap bars as hall passes.

"It's hard to say why administrators don't value the creative teachers, because I don't think I've ever been evaluated by any administrator who has been a really effective evaluator, telling me the good or the bad of what I'm doing. More than telling me, 'you talked too loud for that side of the room,' 'you asked too many questions from the right hand side,' or who have repeated back verbatim exactly what I did in that lesson — that was my evaluation. 'In the first five minutes you went over this and in the next you' — well, I know I did that. I know what I did, but tell me how to improve or tell me what good things or bad that I've done. That's some-thing administrators, I think, should be good at. Most of them are ex-teachers who *should* know what a good teacher is . . . .

"I don't think I'd be in education or be as happy in education if I had freshman history with all the little nerds or low level classes. I like what I'm teaching and I think it can be made interesting to the students. If I were teaching geography or world history or other subjects I'm certified to teach, I don't know if I'd have the same answers for you today. I think we *do* have an overload of bad teachers — some really great ones too. But I think a lot are burnt out. I always tell my students that if I'm sitting here when your kids are coming through, please just shoot me. I think we need to get into teaching and then get out a lot sooner . . . but that doesn't mean you become a damn principal."

Tape #213

*I visited with Ms. J. in the afternoon right after her second graders had
left the classroom. She met me in the office with the message that she just
had to "hit the restroom" and then she'd be ready to talk to me — a
common comment from teachers at the end of a busy day. She looked tired
and showed all of her fifty-three years in her face and sighs, but she was
one of those grandmotherly types that every child should have the pleasure to have in the primary grades. And along with the graying hair and
frameless glasses came a very smart woman who knew a lot about
education, from both experience and research.*

*Ms. J. had taught for fourteen years, was married and had four grown
children of her own. Her school was part suburban and part small town.
As she said, "It had its well-to-do; it had its kids who needed shoes . . . ."*

*Her principals were of both types too. One building principal in her
district had become infamous to teachers that year for his memo about
taking the used staples out of bulletin boards . . .*

"I don't know that I know how any one student learns, but I do know the
conditions that you can create so a person can do their own learning. They
need time; they need time to read and time to write. They need a loving,
accepting atmosphere. They need lots of books, opportunities to write,
things to write with. They need a lot of experiences because they're young
and inexperienced and you need to provide experiences for them. They
need opportunities to talk; talking is a powerful means of assimilating and
synthesizing what they know — like talking with other kids. They need
someone to listen to them, respond to them, person to person rather than
adult to child.

"If you have a strong curriculum, you don't need competency testing.
It tends to break learning down into little pieces. And particularly for
young children who have a much more global outlook of the world — they
tend to deal with the wholes of something. It's appealing to adults for administrators to say, 'She knows what contractions are' or 'she can name
off antonyms.' But children lose that very quickly. It breaks it into too
many meaningless pieces. It's the assumption that if you pass a ten item
test on contractions, you can read and use contractions effectively —
that's a fallacy.

"I think legislatures mandate these things partly due to a historical
attitude towards teachers, that we are not professionals, that we are not
capable of planning and carrying out a curriculum; therefore we must test

and have evidence of those tests to know that teachers are teaching. I think it's been like this all along — the whole set-up for teachers never turned out to be the same setup for doctors, the same setup for lawyers. I mean, lawyers' clients don't have to turn in an evaluation on the lawyer's work, you know. Doctors don't have to pass competency tests to operate. There's just an attitude with a lot of history going into that. Teachers for so long were females who had very little power. School boards were males — who had a lot of power. They said where a woman had to live, what she could wear, whom she could visit, whether she could marry or not — there was a real poor attitude and I think that's not totally gone.

"I think the public attitude *is* changing; I think people are discovering there are many, many committed people who put in a lot of hours, who really care about the children, and who care what children learn. And some of this negative attitude is wearing off. They've discovered we work very hard. Another piece of the history stuff is that we only work nine months. I figure I put in fifty-sixty hour weeks, and when it's conference time — I probably put in an extra twenty-thirty hours the week preceding conferences ... just to get [the reports] written. It takes fifteen minutes to a half an hour a child . . . we do this three times a year."

(Have you ever thought of getting out of teaching?)

"Yes and no — sometimes I get very weary — physically weary . . . like right now. Conferences were last week and sometimes you go home at night and think — oh, for a job where I can just go home at night and have nothing to do. That gets to me, but as far as dealing with the children — not at all. And sometimes, too, a principal can make your life miserable . . . at the moment this isn't true. Some principals are very aware of what ought to be going on in the classroom; they are therefore very supportive of teachers. Some principals are very concerned about their authority, more than anything else. They do not see themselves as partners. I feel the principal is my partner and the principal has particular responsibilities, and I have particular responsibilities and the two of us together focus on those children. And we're here for the children. But many principals don't see their jobs that way. They set up a lot of roadblocks, a lot of nitty-gritty authoritarian kinds of stuff.

"The principal I had in Rhode Island said that you had to have a desk blotter on your desk, two freshly sharpened pencils on the right hand side, no more than three books in a little book rack on the left hand side and nothing more. And I got called on the carpet because we were making a garden and I left the hoe and the rake in the corner behind my desk. And this is what education is about? He'd go around at night to see if you had the blotter and the two sharpened pencils and all that jazz on your desk. But did he ever come in and watch me teach? No. Did he ever sit and talk to me about my children? No. That's sad.

"The principal I had in New York City — now this was in the 50s, before I stopped teaching to raise my children — I couldn't even tell you his name. He sat in his office and when you sent him a discipline case, he'd pat him on his head, give him a lollipop and say, 'You be a nice kid now.' This was in the slums of New York City. And I'm told — he wrote musical comedy! The assistant principal hated children, hated her job, hated teachers, and if you sent her a kid, she beat the hell out of [him]. So you know what you did? You took care of it yourself. (Laughter) The principal I have here *now* I'm very happy with. She's very concerned with the kids and she's very supportive of the classroom teachers. The man before her was very concerned with his own image and enforcing his ideas of what it's meant to be about.

"I read something in the NEA newspaper that in the hospital model, the hospital administrator is a facilitator for the doctors and the nurses. And they are the professionals. And an administrator wouldn't think of coming in and saying, 'What are you cutting there on that person?!' He wouldn't do that. But you would certainly not be surprised if a principal walked into the classroom and said, 'What on earth are you teaching like that for?' They do not see the school setup as that kind of facilitating situation. They see it as a monitoring in the worst kind of way — the school board sets it up to be too. It's unfortunate. And because of that, teachers lack a professional attitude because they aren't treated as professionals. Unions have struggled for tenure because teachers have been dismissed for idiotic grounds and have been asked to work in despicable working conditions. School boards got what they deserved because of the way they treated the teachers.

"I remember once in this district I had a principal tell me I would be moved to fifth grade. And I said, 'Why — are you telling me I'm doing a poor job?' And he said no. 'Am I boring, not prepared' — I went through a whole list. 'No, you're a wonderful primary teacher. But I want you in fifth grade.' He never said this, but he wanted me there because I'm a good disciplinarian. And I said, 'Well, you know that I have children in college and I'm up for tenure; I don't dare resist you,' and he said, 'That's right.' And I said, 'But that's blackmail,'" and he said, 'Well, I'd rather not call it that.' It makes you feel real good. Fortunately, we didn't even have to have another fifth grade so I never had to teach it. In elementary, the assumption is if you're certified 1 through 8, you can teach anything . . . but if you put me in the middle school, I would die. I have no idea how to approach those kids. And I said, 'But if I go to fifth grade, I don't have any experience, I don't have any materials, background — nothing!' 'Oh, well,' he said, 'I know you — you'll work hard.' I'll wear myself out and do the job —because he knew I cared about the children. And he knew I wouldn't have short-changed them; he would use that against me. Now had he approached it another way? Had he said it looks like we're going to have another fifth grade — you're a very capable person and I think you'd be good for it and so on — he could have approached it a lot of ways . . . ."

(Do you think principals see themselves as cohorts or see themselves as something above teachers?)

"Above — and separate from . . . unfortunately. Except for the present principal, that's been my experience. She's from a classroom herself; she's taught — at least more than two years, probably ten, so she had a good perspective on what ought to go on in class. That's important . . . and I'd like to see administrators go back into the classroom on a regular basis. Too many principals from the past — but in the '50s and '60s —came up as coaches. I guess the idea was that you needed that authority figure — I don't know. You get a coach worrying about what goes on in the second grade — they have no more idea about what ought to go on in the second grade than I have on what ought to go on on the football field . And here they are coming in observing me. Well, what are they looking for? They don't know what they're looking for. How can they support me? They don't know! Now they can probably stumble around for three or four years and get a pretty decent idea, but if you've got someone who has been in the classroom at your level, he well understands what ought to go on in the classroom and what kind of pressure and constraints a teacher has. They bring that to their observations, to their contact with teachers, to their support network . . . the expectations they have for the children too.

"The principal we have now is here for the children first . . . even if that's at the expense of a teacher, and that's the way it should be. But she's very concerned about my concerns about my teaching because I think every teacher has a different style, different things that make it work for her or him. She tries to get to know that and offers you support that you need. She's always ready to talk about the children and tries to know something about them before you come in. She's very complimentary and aware of things that I do. For instance, we're working on the writing program in the district and I was one of the presenters. She came! If you do something, she puts a note in your mailbox — I noticed this and it really looks great. She's aware of what her teachers do. What you get from the children may be admiration or enthusiasm, but what you get from her is a professional viewpoint. I saw what you did and I understand what you did and it was good. That's really important. And I really do view her as my partner. But for me, I guess, there will always be some hesitation with principals because of past history.

"I had a parent come in and tell me what reading group her child would go in. 'My child will be in this book.' She has continued to do this, by the way; this year she sent [a note to] the fifth grade teacher in the first five minutes of the year — "'My child will be in x reading group' — I mean, the teacher hasn't even met the kid yet! So I tested the kid and I said here's my results and she said, 'She'll be in another reading group.' So I had the reading teacher test the kid and she said, 'Your results are correct.' The mother still said , 'She'll be in another reading group.' So then she went to the principal and, still not satisfied, she went to the superintendent — and got everybody all fussed up. So the assistant superintendent said, 'Well, the relationship between the parent and the teacher is destroyed, so we'll move the child because there's no way she can work with this.' But this blew my mind; they put the child in the next classroom for reading in the morning but then they brought her back for the afternoon for math and all the other things. I thought — well, if the relationship is destroyed, it's destroyed, but I was to just swallow everything — let this kid go next door against all indications that she belonged there. At that point, I think they were just appeasing the parent. Moving the kid was ok, but this? And in this community there is a lot of that pushy — my child will be a super-achiever. I've had parents say to me — second grade, seven year old kid — 'My child is going to Harvard.' Oh! And they mean it."

Tape #68

He had been a principal for twenty-two years and had returned to the classroom for one last year of teaching science. His hair was graying and balding. He was a pleasant looking person and seemed a pleasant person all-around. He spoke seriously but whimsically too from behind his glasses. He had forgotten that he was to be interviewed. He was apologetic, but he seemed to take for granted his forgetfulness. All in all, his education career spanned thirty-two years. He was now fifty-eight, married, with four grown children.

(A lot of teachers feel that administrators lose contact with what it's like to have been a teacher and forget what it's like to be in the classroom. Did you find that that happened or not?)

"A year ago [I] might have answered that a little differently than I would today when I'm back teaching, because I thought that I really worked at that problem. I was sensitive to and knew what teachers were thinking. I tried to not become so apart from the classroom that I'd forget that, and, in fact, tried to do some teaching each year of some kind — maybe a small unit or a few days here and there. But having been back in the classroom for eight or nine weeks, there are some things you forget exist and some you take for granted. There's no doubt that principals have to help themselves in the area of keeping themselves sensitive to teacher needs. The best thing would be to teach, and I guess I do believe that most principals could take two weeks aside and take a class in their specialty without [interfering with] their time frames or anything else. I think they need some support again from their bosses, so to speak, but I think that would meet that need.

"And class size — I know it's hard to say you've got thirty, now you've got twenty-nine — what's the difference. Saying there isn't a difference between thirty and twenty doesn't make sense. I could even bear where the class sizes are pretty good and I have one with seventeen and one with twenty-four and just some of the things I want to do with them when you get down to the individual or in a group, interactions that are different, so, I guess I do believe, I think, [class size] has to be noticed. I don't believe that they get to everyone. Teachers who are working [with] 130, could work with 100. I do now believe you notice a significant difference."

Tape #140

Ms. B. had a weathered face that reminded me more of the West than North Carolina where I interviewed her. She had taught for twenty-six years and was currently teaching biology in a suburban city high school in the South. She had also taught for several years in a nursing college where she felt she was treated professionally by administration. She didn't feel that way at the high school level.

She had short blondish hair, an aging face at fifty-three, glasses, stylish jewelry and was divorced with two children. Would she become a teacher again if she had it all to do over again? No.

(If you were back in college now, would you still teach?)

"I would have gone into another career. I really enjoyed the nursing school atmosphere where I originally taught. The treatment of instructors is very different at the college level, professional all the way. And I learned, you know, that I was not — I have never really been treated as a professional as a high school teacher. For one thing, I am not treated as though I have any real say; I have no power; I have no input. And I have no feedback, really, except in a negative way. The only time I ever hear from anyone is if something's gone wrong. There is no positive reinforcement for me. And when there is a meeting of some sort, it doesn't seem to dwell on anything that gives me any feeling of doing a good job or even being important.

"I expressed this to my principal the other day, whether he liked it or not. I think it's a real problem. I got that kind of feedback from my co-workers in the nursing school; I got it from doctors with whom I was associated. [They] were very aware of the importance of training nurses, and they were very interested in assisting us in any way. I was allowed, for example, to observe a number of surgeries. And the doctors would go out of their way to be a teacher to me, without being condescending, without being patronizing in any way. They were interested in sharing and in treating me as a professional person. Here, more or less, they're the power structure and we're the laborers. It's definitely that feeling that I have.

"I think in this school and in others — I've taught in another high school — we've been told, 'That's not your decision.' If we make suggestions, we're being put down. 'That's not your decision to make; that's the administrator's.' Or — I wrote a letter to my principal last year and said that I felt that he was not utilizing the staff, with all of its vast knowledge and experience, that it's very difficult to run a school just for administrators, that he really needed all of us, and that if we all were working together, we would pull together, and we would feel that we were accomplishing something. And this year, for the first time — I'm not saying that I did that, because I'm sure that other teachers expressed similar feelings in one way or another — but there is a so-called school improvement committee that is made up of a group of teachers and students and administrators and parents. That's the first indication I've seen of any attempt to try to do whatever improving we're talking about.

"Actually I was prompted to write the letter by a faculty meeting in which we were all severely admonished for whatever some teachers were doing; I objected to being severely admonished when I hadn't 'committed the crime.' You know, I didn't need that put-down and I was very, very disturbed that administrators would do something to us that we never do to students. If we did that, if we did a group punishment to students, we would immediately be called on the carpet, and yet it's all right for him to do that to us. And there were a number of us who were incensed. I was incensed strongly enough to write him a letter.

"In an ideal situation the principal would be knowledgeable about all the curriculum and would be able to — if not personally, have key people who would have curriculum areas in which they were knowledgeable and would be able to understand what is going on in a particular area, like science or math or foreign language, whatever — and be able to understand the particular problems that can come up because of that particular discipline, or the needs that a particular discipline has. I find that most administrators, for example, have no concept of what it takes, in terms of time and effort and equipment, to put together a good lab for students. They have no concept of that. They can understand that English teachers need a lot of time to grade research papers or themes or whatever, but they don't understand that science teachers need time, too, to put together a lab.

(How do you feel about being evaluated?)

"I endure it. I endure it. And I realize that — I've sort of become hardened to it. You know, it's not going to affect my pay, and I know that I'm doing a good job, and if I feel that I'm being severely disciplined or admonished in a certain area or marked down greatly, I have the recourse of writing a rebuttal to that, which I have done. For example — in this school system there is a great emphasis on how things look on paper, from the top administration down, and a great emphasis on how the grade distribution looks on paper, without considering what contributes to this grade distribution. Then you have an administrative policy which says a student who misses six or more days a quarter will fail, unless there is justification, you know, where they should pass — then they tell us, you have too many Fs. So it's damned if you do and damned if you don't. Well, we are caught in those things all the time. And I've been in that spot, too — I have too many Fs, without looking at the record to see, you know, that I have certain students who just don't come or who have never lifted the first pencil and have never done any work and would not, under any circumstances, qualify for a passing grade. But that is not looked at, because that's not the way we do it. That's what makes our educational system rather ridiculous, in a way.

COUNTERPOINT

Tape #161

> "We [teachers] have a natural knack for teaching, but we
> don't always have a natural bent toward articulating what
> we do to another person. That's what a resource teacher
> needs to be."

*Mr. W. described himself as a sort of "touchy-feely" sort of teacher. He
was that rare breed of male elementary school teacher . . . not only elementary, but kindergarten. He had taught for fourteen years when I interviewed him in a Southwestern "big city." But this particular year he was
working as a curriculum specialist.*

*He said basically that it didn't matter if you hadn't taught in the
classroom for several years. That was an "over-used thought." But later,
when commenting on why the public may not see public education as
good, He said, " . . . the farther away from the experience, we can't make
sound judgments on real data anymore." Then at the end he did say that
teachers need to stand up and take control.*

*Had he already moved away some from thinking as a classroom teacher
after only one and a half years away from the classroom? Obviously there
was still a connection.*

*Mr. W. was married with two children of his own, and his hobbies were
gardening and collecting kids' books. He was heavy, with glasses, and
wore a very Western shirt when I interviewed him early one morning
before work.*

"I miss the classroom now that I'm working as a curriculum specialist
this year. I miss having my own group of kids . . . that sustaining love that
keeps you going from day to day to day. I miss seeing one kid change over
a period of time. But I've found myself being made to feel guilty about
being out of the classroom more than I feel guilty. It's a self-guilt that I
think all teachers who leave the classroom to do resource kinds of positions have. They literally feel — even though I have a very good reputation in the district — being out for two years, [that] I automatically have
lost about twenty percent of their faith in my ability . . . just because of
having been removed from the classroom, for just that little bit of time. It's
like since you're not there, you can't really know.

"I think it's an over-used thought. I also see that I do well in my position
and I see a great need — because I'm the only support in our school

district for helping with instruction in the classroom. Teachers are often ill-trained to deal with particular problems in the classroom. Principals are even worse as they often have no ability. They're put into a school with thirty teachers and eight hundred kids and they either sink or swim. And I'm the only person in some respects that this principal has for curriculum. I'm also the only person a new teacher has to go to outside of their building . . . everyone in their building is so busy, and there aren't resources to provide help for them. I think then that I'm needed, and it doesn't take exactly the best teacher — working with kids. Having an ability to work with kids doesn't mean you're good at working with adults too. And I'm finding that I can work well with adults as well, whereas some teachers go into a resource position and they've very good at taking over a classroom and working with the kids, but they can't tell a teacher what she should be looking for, what kinds of questions and strategies she needs to be looking for, the activity structures that I used, what words did I use, how did I interact with the students. It's not something that many teachers are trained to do. We have a natural knack for teaching, but we don't always have a natural bent toward articulating what we do to another person. That's what a resource teacher needs to be.

"Once you're out of teaching for, say — ten years — I do think it makes *some* difference, except I also think you can have an empathy towards what's happening at some level. I think a lot of resource people put up a sort of barrier between themselves and the people because they think that the teachers don't think that they're any good and that they're not going to implement what they're doing anyway. Or you're so busy doing stuff, you'll probably only take a tenth of what I talk about. And so why do I bother? So I see a negativity pervading the atmosphere with resource teachers. But my feelings are that teachers will change as much as they want to change and are encouraged to nurture — to want to see a difference in the classroom. I think by and large teachers are good; they're just not encouraged to be better.

"You're usually encouraged to be run of the mill because no one knows, in buildings, how to encourage them to be better, because administrators are trying to get everybody to be the same, a back to basics, back to whatever our romantic vision of past teaching was. And that's a romantic notion that's never been true. Teachers have always had the same problems we have now . . . they certainly are more pronounced than they have been in the past. But today I think teachers are so busy trying to conform to an image of what they think people want of them that they're not trying to conform to an image of what they think they should be. To me, the best teachers literally capitalize on what they do best. All the studies of teachers who get awards, the teacher of the year kinds of teachers, generally are very unique and in fact, when a teacher has trouble in the classroom, principals and resource people often — rather than capitalizing on their own uniqueness and moving them to become very individual in their work — literally move them to a more generalized mold which is hard for them to fit because they don't really know what it is they're going to be doing.

"I think there're two kinds of public when it comes to looking at teachers. There's the public that you deal with in terms of the constituency of your kids' parents and that public generally has a great respect for teachers . . . . They respect what the teacher has put up with because they know how difficult it is to raise their one or two kids and they see a teacher having to raise thirty kids all year, so I think that constituency is always supportive. But I think there is the other public, the public that has raised their kids or the public that is looking at teaching in the broader scope or also have had maybe three or four really bad experiences with teachers — negative experiences, I guess I should say — they have a generalized notion that teaching is not going well. Teachers aren't prepared, that they don't care and so on. And so that's sort of pervasive in society as a whole. But the parents of your kids appreciate everything you do with kids. They literally want to know that you care about their kid, know what their kid is like, and that you're doing everything that you can do to help the kid. And generally I find that parents are very supportive of me once they know me. If I spent my time trying to keep them away or trying to explain why I can't do things . . . then I think I could lose that. I think in general teachers have great respect from the parents that they serve. It's just the community at large, and again — we build on past experience in our early childhood training. And our prior knowledge and early childhood experiences are what we make judgments on. Most judgments are made from [our early childhood] and the farther away from the experience, we can't make sound judgments on real data anymore. We make judgments on what we thought used to be real and what is perceived to be real now. And that's always going to be a problem.

"But principals can be helping new teachers to progress and become better or they can be maintaining mediocrity. And I think everyone has within him the — ability to remain unchanged . . . and I think that's what I mean by mediocrity. It's easy to take the easy way and not grow and try to change to find what's best for the kids. And principals have a hard task. They're literally the stepchild of education. Everybody yells at them —the

parents, the teachers, the central administration. And everybody is pushing and pulling at them, but there is nobody there to help them to be a
better administrator, a better curricular specialist. So most of them are
very well meaning but none of them have any particular structure of
support. They're either very lucky and make it or they're very unlucky.
Today [1986] we have a Secretary of Education who thinks that principals
can come from the military and business worlds . . . because that's how so
many people have come to look at education — as a business. And what
generally happens with a principal is that they come and decide that they
have to change teaching because things aren't going well and they have to
make it go well. And so one of those methods ideas are used to save
teaching — assertive discipline is going to save teaching, or essential
elements of instruction is going to save teaching, or some program that
costs big bucks somewhere, but it will make it easy if I make everybody
do this and then we can say — we've done our best. And then it's the kids'
fault they're not learning."

Tape #277

Ms. P. was a central administrator in a rural area in the Midwest,
though she'd come from the big, bad city. She told me she had a "global
view" of things and thus was better able to administer and help the
teachers. She had taught for only five years in the classroom and had run
a gifted program for three. She was forty-five and married with two
children of her own.

I liked her and agreed with her some, but she was an administrator. She
felt all adminstrators had a more "global" view of education, that some-
thing happened when you became an administrator and suddenly you
have a whole different view of education. I thought so too. She told me the
teacher who said the state association had gotten some changes in the
state curriculum and requirements for school was wrong and that it was
the state superintendent's office and those administrators who had done
that. She was wrong.

"What do I like about being an administrator? Well, I must immodestly
say I'm a global thinker, a good planner; I can analyze. As a teacher I
would look at things, and I would say, 'Well, it would be a lot better if we
did it this way; it would be easier if we did it this way,' and I was
continually told, 'Those are not your concerns; you are a teacher, and
those are administrative concerns.' And I didn't like that. Especially when
I believed that the people who were telling me that were less competent

than I was to do the job they were doing. At first I thought — oh, I'm going to miss the children terribly, and I cried the day I left the classroom. But as I got into administration and began to learn a lot more about learning theory, I saw that there was a lot more, it seems to me, a different cognitive level of information available to administrators than there is to classroom teachers. At least that has been my experience. I took a lot of courses; I learned a whole bunch of stuff, and I was getting global ideas that explained things that I had been thinking about in a messy fashion for years. I used to think of my brain as a great big gridwork like for a skyscraper and I would fill in a room each time I learned something, and I was filling in so many rooms when I became an administrator. There was access to magazines and to people I had never had access to before."

(What about the argument that once someone leaves the classroom they forget what it's all about and make decisions that are not based on the reality of the classroom?)

I think it's less a matter of forgetting what the classroom was like than seeing a bigger picture. Because you have to remember that each individual teacher speaks from his or her personal experience, which is often quite limited because they are autonomous in their classroom. There are things I understand now; and people who have come out of the classroom to enter a position like mine say, 'My view of teaching has changed so much! These people are still my friends but I think differently.' And I don't think it's necessarily a negative thing. I still remember what it's like to be a teacher. When I observe a class, I sit there thinking — I want to do it; I love it. But I also like getting teachers to cooperate and getting them to improve their lot in the school and that's how I see my job. I chair meetings at which thorny problems are discussed and I'm the one who keeps track about whether we're on subject. And I'm the one who provides the materials ahead of time; I'm the one who reads all the junk mail that comes in the office to find out what's new; and I'm the one who gets the notices of conferences and I'm the one who goes and translates it. I really regard those 125 or 150 teachers as my class. I have a mental file kind of like, of where each one of them is. I don't know all of them, but some of them I know very well. And if I see something and think — well, so and so could make use of this, then I call that one and I arrange for that to happen."

(Who should control curriculum: the teachers, the board, the administration, the students?)

I don't think the board should have anything to do with it. At least around here our board members are not experts on education. They're farmers; they're small businessmen; they're good citizens. Why anybody becomes a board member with the grief they get is beyond me. But I think the board should set policy with input from the administrators and the teachers, which is what they do around here. And I think it depends on who you've got in the administration. If you have a principal who keeps up on what's going on, who has a solid foundation in curriculum — many of our principals were coaches [in] physical education. Many of them have never taught in a regular classroom. I've taken the principal courses; I have a certificate to be a principal. In one course they asked the question, how do you explain the fact that many of our principals do not provide instructional leadership? And I said — for one thing, they're too busy with the manager stuff; but look at what was required to become a principal — one course in curriculum! You can't be an expert in curriculum if you don't take curriculum courses. If your master's degree is in education and you take two more courses and you get a principal certificate, you're an expert in managing a school building; you are not an expert in curriculum."

(Do you think administrators should have the "power" to tell teachers they should teach a certain way?)

"I think there are a great number of options for teaching that are effective; however, there are some that are absolutely destructive, and if I were a building administrator and I saw these things happening in my building, I'd want to have the power to tell them to stop it: shaming children, belittling them, giving them unreasonable homework assignments — those kinds to things are harmful to children. But if a teacher has a good reason for teaching a certain way, then I think that they should be allowed to do it. There is no question that there are lots and lots of ways to teach effectively and some of it is dependent on the cognitive role of the teacher. Teachers around here are receptive to my ideas in general, but I don't try to push them too hard either. Mostly what they do is they say — I want to do this, how can I do it best? And I give them five choices and they pick."

Tape #185 PRINCIPAL

When I asked Mr. L. if he thought teachers should have more control of curriculum and education decision making, he said, "I thought they did." Mr. L. was a principal, not a working teacher, so it was interesting that some teachers in his building thought they did, too. They did not as was evidenced by examples given to me by other teachers in the district. But I couldn't help including Mr. L. since he so typically personifies the principal — and an apparently decent principal at that. He had only taught in the classroom for six years before he was offered a principalship. He had been a principal of some sort for fifteen years. Now he oversaw a large and rich high school in a well-to-do area; he stressed the academics.

(Did you feel once you left the classroom that you missed it?)

"You miss explaining the subject matter that is interesting to you to another person and having them see for themselves the same understanding that you have — I miss working with the kids individually and working with them on experiments and just talking with them in a *what-if-we-do-this* sort of way. Although, I will tell you that administration is a form of teaching. I think that I teach something else — you know, I always did some discipline and some athletics. So I was always teaching, though my subject matter was different. When it comes to discipline, helping the kids with their problems and things like that — I still think that I'm teaching every day. You know, my definition of teaching is that from the time your car comes into the parking lot to the time you leave that door, you're modeling; and that's the best example of teaching I know."

(Why do teachers mention administrators as such a big problem?)

"I think it's the same problem in any position when people perceive their boss as someone over them. The teachers are trained to be experts in their fields and to have someone else tell them or have a direct legal influence on what they can or can't do is a source of conflict just like it would be in any situation, especially when the person may not be an expert in their field. I think that's true wherever you are — you're going to have that. Much more in the professions. Plus, don't forget a lot of us have not been trained in taking direction. We've come from four or five years of college where we've been very successful — you weren't selected for that teaching position unless you were successful — and that becomes a problem. Also, there are no right answers. So anyone with an opinion who wished to express it can either attack you as an administrator or support you and it comes from all different sides so it seems like one person's opinion is as good as someone else's. You never know when there's a right answer. It was one of the most delicate things you can have. I always like to tell my staff that I'm part of the solution, not the problem. I always tell them I'll praise in public and criticize in private. I always value everybody's ideas — that doesn't mean I agree with them. I go with the fact that they do have some good ideas but maybe the time is not right for their ideas. I tell them that decisions will be made —- *I* make decisions — but I always do get input. And so I try to take the onus off of them of having to blame each other for a decision made. They can blame me — which may or may not help. And I try to let them know that I like them personally. I know I often have to make a decision that isn't in their favor. So I tell them, I know this is not a decision that works in your value system; I have to do it this time — here is the reason. Disagree with the reason, but at least I want you to know the reason."

(So you think the evaluation process makes part of the tension between the teacher and the administration?)

". . . it shouldn't. The evaluation process should be kind of a mutual substantiation of somebody's abilities. The goal should be mutual improvement and the way it's set up in this district is a lot of things that we evaluate is what the teachers tell us they would like to work on. We're all hopefully being trained in the same teacher-learning model, so we're all talking the same language. So I go into a class where I look for something the teacher said 'will you help me on this?' Also I've always felt that teacher evaluation was really something of a misnomer; that what I was doing was — I wanted to be a colleague going into the classroom, giving them some suggestions from what I've seen before. I look at myself as a sharer of information. What you do well in your classroom I'll share with another teacher and so on — to me, that's the improvement of instruction. Evaluation to me means whether you're going to hire or fire somebody, and out of a staff of say seventy people here, you maybe get into that once a year."

(Another complaint I often hear is that if an administrator has only been in the classroom six years and that was fifteen years ago — they don't feel that it's valid for a person to evaluate their teaching.)

"I think I'm probably better than anyone they could get in evaluating the interaction in the classroom environment; but they're right when it comes to evaluating the curriculum — ok. But I would tell you that I've seen — just based on experience — I've seen more than they have, and I think I've seen more day to day what goes through the dean's office and what goes through our social worker and our counselors, what goes on at home. I spend a lot of time in the halls of the school just walking and taking temperature — environmental temperature of the kids. And I think that when it comes to evaluating a teacher — of the classroom environment, of how they relate to the kids, what communication — verbal and non-verbal — they're giving out, I can do that very well . . . probably better than any colleague, and be more frank with them. And I usually like to look at it as I observe this and I tell you this for your information — work it around and see how it fits you. I think I'm better at this than their colleagues because of my experience and the training I've had. I've been in classrooms for eighteen years (as a principal); I've seen every subject area; I've seen every ability; I've seen the parents who come and cry, emotionally upset when things aren't right. I think I know through experience and through study — but mainly through experience — what kinds of things work in that area. Curriculum-wise, I couldn't tell a French teacher how to teach French or what to put into it . . . and I've never tried. As an English teacher like you, I couldn't tell you how to teach writing; the English teacher I would hire would have a plan in her own mind how to get from A to B and can work their own plan."

(Can you take a stab at the percentage of what you think are good principals nationwide?)

"Are good principals? Ha, you might think I'm lying when I say you'd like to think they're all good principals hired and selected for that job. It's like teachers — you'd like to think they're all good teachers because they've gone through a process of being hired and selected. Uh . . . I'm not sure; I think it's a success that is probably situational. There are definitely mismatches for that position. I know I'm skirting your question. I don't have an answer for you. I can't put a number on it. I know what happens probably when they say that principal is no good is that that person probably is not good for *that* situation. You do not become a principal because you are an unsuccessful teacher or assistant principal or whatever jobs you had prior to becoming a principal. I spent six years as a teacher and approximately another sixteen years as an assistant principal and I went to a lot of schools, and each of those experiences was successful for me. At least you go through them — and then you were selected to be a principal just as a teacher is selected for a job. I don't select unsuccessful people. Now granted, some principals do become bad principals because of personal problems. It's almost like being in a war where they say there's a bullet out there with your name on it. For a principal, there's always a parent out there with your name on it — right on the forehead. (Laughter) It's just a matter of you just picked the wrong person to get in a disagreement with. I think success is so situational."

(Do you think that public education by and large is successful?)

"It depends on your definition."

(By your definition.)

"Yes, I think we do a good job — now this is for our school here — we do a good job of keeping our students doing a total job of learning until they're eighteen."

(Would you go back into education?)

"Yes . . . I think I'd do the same thing I'm doing now."

(Become an administrator . . .)

"Well — I think so. I like to be a principal in a building. I like being in the building. That's why I think I'm still a teacher. Sometimes I teach teachers. Well — really I explain to them our position or how we do something or policy. But I still think I'm teaching every day. And I know I've never left that. And I always like to get out in the building because I know there's always something new happening. So to answer your question, yes, I think I'd still be a teacher."

COUNTER-COUNTERPOINT:
THE HORROR STORIES
Tape #110

You want administrative horror stories? By the time a well-dressed Ms. S. was finished talking to me in her classroom during her free period at the middle school where she taught eighth grade English, she was in tears. She had retold a story to me about administrative non-support, and tears finally came brimming out of her eyes when she said she just didn't know if she could stay in teaching. She had gotten out once before. Now, after sixteen years of teaching altogether (and one as headmistress of a small private school), she was at that point again . . . and again . . . and again. Teachers are constantly being treated unprofessionally by administrators whose jobs basically should be to facilitate the teachers' jobs. Every teacher has his or her administrative horror story. ". . . and I've had nothing but master teacher evaluations."

"First I started teaching, and then I got married and moved out of state, and that put me in another grade level. And then when I came back to teach here, when my husband went to Viet Nam, that put me in another grade level. And then I resigned after seven years of teaching. I needed to get out. Administrators burn you out. It was time to get out. So while I was out, it was the perfect opportunity to have children, and I stayed home while my two children were home. And when I came back to teaching, six years later, we had what was called a surplus of teachers in the buildings. So if you're low seniority, which I was, because I'd lost all my seniority when I resigned, then you get bumped around. I went from fifth grade to kindergarten, from kindergarten to fourth, and that kind of movement, you know. Oh, it was a terrible amount of work, like being a first-year teacher each time. However, you're never stale. There's a lot that can be said about it. At the time I resented being surplus, when I worked my tail off and then they'd tell me I'm surplus. And then I get into kindergarten and I have absolutely nothing for kindergarten like they teach it here. It was very difficult. I worked every night and every weekend. If I went anywhere, I took my work with me. When my kids were playing soccer, I had my kindergarten work. Whether it's cut and paste, cut out, you know, everything — you don't find a lot of supplies for kindergarten. A lot of it's teacher-made. So you just take your little bucket of cut-and-pasting glue and yarn and sequins and buttons and everything you need. People thought I was a little bizarre at first, but they got to where they asked if they could help at the games. 'Let me cut something out.' So I started carrying extra scissors, and you know, it worked to my benefit!"

(How did you get to the seventh grade level, teaching English?)

"Why did I come to middle school? It was either middle school or get out of education. I became very frustrated with elementary education. There is no discipline in elementary. You do not have any support system. Johnny's always right . . . according to parents and most of your administrators. 'You need to show more patience.' I mean, if they lived with the kids six hours and fifty minutes, they would lose patience too, especially after you've put up with it for a semester. And you have conferences, and if the child isn't learning or he isn't doing his work, it was not 'why isn't Ricky doing his work,' it was 'why can't you *make* him do his work; he sits there all day.' And then when you would try to say, 'All right, fine, but why didn't he do what he was supposed to last night?' — 'Well, I can't *make* him.' They have three kids at home, maybe five; some rare exceptions, eight. They don't have thirty-three sitting in that classroom. And yet we're supposed to be God. You have conferences with parents; the administrators you expect to support you, and they don't. They will tell you one thing before the meeting — yeah, they'll support you and all this. You sit in the meeting with the parents, and it blows out right in front of your eyes. You don't say anything because the parent does not need to know the dissension within the educational field.

"I was at one school and I had a child who refused to work, all year. I had conferences with the mother and everything, and it's 'why can't you' — she had two children — 'why can't you make him learn; why can't you make him do his work?' But yet when he would go home to do something, he came back with a blank sheet always. She didn't have time. She worked. And she had other children. She had *one* other child. I had thirty-three sitting in my room. So we had this conference and all this, and I documented every paper he didn't do. I made copies. I kept the originals, sent mother a copy, counselor a copy, principal a copy. At the end of the year I had a folder probably four inches thick, of every paper that child did not do, with his name on it and why he did not do it. I didn't want to hear ... 'I lost it,' 'I can't find it,' 'I don't care' — you know. I may still have that file in my basement, because that kid's not coming back to sue me, that I didn't try to teach him. I wanted to retain him.

"Principal: 'Well, I don't know, I don't know, I don't know.' Counselors: 'I don't know, I don't know.' So if you can get the support of the parents — I called the parent in and I got her support. I even got her to agree with it in written form. Ok? The next year a new principal comes in. File, four inches thick of the reasons why that child is retained. What'd they do? Put him in fifth grade. 'Not enough evidence.' Now you tell me that's not disgusting. It's time to get out, when that teacher has no backing. I sat with the kid, worked with the kid, nagged the kid, bragged the kid, did everything. I just could not reach him. True, I was a failure with that child. But he knew Mother wouldn't make him, and he knew Mother blamed the system. He failed in the Catholic school system and they tossed him out. Then he came to the public schools. So it's all the educational system.

'Why can't they do for my child?' But she didn't do. And then when you go through all this, and you even go to the trouble to log it and document it, and they pass them on — I was ready to get out. My husband, being a counselor, says 'Don't give up; you have good potential.' I am a good teacher. I work hard at it and I care. So I came here three years ago, in a burned-out situation, and was totally revived.

"I think a lot of the problems were highlighted when teachers started gaining rights through the unions. Until then, they had no control. They couldn't grieve in a situation. Believe me, it was truly needed. Because you have principals, who have their little groups, and they can say all they want to [to deny it] — it happens, in every school. But teachers need unions, and I think that's when they started splitting, administration and teachers. When teachers found out 'My god! I am an adult; I have rights. Mercy!' You know, they never realized that until they got into a union and found out. It can give you time for free lunch. It can give you potty time. And they cannot force you into hours and hours and hours of meetings. That has made administrators less comfortable; I think it makes them defensive.

"And I was an administrator — at a private school I was what they called a headmaster for one year. There was no gratification in being a principal. The contacts you have are usually with irate parents, discouraged, problem children, never in happy situations. Everything seemed to be more on the negative, and you didn't relate with children that much. And, to be perfectly honest, if I had to choose between being continually around adults or teenagers, I'd choose teenagers.

"But I've had an awful year this year, because I've fought the school system all the way to the superintendent. Over what? Taking a group of students to New York. We took them last year, and they were perfectly happy. They thought it was wonderful we went. We spent our own money. We had to take sick days or personal days to go. They would not give us professional days. The teachers paid their own way; we took sick days, personal days, plus we supervised kids for five days. Ok? I asked for professional days for my teachers. I planned this trip. One of my bright ideas. And last year I couldn't get them. It was late in the year; I accepted that. This summer, I worked all summer on a curriculum for this trip. I mean, we've got booklets for these kids that go with science, social studies, math, and the language arts. So I asked for the professional days the second day school was in session. I did not get them. They told me last year I couldn't have them because they were all gone. This year they told me they didn't think they were going to get any. Okay, I'm on the association board. I found out they reinstated four hundred professional days. I came back, had all my teachers sign up for professional leave. They denied them. They weren't giving trips for teachers this year. And I thought, hell, if you're going to deny me this year without a fight.

"So I called the [administrator in charge of middle school issues], and he informed me he 'didn't talk to teachers.' If I had a problem, tell my principal and my principal would relay it to him. That did nothing more than make a volcano erupt. So I came back and I wrote a letter to the big honcho underneath our superintendent. I got a letter back guaranteeing me I could have those days. Resubmitted. Denied again. So I wrote a letter to the superintendent. I happened to be at a local board meeting. Three bigwigs underneath the superintendent were there for a discussion. And the big honcho who promised me the days said something about the morale of teachers was higher than he had ever seen it in the system. And I asked to address that remark; I gave him a log of everything that had happened, plus the fact *you* promised me the days and you reneged on them. So I have a five-page letter to the superintendent. Right after the meeting they guaranteed me I'd have those days. And I said I am sorry, but I don't accept anything unless it's in writing. I've been guaranteed verbally by you before. I sent my letter to the superintendent. I got back a letter that was just a slough-off letter. I hope your problem's taken care of. This is from the superintendent!

"Now that's what causes teachers to burn out! All the way up the line. But yet if it weren't for my kids, sitting in my room, I wouldn't have a job and [the administrators] sure as hell wouldn't. But they forget why they're there. They've got the big salaries; they go to the big workshops and the big conferences, and that's just like this middle school guy says, 'Oh, we're going to use this money for conferences.' I went to the middle school conferences. The president of the middle school conference said, 'How many of you would be interested in partying next year all the way to St. Louis and back for the conference, because that's where it's going to be next year?' Partying! Professional days will be given for partying to a middle school conference, and I can't take my kids to New York with professional days. That's true. I've got every bit of it logged, verified. I was ready to go to the papers. And I think Mr. Big Honcho knew it.

"Finally they approved it. Finally. But I told them, I won't stop at the superintendent. My next step was school board, media. And I would have been on local news. And I'd dare them to try to fire me, because I'd sue their butts off.

"I'd say we've got enough principals that need to be kicked out, just like these deficit teachers. We have an awful lot of inadequate administrators.

"For example, I had a student this year, at the end of school, defy me; totally defy me. Whether I told him to sit down and be quiet, go to the office, go stand out in the hall — eleven times. I called the principal down. I couldn't get him out. He's six feet four inches, three hundred pounds. You can see his stature compared to mine. And he refused to do anything. Called the principal. It was the end of school. She says, 'Oh, I've got to go make announcements' — over that thing — 'so I'll be back.' She couldn't even get him to shut up. She called the parents. Couldn't get ahold of the parents. Next day the parent comes in and paddles his butt. That's what the parent should have done anyway, but the school did nothing and he was back in my room fourth period. They go into ISAP [In-School Adjustment Program], it's a big joke. 'Where have you been?' 'I'm in ISAP today and tomorrow. Ha, ha, ha!'

"And after that process they're supposed to be suspended. Kids don't even care if they're suspended anymore. All these central administrators have told [the principals] hold down on the suspensions. Jody had been in so much trouble, already had a bad record, and yet he defied me eleven times and was back in my class then the next day. Tell me that's not disgusting. You're looking at a Jody Nelson outfit. This is what I bought after I couldn't get any gratification at this school for discipline. This is an original Jody Nelson. He cost me two hundred dollars. Well, I bought two. And two drinks. I couldn't get anything from the principal.

"I work damn hard at being a good teacher. Well, my God, sixteen years, and I've been whipped sixteen years. How many battles do you lose? I would have walked out this year except for my counselor, my husband — he is a counselor. And he uses all the counseling techniques on me. But they're going to lose a hell of a lot of good teachers, like me. And I know I'm good, because I work hard at it. And I've never had anything but a master evaluation. But they're going to lose so many, and it's going to be so sad, if they don't straighten up. I'm very feeling about education. But they won't do it, they will not do it, till it gets to — crumbles. I tell you right now, anybody that talks to me, I'll tell them: Are you sure you want to teach? And if you want teaching, do you want public? And it's not the kids I'm talking about, it's the administration; the bureaucracy. They've forgot why they're there. We fight for why they're here, and we're losing. They've got all the power; they have all the money. We don't have

anything but a lot of frustration. And we have the heart of the business —
the kids. They don't have that. It's sad."

Tape #254

*I only got to talk to Ms. M. for about five minutes . . . and then I was
kicked out of her school by her principal. Even though I later got back into
the school . . . it seemed symptomatic of what's partly wrong with public
education — everyone is so scared. Ms. M. actually bent down and
sneaked back to another table in the faculty lunchroom when her principal
came in and asked to see me. She was that frightened of her own boss. Her
principal was the type of female administrator who gives woman bosses a
bad name. In the hall as she was telling me I had to leave, she stopped
another teacher of her staff and asked her if she had left the building —
she swore she had seen this teacher's car not fifteen minutes ago. I wanted
to slug her and then remind her that this other woman was a professional
person who shouldn't have to be kept in a building unless she had
permission to leave. What school administrator has the right to tell a
working professional teacher to whom he or she can talk during their
lunch break? And if the schools really want to work, what have they got to
hide? Do schools really want people to come in and see how well they're
doing? Not the paranoids in this upstate New York city school district.*

*By the way, Ms. M. was forty-one, had taught seventh-eighth grade
math for twenty-two years, and was teaching in an inner city school.*

"The major problem in an inner city school is discipline. I just went
nuts a few minutes ago with the teachers at the lunch table . . . that's why
they were laughing. I had this child enrolled that will not listen at all. You
know — won't do the work. I've tried ignoring her; I've tried writing her
up. I've tried being nice to her. And — she will walk out while you're
teaching. She doesn't have the homework, doesn't have the book. And she
answers you back . . . she's fourteen. There are two or three of these in
every single class, but this kid has just gotten to me in the last couple of
weeks. So they told me to keep an anecdotal record of every single day, so
I did for two weeks and then for the last week I've totally ignored her. She
can jump up and down, do whatever she wants . . . I'm going to just
pretend that this child doesn't exist in this room. I did that for a week and
that didn't help, so today when she walked out again, I calmly walked out
into the hall, and said, '_____, when you're finished playing in the hall,
please go to the principal's office.' And I closed the door because the kid

goes nuts when you talk to her. The principal came in and asked me where _____ was and I went nuts on the principal. 'I don't know where she is,' I told her. Here's a list of the things she does . . . here's a list of the things that I've told you have been going wrong. I have been telling you people this over and over again. I don't know what else to do. I mean — I'm at my wit's end. So finally today the assistant principal came in and said that they would have a counseling hearing for _____. (Yelling) That was after I went completely crazy and for three weeks went home and screamed at my husband over this kid. Plus, for a week of trying to ignore her, I felt that this wasn't —"

Tape #87

I interviewed Ms. Q. in her living room; she sat on a pillow on the floor across from me on the couch. I didn't have to ask any questions; she had already thought out a short outline of what she wanted to talk about. What I found the most interesting was her own personal horror story with an administrator.

She had taught French and Spanish for fourteen years at the high school level, two years in parochial schools, one year in a very backwards rural district, and the rest in middle class suburban districts. She was thin, thirty-nine and single.

Before I left, she pointed out that she waited tables to make extra money to buy her cars and pay for her flying. She noted that she could make more money on tips from a good Friday and Saturday night and Sunday afternoon than in a full week of teaching . . . and she had a master's degree plus thirty hours.

Ms. Q.'s was the quintessential administrative horror story.

"In the thirteen or fourteen years that I have taught, I have seen behaviors such as cheating totally sanctioned by parents and administrators and by some teachers — teachers that aren't necessarily the strongest teachers but that want to be the most popular teachers. They know what's going on and they might not necessarily approve of it. I have taught with teachers that know that cheating is going on in their classroom and some of them have even encouraged it in an indirect way because it makes the grades higher. I have seen parents say, 'Well, if you motivated the student, he wouldn't feel like he had to cheat. It's because you're not doing your job that that student feels like he had to cheat.' Not, mind you, because the student is out until 10:00 or 11:00 on a basketball team or working at

McDonald's until midnight and getting up at 5:00 the next morning to get ready for school. [Reasons] like that don't cut it with the parent, but when you call them in and say, 'Look at this little cheat note that I picked up from Johnny,' and [the parent] says, 'Well, he tells me you're a lousy teacher and you're not motivating him and that's why he had to resort to methods like this.'

"I know at my other high school one time there was a teacher committee formed for looking into the cheating problem. It turned out there were a number of teachers there who were very concerned about the cheating problem at that high school. We all did not get to express our opinions about it as it turned out because, after about the third committee meeting, the principal brought in a group of students and he had the students berate teachers, those who were there, present at the meeting and those who were not. 'If these teachers taught better, we wouldn't feel like we had to cheat. Teachers should tell us exactly what is going to be on the test, rather than to just say study Chapter Fourteen. We know methods of cheating; teachers are so stupid that they permit this to go on in their room.' Teachers were made to feel — first of all, why bother ever even complaining and why bother requesting a committee to study a problem again because it's no use — no good has come out of it. Secondly, their self-esteem was lowered by this. So when I say cheating on the part of the students is sanctioned by parents and administration and by some teachers, it's because some teachers see that if they permit a student to cheat, that they're not going to have a problem with that kid. That kid is going to maintain a good grade. Then they are going to allow that to happen and I've seen that, too . . . .

"I was in litigation for three years [over a situation where my principal tried to fire me due to my run-in with a county sheriff]. Meanwhile, my principal was calling private meetings with parents and making references at faculty meetings. I was barred from faculty meetings and he would talk to the faculty about me. He would, under the threat of insubordination, order me to stay in my room. I'm serious. He did this during PTA or PTO, whatever. The open houses — when he would have the parents down to the gym ten minutes before open house would start and then he would introduce the whole faculty — under threat of insubordination, he would order me to remain in my classroom so that I wouldn't appear as a member of the faculty. That went on for two or three years. What I went through there, and I'm sure there are a lot of other teachers in the state that have too . . . incredible.

When I was going through the lawsuit with T. [her principal], he was going to come into my classroom to evaluate me — I have always said that my classroom has an open door, 'Come in any time you want to; you don't have to forewarn me; don't do anything; just come in; I don't care; I'd love for you to see what my kids are doing.' Well, he was going to be coming into my classroom and the day before, unbeknownst to me, he called, I would say, about a half a dozen kids out of my classroom in a French class which was very small and I found out that they had spent my French class in his office the previous day. Well then, the following day he came in to observe my class and I taped it because I knew that he was going to be observing. I did not say to the kids, 'I am going to be taping this class.' I was a little deceitful. What I said was, 'I'm cleaning tapes — I'm erasing tapes over here so if you see me go over to my cassette recorder, don't worry about it, I'm trying to get some clean tapes.' I was not cleaning tapes. I was taping my class because I wanted my attorney to be able to hear what was going on. In mid-sentence of an instructional statement — I had bright kids — 'How many keys are on a French typewriter?' 'Miss Q., are there four words for 'cat' in French?' 'Miss Q., how many pages are in a French dictionary?' I would only be able to get to mid-statement and I could tell this was set up because these kids had *never* behaved this way. The kids that were doing this were the kids that were in his office the previous day. So at the end of class I decided, 'What the hey.' I walked over to my cassette recorder and I said, 'Oh my gosh. Would you believe I've got it on recording? Now I'm going to have to erase them all over again.' Well, these kids about fainted. They paled. In fact, one of them, Keith, the next day said, 'Miss Q., did you know that it was illegal for you to have taped us yesterday?' And I said, 'Oh, goodness, I had no intention of taping you. I was just cleaning the tapes. I told you that.' 'Well,' he said, 'that really wasn't right. You shouldn't have done that.' And he had been one that had asked me how many keys were on a French typewriter or something to that effect, rude questions that were constantly being thrown out to spoil my train of thought so that the instructional procedure would be interrupted continuously."

Section 10:

SOCIETY

While I was editing this section and thinking about what to write for its introduction, a friend who works at a home for disturbed youth told me about one of his charges' experiences from the day before. The boy is thirteen, and they had to tell him that the courts had decided that he wouldn't be allowed to see his mother anymore. The mother abused him, mentally and perhaps physically. It was known by the court psychologist that she slept with the boy at times when he was home; she also told him that he was going to grow up and go to jail "just like his father." In fact, she usually openly disliked him because he was blacker in color than she and her other lighter skinned children. Once, when the home had called to arrange a weekend visit with his mother, she had told them no, she had to get her hair done that weekend.

As one teacher told me, "It was easier to teach forty-two kids in the '60s than it is to teach thirty today." Our changing society — less responsible, less caring, less willing to sacrifice — is today one of the largest negative influences in public education. Not only do schools reflect the society in which they exist . . . but they have to deal with those very same problems of which they are a part. The better parents make mistakes and send their children to schools to get fixed; the worst parents do horrible things and send their kids to school to get them out of their hair. Either way, we must try to "fix" them, because these children must work and exist safely with other children. It is a different world than it was yesterday; it's a whole other universe than it was twenty years ago. Children may always have certain behaviors that don't change, but the environment in which they act out those behaviors has; and this, in turn, has greatly decreased their possibility for success in growing up and in academic learning.

How do you tell a thirteen year old boy living in the confines of a group home that he can't see his mother anymore? And then — how do you teach him?

Tape #109

Her father had taught in a one-room schoolhouse when she was a very small child.

Ms. L. looked like she had been on the front lines for the twenty years she had. She was tall, more or less blonde, and had a take-charge attitude. She taught in a lower socio-economic middle school. It was, she told me, the very school that had started an infamously messy desegregation suit that wracked the city she was in twelve years before. She was fifty-three, married, with four children of her own. She taught English.

She summed up the two aspects of one of the largest problems facing the public education system, which as a matter of course reflects the society in which it exists: parents and kids.

"My father was a teacher when I was a young child. He taught in a one-room school down in _____ County, Kentucky, in the western part of the state. It was in the country, very small, and had grades one through eight. The older kids helped the younger kids. What they did was a lot of the open-classroom concept that we talked about years later. I know; I talked about it with my father. He told me that really it wasn't anything new; that in fact, that's what he used to have. It's a one-room school, where you had all the grades going and [doing] different things, and the older children assisting the younger ones. He taught all subjects. You know, you had four or five kids in each of the areas. And a lot of this global kind of teaching and concepts. I can remember going to school with him when I was a small child, very small, and I know he was very active in trying to improve working conditions for teachers and what was happening. His whole family was very education oriented, so we just sort of fell into teaching. I have three sisters. The four of us have all taught school, and three of us are still active in it.

"What's wrong with public education? Lack of parental support, lack of discipline, inadequate funds. Schools are trying to meet all the needs of children, social as well as educational, and we aren't equipped for that. We're not properly prepared to deal with pre-suicidal kids, kids on drugs, the many, many problems they bring to school, the one-parent problem, with families where the parent has to work; they are never able to come to school. I'm not sure you can say one is the worst. I think many of them fit together. The fact that you have so many children from — in our particular situation, from low socio-economic status — whose parents work, whose parents are never home, who aren't disciplined, aren't supervised. They come to school and it's a social setting for them rather than a learning environment. There's no one who really cares whether they learn or not. It's — 'you take care of them while I have to work.'

"There used to be a very strong parental support for education and for the student and the school; and the desire for parents to want the children to succeed and to make good grades [and] to learn as much as they could. I think it has changed. But I started off with it; then there was a period of time in teaching, in the twenty years I've taught, where it was absolute chaos in the schools, where you were physically afraid in some instances, back during the desegregation times. When this became the middle school, the first year we thought we were successful if we ever got all the kids out of the hallway. That's not true here today. So we've gone through a period and we've come back. But when you have kids who have no self-respect and you have to start with teaching them that, then it's more difficult to teach.

"I'm sure a lot of it has to do with drugs. A lot of it has to do with the break-up of the family unit. A lot of kids that we finally have in school, that are having some problems, are kids who did not have a good start in life, who probably never had prenatal care, who haven't had adequate diets or adequate taking care of since that time. And then you get them here and they have all sorts of problems. If I could write a philosophy of education and could start back with a model, I'd spend the first two months of the school year working on the child's own concept of what he or she is all about. So many of our kids have a poor self-image.

"But we still have every kind of drug problem in the middle school setting. There is alcohol, marijuana, speed, pills. One group we had was getting high on an over-the-counter drug, because if you take enough of them, they'll get you high."

(You've personally had these kids and dealt with these problems)

"Oh, yes. I'd say the percentage of kids who have experimented with drugs in this school — fifty wouldn't be too high . . . with some kind of a chemical or drug abuse. You notice an effect in the classroom. When the kids come — some of them fall asleep, some of them are hyper, some are spaced out. And what can a teacher do about that? Not much, unless you're willing to call the parents; you can suggest — I have suggested — that they take them in for a complete physical. I've talked to them about the fact they fall asleep in class or are not attentive or have problems concentrating or have problems getting things done. You can suggest this, and that's about all. I've had parents come in and tell me, 'I want you to understand that my child is pre-suicidal and is under treatment.' *I'm* not trained to deal with pre-suicidal kids. I'm not trained to deal with kids with drug problems. My training doesn't extend that far. And yet you do it every day. Emotional problems. We've had students in this middle school who have tried to take their own lives. And I see more of this now than when I first started teaching. A lot more. Before, you wouldn't mention drugs in a junior high setting.

"I invited a college professor from U. of __. to come and take my class for a week. And he took the challenge. And I said you can't come for one day, you have to come for a whole week and stay every day. And at the end of the time, we talked. I said, 'Well, tell me, what was your experience?' He said, 'Well, I'll tell you one thing, I had to throw out a lot of my concepts.' He says, 'Teaching has changed since I was in school and I had to do a lot of things differently. And some things I did just simply to be able to survive in the classroom.'

(Do you think society has less respect for teachers?)

"Definitely. We have become the whipping boy for what's wrong in this country — not just what's wrong with education, but 'why can't Johnny read,' and 'why do we have so many illiterates,' and 'why aren't businesses attracted and kept,' and 'why can't we get in new industry,' and — the easy, easy target has been to blame the teaching population. We have become the whipping boy for a lot of social ills, and we don't deserve it. When my father taught school forty years ago, the teacher in the community had a great deal of respect and a great deal of support by the community and was looked up to. Teachers burn out easily because of the inability to control the students or the problems they have and the kids not wanting to do the work, and all of these things combined, and the low self-esteem, the low income, and the fact that we are not treated as professionals — teachers burn out. Teachers say, 'Well, if I had it to do over again, I wouldn't go into teaching.' I don't happen to feel that way. I like what I do and I like working with kids. And I've had opportunities to do other things. But I don't think you can attract a lot of our bright kids to come in.

They say, no, I can make more money. I have four kids of my own. None of them have gone into teaching."

Tape #39

"Children learn at three years old that adults are assholes."

Ms. A. described herself as "hard-assed." She was forty-three and teaching her sixteenth year as an elementary school art teacher. She was — outspoken. She lazily combed her hair through the first part of the interview and told someone afterwards that they should be interviewed, that all I did was sit there and say "yes" and nod. She was attractive in an artsy way, long streaked hair. Her hobbies were scuba diving, painting, and singing. She was married with one kid and she taught in a poor school in a mainly suburban school district.

The next day she dropped into the room I was using to interview to see how it was going. She told me it was a little like therapy to talk to me yesterday and wanted me to know how much she enjoyed it. If she knew as much about getting kids to like her as she knew how to get men to like her, she probably was a terrific teacher.

Still, amidst all her color, Ms. A. saw the parent problem of education very clearly.

"The problem with public education is the parents. It's very simple. Because we really can't do very much about it. We're doing a fantastic job. We're doing an unbelievable job because not only are we teaching the three Rs, but we're also teaching morals and giving these children, poor little things, a sense of worth and making sure they get fed and making sure they have the right kind of clothes and it's just — it's a horror of our society, that people are not aware enough and don't believe in themselves enough to push forward their ideas onto their children. They are so unsure of themselves in this world that they push nothing forward in the way of ideas so what we have going to school are little, tiny little things that really don't know the difference between right and wrong. I really think it's very different from twenty years ago."

"There was a moral code twenty years ago. When I was in high school, we had a little test that went around that all the girls took. Question number one was, 'Have you ever kissed a boy?' and question number ten was, 'Have you ever gone all the way?' and it was very exciting. You never told anyone your answer. That was a very racy thing to do. But times have changed and that's terrible. In those days, there was a set standard and everybody knew what you weren't supposed to do. People that didn't really have any intrinsic moral ideas knew what the standard was so at least they could tell their children that 'you're not supposed to do this,' and 'you're not supposed to do that.' But there's been a breakdown and people don't trust themselves anymore and they don't give any moral standards to their kids.

"Now, schools shouldn't teach values; however, no one else is teaching them values and the thing that happens is that you get a class of children and you'll have someone steal someone else's thing and no one knows whether it's right or wrong so you have to sit and you have to explain why morally you should not steal. The fundamentalists, they don't want the schools' morals to conflict with their ideas and the liberals say that education is for education and I agree with all that. But, if it's not being done anywhere else, it has to be done in the school, for the simple reason that the children have to function in a moral framework. You can't have twenty-five children in your class learning unless you have some kind of moral code with which to keep them as a cohesive group. It's practical — it's got to be done.

"But yes, the schools have taken on too much of the parents' job. We should not *have* to teach morals. We should not *have* to teach values. We should not *have* to teach sex education. We should not *have* to feed children — we have a nutrition unit that the kids do every year and the teacher says, 'Who ate breakfast? Who didn't eat breakfast?' And you get five or six kids in every class that say, 'I wanted to eat breakfast, but there was nothing in the house.' Why is that? It is because Mommy's working the swing shift and Daddy's in jail and there is nobody to feed them. Or, there's no milk. I can't tell you how many times children eat Frosted Flakes with no milk. By ten o'clock they're hungry, and you say, 'What did you have for breakfast?' And they say, 'Frosted Flakes.' And I say, 'Did you have any milk?' And they say, 'No, there wasn't any in the icebox.' And that's what you are confronted with.

"I'd also like to see a full-time psychologist at every school. There are so many kids with problems that I have heard two psychologists say within the last two years, unless it's a chronic case, 'Don't refer them to me. I've got too much of a load.' For example, there was a little boy that was thrown out of my school last week for molesting a little girl. He's going to rape somebody. He's a very sick little boy. He's got to wait three weeks to see the school psychologist and then his mother is very recalcitrant when it comes to helping him, which is one of the reasons he is so sick. So she's not going to push. If there was a full-time psychologist in the schools, because of his lack of moral training, etc, he would have somebody there to talk to when he needed it. I think it would be very beneficial to society. But I don't think you'd be able to measure it very well, so it's probably not something that they'd do. Still, if they just had somebody there to talk to with these poor little things with their day-to-day problems — when Daddy comes home drunk and beats up Mommy, and when they have to move at night because they haven't paid the rent.

"How much of that can a teacher do? Very little because our job is really there to teach the children academic skills. But if they just had somebody there to help them, tell them what the right thing is and guide these children that are going to end up, without some help quickly, in our penal institutions — maybe that would help some."

(What would you say to teachers who have said that they don't feel that they are as respected today as in the past?)

"First of all, I've taught sixteen years and I'm forty-three. I started at twenty-five so I should have taught, maybe, twenty. Let's say, let's take somebody that's taught thirty years. They started teaching in '53. They were aware of the war and when it went on. The laws and the morals of this country were very different in the late forties and fifties when they were receiving their education. They had very high moral standards; people knew what was right and wrong. Then there's television. When you went in as a teacher, you were very respected. Children were very naive and you knew what was right and wrong and we were the best country in the world. What happened between the '50s and the '70s? We became more of a world community and we also got television. Television did a very interesting thing to children. There are no naive children in this country anymore. There are dumb children, but there are no naive children. Children learn at three years old that adults are assholes [because of television]. So when they get into the classroom, the teachers don't get the automatic respect that they did fifteen or twenty years before. Then they think that it's because of the children and it is, but at the same time the children know that adults are assholes and they are desperately, desperately trying to find a person of some worth. So if you show them that you have worth and that they can rely on your word and you mean what you say and you are strong and you are interested in them, they will do anything they can. The respect is there but you have to earn it as a teacher today. It doesn't automatically crawl in your lap. The people that I know today that say they don't get any respect from the kids are people that were brought up in a different world in a different generation and they don't understand that you are judged on you own merits, not on your position."

(What would your perfect school be like?)

"I'd like to teach in a school where the parents cared about the kids. Where all the parents cared about the kids, because that's the heartbreak. It's teaching a child whose parents really don't care. That's the sad part."

(Do you really notice that large a difference between kids who have caring parents and kids who don't?)

"Oh, sure. Absolutely. Look at three different children. Mary, whose parents really care about her and she's never a discipline problem; and when you call the parents up and say, 'Mary didn't finish her homework,' then they help her with her homework, and she comes in the next day, and if they are caring parents and they aren't real pushy, Mary's probably working as hard as she can. Then you have Joey. His parents don't give a s___ about Joey. Joey knows it and if you call them they say, 'That's your problem, not mine.' They never fix Joey breakfast. They don't dress him. He comes to school and you wouldn't believe what stuff — the cat p___ all over his coat and he comes in and you think, 'What is that smell?' No one cares about Joey and everybody knows it and Joey is going to be a very sad adult. Then you have Tommy and Tommy's parents: they tell you that they care. Oh, they care. Tommy couldn't have done that because Tommy's been saved. He's seen the Lord and he's been saved. Their punishment, 'Well, what do you want us to do. Well, we might be a little too busy to do that . . . . Tommy's going to get punished, but he's not a bad boy because he's been saved.' Those are the little boys that end up in jail."

(What would Tommy be like in class?)

"Tommy's a real little s___. He's sneaky; he lies a lot. He's a discipline problem. He bothers the other children. The other children hate him."

(What about the other, Joey? What would he be like?)

"He would probably be the leader of the gang. If he has any strength about him, he would be a leader in the class. He is the hoodlum. He's the one who gets arrested for car theft and after doing time in a training school, maybe he'll be a fairly decent citizen but he'll always be a very lonely small person."

(Can a teacher make any difference in these kids' lives?)

"I can't. I don't see them enough. I know some teachers who have made fabulous differences in some children's lives. They have to be their classroom teacher. They have to really care about them. They have to be able to learn to take on the responsibility of talking to them after school, maybe having them spend a weekend with them once in a while.

"But all of a child's wants, needs, ideals, morals are set within the framework of the persona of the parent. A child will turn himself inside out to make himself acceptable to a parent. If the parent doesn't care about the child, then he doesn't care what he does in school, but that's the child's future. What you do in school is what you're going to become as an adult. So if the parent doesn't care about that, then the kid doesn't care. He says, 'Hey, look. I'm not supposed to care about school. I won't. I will watch television' So there goes the kid . . . ."

Tape #222

Ms. K. was jolly, black, and large. She spoke with me in the association office in a large northern California city. She had taught for ten years, was thirty-nine, and still was happy about what she was doing — even in special ed. She taught at the grade school level, and she too saw parents as her largest problem as a teacher.

"I had a lot of people say — you're so bright, why would you want to work with all those slow children? But I felt that that was more beneficial to me. I would rather get that — 'aha' from someone that no one else could get it from . . . .

"But I would say the biggest problem is lack of parental participation. Because it just makes my job much, much harder. This year I've been working on getting parental participation; it just makes it an easier year for me. Homework comes in — we don't have to go through a lot of — 'well, my brother ate it' and all those kinds of things. And I know there's a real problem because a lot of their parents can't do their homework or can't read the assignments themselves, and they don't want to let their kids know how little they can do, but I try to impress upon them that the more they see, the more they realize the need for learning these things. A good example of lack of participation is a boy I had a few years ago. He was very bright but acted up all the time. His mother only came up to school once, because the social workers were on her tail. We had several different phone numbers for her and when you called it was always, 'we've never heard of her; we've never heard of her.' And he would just leave school or have a tantrum and you couldn't tell anybody; you couldn't call anybody. She didn't care, you know — just total lack — this kid was raising himself. She finally shows up; she gives me her working number and then the first time I try to use it — it's the same thing all over again. But — graduation, he comes in a stretch limo! Eleven years old! Now she'll do that — chauffeurs, the whole bit. He's graduating from the fifth grade! (Laughter) Quite frankly, I pulled her aside and said, 'What are you going to do for him in middle school and high school graduation? I mean, this is a hard act to follow.' 'Well, if he does his days in school, he'll own one of these.' Yeah, sure, right! Who knows if she was serious . . . .

"I think today most parents don't participate as they could, but I don't think that's the way it's always been. My mother was very in tune. I would be in mortal fear to have anybody call my house and tell them anything — even good! (Laughter) I think each generation changes. I think maybe it's a lessening of values. I do think there is more parental participation at a suburban or private school — it's almost a prerequisite. Even these alternative schools we have in our city — the very first rule is that the parent must participate. They even give them X number of hours — if not, they don't get to go to the school. And in public school, we have to take everybody; that's why there's a big problem. And you can try to coerce or blackmail or whatever you want to call it (laughter), but the bottom line is — they don't have to. We have to teach them anyway.

"I sit down with each of the parents from my room and try to talk to them to get them to see how important it is to participate, because if I don't, I'm just spinning wheels in whatever I do. I even give them my telephone number. I try to impress upon them that I'm not running a babysitting service, to be dropped off in the morning and picked up in the evening. And I think the kids, within a month or so, tend to tune into that. They go back and tell their parents, 'Hey, I've got to do this; Ms. K. said so and so and so.'

"And most of my kids aren't living with their parents — they're living with caretakers. Grandma, who is about sixty now and she has her own house. She has a car. She says [to the parents], 'Hey, you're not taking care of him; I'll raise him.' She's not working so she's there; she has the common sense. And the kids realize that their parents aren't taking care of them. There's nothing really worse than knowing a drunk mother doesn't really want you. And then you come to school and you know the other kids are going to talk about this. One kid says, 'Well, at least my mother comes and picks up my report card; what does your mother do?' And when you're ten or twelve, you're at the age where you realize that she's just sitting at home . . . I think if I weren't working on this, zero percent of my parents would participate. But by working on it, I had seven out of eight sets of parents show up to pick up their child's report card this year. Now for the potluck of the whole school, my room had the highest percentage — four students. Now out of a school of 450 students, fifty percent is the highest! What does that say? Rooms of twenty-eight and thirty are getting one parent, two parents. I had eight kids and I got the highest score. That's a good commentary. And we're a racially mixed school; we're black, Latino, Chinese — a bit of all. And we even had busses — we paid for busses to go to where they live since our kids are bussed in. But we went to certain pick-up points for the parents to pick them up and bring them back home . . . and no one showed up for the busses. So that's two or three hundred that we just blew.

"Without parent support, it makes it very hard to educate their kids — you have no feedback; you have no support. I mean, it's like a one-way communication. You talk out, but you don't know if your receptions are being made or not. Of course, if you say enough to a child, over and over, some of it's got to sink in. But no parental participation sets up a pattern for middle school and high school. I mean — you know the classic school story. A kid gets to eighteen and can't read and the parent comes in and wants to know why his kid can't read and he's eighteen. Well, why did it take you until he was eighteen years old to find out he can't read?! But they don't really see that. They just want a finished product. They want to drop him off in kindergarten and pick him up in senior year. (Laughter) And I think that transcends race and even economics, because the class that I'm focusing in on now is really the middle class.

"The middle class parents are not doing their jobs either. Even though they push education, the only thing they know is to go to school. These kids don't know how to shop; they know nothing about finances. They get chauffeured to school and back; they don't know how to catch public transportation. I think they're totally not prepared for real life. You know, a lot of people think it's only the welfare kids. But when you're in a public school, you get everybody. And listen, with those kids — if I go on a field trip and they don't listen to me about getting in the car — they won't be able to get home! And I mean, that's sad if your mother's driving a BMW! And you don't know how to get home . . . . You know, you've got fifty dollar jeans on and sixty dollar tennis shoes (laughter). In the past, there were certain things you learned at home and then went to school and it was reinforced, but now I just don't see it.

"What do I say in defense of public education? Well, I tell people that I'm a product of it and I've done well. I'm successful in a good career. And I'm from a real tiny, tiny town where racism was abundant. We had everything going against us, but they did focus on education and I took advantage of it. And if you were one who listened . . . and sat down, they gave you everything you needed to be successful. And I feel like that is really the job of the teacher — to teach, given half of the supplies and three-fourths of the books and a little parent participation. You know, I purposely don't send anything home over the weekends because two or three days at home is just too long. You won't see the books again. 'We had homework?! What's that!' I've even typed up the whole thing on a list and sent it home. Then I've had parents say, 'You know, he doesn't have any homework.' And I say, 'Really? What school have you ever been to where they didn't have homework?' I mean, the parents really literally act like they're the children. Whatever the child says, they accept! 'Well, he told me!' I say — 'He did what?' 'Yes.' 'Well, this child is ten — what are you going to do when he gets to sixteen?' (Laughter)

"Parents come in and ask what they can do to help their kids, and they want to hear something that will cost them money. I tell them — number one, start talking to him. He's learning a vocabulary that he doesn't use anywhere but in here. It doesn't have to be highfalutin — you can talk about your favorite soap opera. Just so you're saying something more than get up, hurry up, shut up, go to bed . . . . But *they* want me to say, 'Send him to Dr. So and So from four to six in the evening.' They want *somebody else* to do it. And I would think that only forty percent of the kids leave high school knowing what they should know. So if I could, I would make parent participation mandatory . . . I mean, you can put band-aids and band-aids and throw money, but if the parents don't care what goes on from 9:30 to 3:30, it's not going to happen. Because that lack of whatever comes over to the student. He knows — 'Hey, I don't have to do this. Who's going to make me?' And now we can't touch them, you know, with this child abuse thing. I used to say — if you're not going to be afraid of your mother, you'll be afraid of me! But you can't do that now. Our hands are tied. So what do you do? Call their parents? Maybe there's no phone or you get that grandparent we talked about — you lost that. Ok, detention. But you can't have a detention anymore; these kids ride the bus; you can't keep them two minutes past school. Then you start thinking —

well, I'll suspend them. What is suspension? They're looking for it; now they can stay home and watch TV and VCR and really don't have to be bothered with you. So you're really in a dilemma without parents.

"My father had me work in this factory in the summers when I was a teenager and he did it on purpose. He wanted me to see what I would have to do if I did not have an education. And he didn't have to tell me anymore about going to school and stuff, because that was hard work. I couldn't believe how these people did it for twenty-five or thirty years. It cured me! (Laughter)

Tape #226

Mr. S. taught at the academic high school in what was an otherwise fairly inner city school district in a northern California city. He admitted that he taught in a special situation and wasn't sure how he would feel about education if he taught in something different. But he pointed out the minuses of the situation as well as the pluses, how all levels of society can be detrimental to education.

He was friendly and bearded with glasses and very casual dress. He was forty-three and divorced with children of his own. He taught high school math and had done so for twenty-two years.

"I do see a lot of grade consciousness that is just truly unbelievable. A poll revealed that seventy-eight percent of the students cheat at some time in the school. The competitiveness is really all for the grade. That's one of the reasons I have small classes; I happen to be a tough grader and kids pick their teachers at our school. They all think that I'm a very interesting teacher, but given the choice, they would all rather take Mr. X., where they are assured of getting the better grade. There's always studying going on all over the place in our school; the library had to be expanded; there weren't enough chairs . . . our students carry their books home; they are prepared; they've done their homework. It's another world. And the kids realize that they have to be the ones to do it.

"The whole atmosphere is just kind of that way. There's great parental pressure put on some kids; I remember I gave a child a C. At 9 o'clock I told him his semester grade was going to be a C; at 10 o'clock I had a call from the parent, wanting a conference about that particular grade. I mean, you're talking immediate kind of stuff. "Our department has a problem getting on a uniform grading scale. Nineteen teachers once graded the same geometry proof and the grades ranged from an A to an F. And there were strong proponents why it should be one or the other — it was completely subjective. I think that's really appalling. Our math failure rate on the state test is about nineteen percent. So we feel we do a good job, but nonetheless there is grade inflation. And yet, it's kind of justified because with these kids, if they went to the other district high schools, they'd almost all be getting As.

I do have — some of the weaker students, their parents don't seem to respond when you send home notices. I've sent home thirteen this year and so far I've received one response. I find that somewhat mystical. I agree that a lot of what a kid does in school comes from the environment at home and I'm really spoiled there. About sixty-eight percent of our school is Oriental, and as far as most of their families are concerned, education is an important part of their lives. The desire to achieve and I think the support they get from home is definitely higher.

Tape #162

> "I got assaulted by a kid, and when I went to get the kid
> changed out of my class, I had to go find a teacher who
> would be willing to take him . . . . I told the principal that I
> did not want this kid in my class . . . by now, I really
> actively dislike this kid anyhow. And she said, 'Well,
> nobody else wants him either.' "

She was twenty-six and had taught for six years at the junior high and elementary school levels. She originally taught music at the junior high level, but the year before I interviewed her, she had been corralled into teaching English also . . . as they needed an English teacher for two extra classes. Her school was poor urban in the Southwest, with lots of poverty and little parental support.

"In general, I see the absolute lack of support from *parents* as one of the biggest problems in education. I shouldn't say absolute — a big lack of support from parents. I know that I contact parents and I say, 'Your son is coming into class late every day; he doesn't bring his pencil; he doesn't bring his work; he is disruptive, talking out, bothering other students. I would like your help in helping me solve this. I've tried moving him, I've tried keeping him after school for detention, I've tried talking to him — mind you, none of these seem to have had any effect. What do you suggest?' 'Oh, I don't know; I just don't know what to do with him. He's your problem from 8:30 to 3:30. That's your job — is to deal with him.' I feel like — first of all, I'm only twenty-seven; none of these kids are mine. And second of all, you've had this kid for twelve years and I've only had him for one semester, and I'm expected to change his behavior like that.

"Another example is this year we started having conferences with the parents of children who are in danger of being retained. And out of the twelve conferences I had scheduled for kids who were failing in my classes . . . I think I had four parents show up. And I know that if that were my kid in school and in October the school called and said your kid is already in danger of failing — I would *make* time to be there. I cannot believe that most of these parents couldn't have found some way to get one of them here. They were contacted about the conferences and told to call if they couldn't make it; none even bothered to call if they weren't going to show up. And so there you are; a teacher is trying to develop an intervention plan for this kid and there's no parent there. And a lot of this stuff that has to be done for this kid to start achieving has got to be done from the home.

"This is a very poor area. For my concerts — well, band parents tend to show up more. They hear the practice at home; they laid out big bucks for that instrument. But it's amazing to me how many of my kids have to walk over here at night for a concert because their parents won't bring them. There are kids that I have to pick up because their parents won't take them. I would say that usually maybe ten percent of the parents show up from my group. And in the classroom? You say, 'I'm going to keep you after school,' and they say, 'Well, I'm not going to come. My parents told me I don't have to come. She said I didn't do anything wrong so I'm not going to come.' When you've got that kind of situation . . . I have a theory that parents are like this because they're the kids of the '60s and the ones always knocking authority and the teacher is rotten and everything sucks. I feel like maybe they had that attitude when they were in school and they still have it now. And in my classes, I have an immense number of kids that come from one-parent homes. Mom's working and working and working and she's not around to supervise.

"It's really strange that in this state everyone is suddenly really concerned over the ratio of teacher to kid in day-care centers. They've just legislated a five to one ratio. And yet in the classroom it's ok to have thirty to one. I think if you want quality education you have to lower the class size. It doesn't occur when there are thirty-five kids and one teacher. I had a kid they put into my seventh grade English class who couldn't write his own name. His father worked for the carnivals and they traveled a lot so he was never in a school long enough to learn — anything. So they put him in my class. He wasn't able to qualify for LD [learning disabled] and not EMH [educally mentally handicapped] so I've got him with my other thirty and I'm supposed to teach him to read and write while I'm teaching everybody else about prepositional phrases at the same time. You could group better for no more money except you'd probably get sued for having, say — all your Hispanics in C classes and saying they're being discriminated against . . . or whatever."

(Would you become a teacher again?)

"No. In college, they don't tell you what it's really all about in teaching . . . they're afraid you'd quit. They tell you about this ideal situation where you have thirty little angels and none of them are on drugs and all of them want to learn and none are being abused by their family and none are just plain mentally disturbed. Everybody is perfect. I don't think the ideal experience is the best thing because it doesn't really prepare you for what it's going to be like when you're dropped into your first classroom and you have to decide what you're going to do.

"I think teaching is the most important job in the world, and I would say that even if I weren't a teacher. Because, what the world is going to be like tomorrow depends on what the teachers are doing in the classroom today. . . . But my husband says that the reason teachers don't get paid any money is because they're not *making* any money for anyone else. The way you make money is to make money for somebody else, and those teachers just aren't making money for anyone. Parents and people in society just don't realize that being a good teacher *is* ultimately making money for others . . . but they don't see that."

Tape #141

Ms. C. was fifty-six with white hair and looking all of sixty-five, for sure. She had a slightly worried, slightly puzzled look, but her face was warm and friendly, especially when she smiled. She started teaching in 1951, had been teaching for only nineteen years as she had taken years out to raise her own two children. She taught math.

"When parents come to see me now, they don't come to see me about why their son or daughter is not learning . . . they come to see me about why they're not getting a certain grade. They don't come and say what can

I do about this student at home to improve his grades, but — why is he not doing very well in your class. They want the good grades . . . but they don't seem to be putting the emphasis on learning . . . ."

Tape #131

"What can you do with an unmotivated student?"
"Nurture and wait."

Ms. S. had spent several years working full-time as a secretary . . . she knew there was something more. Now she had been teaching high school English for three years, and although she had her doubts about the whole system, she had no doubts about the fulfillment of the job. She was doing more than a secretary.

Ms. S. had come to be interviewed in the middle of the day during her free period during exam week . . . now, that's dedication. She was pretty, thirty-one, with two kids of her own. Her hobbies were running, reading, playing tennis, and needlepoint. She taught in a Southern middle class high school.

I knew she was a dedicated teacher.

"I think the recent attention from the media on the profession has had a garbled effect. On the one hand, I think people see that we need to do some things to make it better. And on the other hand, I think it's lowered what respect there was a . . . a little bit. Still, I think my students judge their teachers on an individual basis. I think they really despise the teachers who don't do their jobs. And the ones who do, they tend to like. They tend to be able to see if a teacher's on the ball or not. They know who's working and who isn't. I just did a survey on who wanted to be a teacher because there was a scholarship opportunity, and out of eighty-three students, only one girl said that she'd be interested in that scholarship. I think it's because of the pay . . . and students seem to be interested in making a lot of money as opposed to doing things to help the world today. They tend to have these little pin-striped minds . . . I'm trying to decide if it's my own personal bias or if our generation really was more willing to go out and help. And I really don't know . . . maybe it's because there aren't any big social issues that are impinging on our conscience today. We get so concerned about economics and can I feed my family and have enough money to have two cars. Kids really are concerned about getting a good-paying job out of college. I just reviewed for their exam with them and I was trying to tell them what was on the exam without telling them the exact questions and it really frustrated the hell out of them. It was like — 'Don't play games with me.' And they said, 'We've got to make good grades, because we've got to go to a good school, because we've got to get a good job.' That seems to be the overriding factor. It bothers me a lot that they're looking more at the grade than the overall academics — although I can accept it and try to change it within my context . . . which is limited.

"It seems to me that my students' biggest problem is that they're getting jobs at say McDonald's and working thirty-five hours a week. And they say, 'Well, I can't do my homework. I had to work until midnight last night. I had to close.' And they're taking these jobs so they can have these material possessions now and they're sacrificing their future for that. I have one girl who wants to be a nurse and she works at Kentucky Fried Chicken every night till 11:00 or 12:00. And she's making an F . . . this is the second time she's made an F in my class . . . how is she going to get into college? She may be getting some material possessions now but . . . it's really difficult for them to think of long-range things.

"In my classes I have two mothers. Maybe more that I don't know about. And that's a really big problem. And I had a boy at the beginning of they year who drank Wild Irish Rose and gasoline to try to kill himself. And I was really sad about that, really sad that he felt so little of himself. And I have another student whose poetry is so descriptively suicidal and in such gruesome detail. I talk with him and he laughs it off. And I finally said to him, 'I really need to know what you're thinking;' and he said to me, 'Some people do it and other people write about it.' And I thought — ok. I do feel that's a part of the teaching job, to get to know the kids and deal with them if they want you to. It's probably the part I enjoy the most. Although I try really hard to remember that my primary job is with the literature and the writing. But I don't mind exercising the parental part of me, the part that can nurture and encourage. And it's all mixed up anyway. It's too difficult to separate it . . . .

"On the good side of public education is that we're educating every-body, unlike in the '20s and '30s. People would drop out and go to work in the mill like my grandaddy did. And now, people are going further in education and hopefully they're developing their thinking skills so that they can make more discriminating decisions when they vote and when they participate in the government. We'll have to see in years to come if we've been effective. I think ninety-five percent of the kids leave high school having gained what I think they should gain from high school. And I base that on hearing people, even people who did a really sorry job in high school, look back and they'll say, 'I had an opportunity there to do something . . . .' Maybe I have a real loose opinion of success, but I think if a person looks back and says, 'I think they were really teaching me something; I had an opportunity to make something of my life and learn something,' then they've learned a lesson. They may not have learned what they should have learned, but they've learned that they should have learned it. It's like a seed that was planted, anyway, that came to fruit many years later. And that's ok."

Tape #179

" . . . in case after case of kids who have problems in
school, behavior or academic, I have yet to meet a kid that
you can't make some progress with when you meet him
eyeball to eyeball."

Ms. H. was professionally dressed, dark hair and glasses. Indeed, she had taught at the college level in community colleges. Now she was in her tenth year of teaching at the high school level. She was working at a very upper-middle class suburban school district in a large Western city. She replied to all my questions with thoughtful answers that did her district proud.

Ms. H. was married to a musician with whom she sometimes sang professionally. Her other hobbies included gardening, cooking, and reading. She had no children . . . but she understood them. And she understood that they changed with the years. You can't tell me that a kid brought up on MTV isn't going to be fundamentally different than a kid who grew up watching American Bandstand . . . .

"I think public education offers the opportunity of an education to everyone and I think that we need to do that and not just have it something for people who have money. And I've taught in private schools too so I know the arguments on both sides. I relate the differences between public and private schools to size more than anything else. I taught at an all-boys private school, and there was a total of 150 students in grades nine through twelve. I think they got a better education and not because it was a private school but because there were smaller numbers and they got a lot more individual attention. I think public schools could do the same thing if they'd just trade the numbers in and not have schools of three thousand where students are just numbers in the halls and in the classrooms. I think we may see fewer kids in classrooms in public education someday; I mean, even in my own twelve years I've seen a lessening of the numbers, say, in writing classes. Some people are starting to say — yes, it makes sense that you would have fewer students in writing. It's nowhere near what it should be, but I think we're making progress.

"I think my idea of the perfect school would be a little red schoolhouse. . . . (Laughter) You look like you're going to throw up! (Laughter) In this sense — numbers is the reason; I think we just need to get smaller. It just gives kids more attention. When I go back and think about my private school experiences — I taught the seniors and the sophomores . . . but I knew the juniors and the freshmen. The kids felt a part of that and I think there were all kinds of positive things that came from it. And they helped others with their work. But these kids, you put them in small groups, and you have to go introduce each of them . . . . I'm always amazed that at the end of the semester, they leave here sometimes not knowing who the person behind them is.

"If I had unlimited money to spend on education, I would put it into hiring teachers to get class sizes down. I don't see materials as being as big an issue as the numbers. To me, numbers is the big issue. Because in case after case of kids who have problems in school, whether behavior or academic or whatever, I have yet to meet a kid that you can't make some progress with when you meet him eyeball to eyeball.

"I do notice a goallessness in many students, and I think a lot of that's due to the atomic age . . . a lot of them just say — 'What for? We're not going to be here after we're blown to bits!' It's kind of like live for now because the future's so uncertain . . . I see a lot of that. And yes, I think kids today are more into material things than humanitarian things. In my sophomore writing class we do some values clarification in their writing journals with instant writing topics type things and it's always things like — if you had three wishes, what would they be and with these kids it's always the Porsches, the millionaire for life stuff.

"I think it goes back to the loss of the family. It's a depersonalization. We no longer have that closeness, you know; and we no longer have that stability of relationships where your father and your mother were there, and you knew they had unconditional positive regard for you . . . or whatever the words are . . . they were going to love you! Yes, that means love. (Laughter) And when the people are not there to provide that love, I think the tendency is to go to *things* to try to get that satisfaction. So people, I think, have filled those spaces where in the past people have been . . . with *things*.

"And I always have this heated discussion with kids in my writing class about I don't think kids should work while they're in high school. They have the rest of their lives to work so they ought to be out there enjoying every moment of their teenage years. And they just think I am crazy and really out of the Dark Ages. And then I say, 'Well, why are you working?' 'Well, I have to.' 'For what?' 'To pay for my car.' 'You don't need a car.' 'Don't need a car?!' And so they want all those material things, and in my estimation the kids here aren't working for the basic necessities. Most of these kids do have parents who will provide them with the basic necessities. But we're talking about the extras. They want the latest outfit; they want the biggest speakers, not just a radio but — "

(If I were a parent and I asked you what you thought the major problem of teens today was, what would you say?)

"I'd say the lack of stability in their lives. They get into other problems because of that. I wouldn't say drugs is the major problem; I think it's a symptom of the problem. I'd suggest to parents to just talk to their kids. What these kids tell me sometimes makes me think that they don't even see their parents, let alone communicate with them. I had this one student last year who said that he and his sister shared the basement of the house and the parents live upstairs and seldom the twain shall meet. I said, 'Well, what about dinner? Do you ever sit down and have dinner together?' And he said, 'Well, sometimes, but mostly we just kind of go out and get our own Burger King and things.' I said , 'Do you like that?' And he said, 'Yeah, it's pretty neat; I can come and go as I want.' So I think that's the number one place that parents can really help, just to talk to their kids, about what they're thinking and how they're feeling. I wonder why a parent would live like that . . . what's the point of having children if you're going to live like that?

"A lot of time there's only one parent or both parents are working and the kids are involved in all this stuff that goes on after school and a lot of times they just see each other in passing. And I think it's kind of common to say to kids, 'Well, did you talk to your mom about this last night?' And to hear — 'Well, I didn't see her last night because she came in after I'd already gone to bed.' They miss connections. So I think a lot of kids' problems are that parents don't even know what they're doing, let alone how they're feeling inside of them. They can't account for where their bodies are, let alone where their hearts are. I think the number one thing for a parent to do, then, is get in communication with the kid. And maybe from there it's to provide a structure for the kid, a structure for study. I find a lot of adults don't even know how to structure their time. It always amazes me when on parent-teacher conferences the parent looks at the grades and says things like — 'God, these vocabulary grades are terrible; what can we do?' Five to ten minutes a night; we're not talking two hours, but every night. Consistency is what they don't understand. I would say certainly under fifty percent of the kids do their homework, probably more like twenty or thirty percent. And with a major assignment like a paper or something — a little bit over fifty percent. And I've done everything from not counting late work to giving it lower grades."

Tape #199

> "I'm almost fifty years old and there's hardly a week goes
> by when I don't feel inadequate, defective as a teacher . . ."

She was forty something and had taught for thirteen years —two years before 1969 and the rest since after raising her own family. She had a unique view of two different teaching times with no gradual change in-between. She was teaching now in an upper-middle class suburban school district in the West. She taught high school English.

"I taught for two years in the early '60s and it was before all the protesting and upheaval in the school; it was really a very lovely time to teach. Then I stayed out for fifteen years because we moved and because I had two children. But when I started back in — subbing — people who had stayed the whole time told me that it was so much harder and I would find it so much more difficult. Still, I saw what they were doing and after a while I saw that I could certainly do it as well as they were, so I decided to go back. And yes, there are differences between now and then.

"The whole attitude that the student has control and right or privilege to claim to question teachers, confront them in a really aggressive way was really non-existent as I remember it. It was a much more loving relationship and a much more friendly relationship. Students trusted what we did even though what we did wasn't all that great sometimes. It was kind of more — the natural way of things. And I just felt that it was a lot easier relationship with students. When I came back, we were into this aggressive defend the grade, argue for the point, prove all of your rules, and that had become the natural way, you know.

"The subbing I did when I first came back built up my confidence, however. People requested me and thought I was good, and I saw the work that many of the teachers were doing — many of the ones I was substituting for — I thought much of it was incompetent. I felt that I could do as good if not a better job than many of the teachers that I was subbing for. I had many discipline problems as a sub but it depended on the school and the classroom environment that the teacher had already set up . . . a lot of it is what you walk into.

"And basically I do think I'm doing better than most of what I saw then. A lot of the differences were a matter of our own backgrounds. I was in school in the late '40s and '50s — I was out of college in 1960. I was trained in a more rigorous background, especially in English. A lot of these people were schooled in the 1960s and '70s and had a more free flowing or whatever you like, more what feels good — and so in terms of my knowledge in content, my knowledge of grammar and composition was much more accurate than what I saw. I saw gross problems in spelling, teaching of usage and all that — not always, but occasionally you'd see — this teacher is wrong; she doesn't know what she's doing. And yet the young teachers that we have coming in, although we get to choose from the best, are very, very bright and will make excellent teachers . . . if they stay in. So I wouldn't condemn the younger teachers . . . .

"I think one of the goals of a public education is still to provide a common background for us as a society. As Americans there are certain things we've inherited in our history and in our literature that teach us about ourselves. And there are points of reference that are used in our culture; one of the goals of public education is that we share that, that we have done that, that we have read some of these people and maybe have some sense of who we are. Even the Puritans — I think it's very important that American students today have read about things like that and have read some of the common literature no matter what part of the country they are in.

"And when parents ask in conferences, as they did a few times last week, what are your objectives in this class — that's what I tell them. We need to have a common background in America. We need to have a literature; we need to see the values and the characteristics that have made us the people we are, see the threads that we've come from. And parents usually say — that sounds great! I sure hope my kid's getting it!

"Have students changed in their writing abilities? Yes. I say this because I have saved some things from back in the '60s when I first taught and I've talked about this with other teachers. I think the good students, with the high abilities, are probably stronger — they're writing better; they're reading at a higher level — they're at a higher level. I think probably the average and below average are a little bit weaker. In comparison — I saved some things, especially some papers from a remedial reading class I taught long ago, and these were the lowest ability, and I read those a few summers ago and their writing was so much more accurate and clear. Our average and good students today have so many more mechanical errors — it makes me wonder . . . . My natural feeling is that the good students are probably stronger, but the average students are probably sloppier.

"Also I'm always shocked by what's happened to the family. I was so naive when I first got back in [teaching] because I always called parents by their children's last names, and you're always shocked because it's some completely different name! I grew up in a small town and I'm used to families eating together and spending Christmas together and blah blah blah. And you're always shocked as an older person, perhaps you are too as a younger person, that your lifestyles are so totally different; you feel like you have nothing in common. I see that affecting their class work. I think they're so caught up in trying to survive just cold emotions that they can't possible pay attention to what's going on in the classroom. I think the whole adult society has entirely copped out on helping children. Their main function is to help adolescents to cope, and we have masses of adults who have not been able to do that. They can't cope with their own lives, let alone teach their thirteen and fifteen year olds how to cope, how to make judgments, handle whatever the daily problems are. I've had six or seven girls this year already try to commit suicide — which is amazing that I've heard about that many. And I've had innumerable numbers of kids that I've heard about going through drug and alcohol problems and you've seen us — our school isn't a ghetto or inner city or anything that would fit any kind of cultural reason for that — other than you've got all these little lost souls out here, trying to figure out how to survive in the world. One is on my mind because I just talked to a psychiatric nurse about her; she just came back yesterday. It was all a matter of her family.

"I think schools have been forced to take on families' roles. I think all of us feel guilty; we feel overburdened; we feel defective. I'm almost fifty years old and there's hardly a week goes by when I don't feel inadequate, defective as a teacher, and I know other teachers feel that way. I think that one reason is that we can just barely do all the things that we are expected to do. Our minds and our hearts tell us that we need to be individualizing;

we need to be motivating; we need to be listening for all these emotional problems; in addition to trying to do a superbang job with the content. And I just feel that — we're in a box. We're not going to feel we're doing a good job."

Tape #134

I'm not sure that I'd ever really sat down and talked with a good ol' Southern boy in my life . . . But Mr. H. was not only a good ol' boy, he was a high school football coach in a Southern city small enough to care about their high school football teams. On top of all of that, he was a PE teacher . . . and at forty-one had taught (and coached) for nineteen years. I asked the first question and he began talking, some down home bull and some right-on perception, especially about students today.

I think I rather liked Mr. H. in some ways. At least he was the only interviewee to have the gumption to say anything negative about my earring.

"Number one, the 'I' concept has to change. Not *I, I, I, I, me, me, me, me* — you know, this kind of thing. If a kid has an awful lot of ability, and I mean a lot of ability, you have to knock out the *I* and the *me*. If the kid doesn't have any ability at all, you have to build that up in him. You have to bring the good to a level socially with the bad. All right? And then I'm not talking about his talent now. I'm talking about his concept of himself. I don't mean knock him down. I'm talking about he's got to learn to live with other normal people. He's got to become normal instead of stuck on himself. A kid down here, with a low evaluation of himself, he's got to come up. When you can talk to a teen and that kid knows he's contributing something, regardless of what it is, even if it's holding a [tackle] dummy, and he's just as important as that star in somebody's eye, then that kid's going to want to come to school, he's going to want to put out, he's going to want to see if that will work in that area. And when he sees that it does, that people are treating him equally with the brain children, he can make it. Anybody, I think, can make it if they just feel good about themselves.

"Now I've been on every level, and I've been in different areas. I've taught in three states. I've taught in small towns, taught in rural, and I've taught in the inner city, on every level. Kids in the city have jobs. All right? The lower-middle class whites treat their job as being the only thing that's real. A kid comes to school, I mean his excuse is, I've got to go to work. I didn't come to school because I had to work yesterday. My dad wouldn't let me pull that when he was making fifty-two bucks a week with five kids. But now, that's real to them. The only thing those kids ever see that's real is how their parents treat their jobs. So therefore, they're going to get a job, because then — you know, that's instant acceptance. I'm in a real world. I got to be at whatever Fried Chicken at a certain time. If I don't get there, I'm going to get fired. To hell with science class. They get out of school early to go to work. These people in these areas that run these fast food restaurants and all, they'll work a kid fifty hours a week if they can.

"So a kid works forty hours a week, attends school and doesn't study, and can't call his girlfriend. Friday night, Saturday night comes. He's got his one day off a week. He doesn't have a social life. He goes and gets him a stash that puts him in another world. Finds him a girl that'll do the same thing, and they go off in their little dream world. And it's not a real existence. That's the tragic thing that's going on out there. The kids can't develop. Number one, both parents aren't there. Number two, they don't have time to grow up anymore, because of this working thing. They can't do anything or they can't accept not having money in their pocket. Even poor people can't. Got to have some money. So that dope, whether it's marijuana, cocaine, liquor or whatever, is their quick way to become socialized on the weekend. And it's a never-ending thing. Before long, they turn into trash."

(What percentage of kids are into drugs at the high school level?)

"I'd say sixty-five percent, on a regular basis. Yeah. I'd say, experimental, experimentally, ninety-five percent."

(What keeps that thirty percent or so from getting into it?)

"If a parent's interested in his kid — and I don't know why I say this, but it's always a common denominator — church has something to do with it. A kid that's brought up in the church — and I'm talking about Carolina and the South (I don't know what it's like up north). A kid's brought up in the church, especially in the small communities, he can't hide. And the church will take up a little bit of their spare time, you know, and work with the parents. I felt like my job in coaching was reinforcing what parents were doing with their kids. I've taken a lot of pride in that. And a kid's got a problem, the parent comes, the kid comes, before long, I've backed up the parent. I'm not going against the parent unless the parent is trying to hurt the kid. Before long, that problem always takes care of itself.

"God, I feel sorry for kids just having one parent, I really do. Because they don't get to go fishing, you know, and they don't get to do anything. They just find a way to get a car, get a woman, and get a job. And then after they do that, they're divorced, most of the time. They won't commit themselves to a marriage.

"I think it's just pure laziness. They will not make the commitment to work for it. Yes, it's because they saw their parents not doing it and their parents lived and they survived. But god, my mom and dad hated each other for twenty years. Always fought like cats and dogs and everything else. But damn, they stayed together. And they told us why. Said hey, she can't make it without me and I can't make it without her and you all. And if we split up, there's no way that this family will stay together. And they were right. I can't imagine what it would be like. We were very poor and [my father] still wouldn't let me work. I thought he was the dumbest guy in the world at the time. I didn't know he was programming me. He had a third grade education, but he realized that he was not going to let any of us get caught up in that type of society and end up like a lot of the people did. See, back then there was another animal that doesn't exist now. Labor supply, back then, meant that we don't want you graduating, we don't want you to get a diploma. We want you to live in this community and come to work at this plant. And as soon as you get fourteen, we'll get you a job so you can quit school as soon as you can and become part of the labor force and live here and raise your kids to do the same. Then all of a sudden the law says, hey, no way, José. And then they had to stop it. Education started coming in. And that's where I first saw the value of an education."

Tape #175

Mr. G. had taken a sabbatical once several years ago to travel around the nation and make slides of America to use in his American history course. The school district had even granted him a paid leave of absence to do it . . . he taught American history for one year after that and then was given other classes.

Now, at forty-one, he was completing his fourteenth year of teaching. He had also spent several years in the Air Force. We began talking in a teacher's lounge so he could smoke and then moved to his classroom so I could better hear him. Before he left, he showed me his next lesson's main point by pointing out the questions he had written on the board. He said he tried to get kids to think about history, not just memorize things. He even came back into the room after he left to point that out to me.

He was married with one child and taught in an upper-middle class suburban high school in the West.

"What's wrong with public education? Probably the lack of esteem that it has today in our society. A lot of people would cite salary as a major indicator of that, and I think that is accurate — probably a legitimate way to show exactly how most Americans view public education. I think lack of respect for the profession, and for public education in general, is probably the worst part of it. I think the students think that also. I've heard students make the comment every year — 'Gee, who'd want to be a teacher; you guys don't get paid anything.' I've had townspeople and neighbors say, 'Oh, you're off for the summer now.' That kind of comment I think belies a hidden kind of disrespect. They don't seem to mind that their doctor can travel to South America or wherever for three or four weeks or that they drive an Audi or whatever, but for a teacher to have the summers off seems to be more than they can handle.

"And as our public has become better educated, thanks to public education, the value of that education has gone down. Too much of a good thing, too easy. In the 1800s, when the average person dropped out of school somewhere between the ages of eight and twelve, certainly the educated person in the community like the teacher was well respected. Now people have degrees and hold these in less esteem . . . I would say it's just because we've done our job too well, perhaps, that we don't impress people too much anymore. But I think there will always be people who want to teach; that's something very common in the human race — the desire to pass on the knowledge to another generation. That's why we have — 'progress.'

"And probably the best defense for public education is that it is one of the most equalizing forces we have in society. It helps equalize various groups in the society economically, politically — it's the social mobility idea. And so public education provides the opportunity for people in this society to move up. When that's removed in a society, then there's a lack of hope in that society. And I think that's where trouble really begins. Check the roots of many revolutions — they usually have to do with the frustration of a large number of people who have no future. And in the U.S., perhaps among certain minority groups, there's that frustration because the system isn't flexible enough to adapt to those groups to bring them into the system, or maybe their own culture prevents them from adapting to the educational environment as it exists.

"But ultimately education coupled with a free system is the great equalizer. When the system breaks down, which it has on occasion or in certain areas, then we see that kind of social unrest or we see an apathy set in. The ghetto kid may not see economic possibilities due to poor education — why show up day after day in a place that's not pleasant and ultimately you don't see anyone who leaves that high school any better off than those who dropped out.

"If I had the money I'd spend it on smaller classes. Kids learn better in classes of fifteen - nineteen or so. Then I would also put the money into smaller buildings, no more than four or five hundred students in it. When you get a large building, it generates a sense of anonymity and alienation amongst students and faculty members that I think is hard to overcome. That's probably one of the problems with major cities, that people have no sense of community, have no sense of belonging. We have a severe case of alienated people. To compensate for this, we need to generate it in small institutions where we can. And I speak from experience, from watching this district grow from one high school with eight hundred students to now three high schools and twelve hundred kids in this building. I don't know all these kids; they don't know me, and at one point we did. And I think that has a big bearing on whether they feel they belong here and what their responsibility is to the school and mine to them.

"Probably the biggest challenge that education has, in my mind, is to remember that the primary job we have is to teach kids how to think, how to make decisions and how to analyze them and evaluate what's in their lives. Because of all the changes and the rapidity of change today, anything we teach them in a content area is apt to be obsolete rapidly. So we need to give them the tools to — evaluate; and I think that we need to have a little courage so that we don't get tied up with conservative 'back to basics' or people who would attempt to turn back the clock to nineteenth century nationalism or something where you keep things out of the classroom because it's not morally right. We've come too far to go back to that. I think as individuals, many teachers do teach students how to think, and if we keep the standardized test people from destroying creativity — thinking is a creative process — we'll be all right."

Section 11:

MONEY

What other society has thought that a lottery is a good way
to support education?

*No matter what the conservative politicians say, money is one of the
major problems of public education. They constantly say things like, "You
can't throw money at the problem that is education and expect it to get
better." And of course they're right; you can't just throw money at any
problem and expect it to get better, but if they had a good aim, there are
a lot of targets that could be hit with that money.*

*Money impinges on everything. Teachers' status is low because society
perceives them as people not worth much — after all, they're not paid like
doctors or lawyers. But who would argue that they're not more or at least
equally as important as a doctor? Equally as important as a lawyer? To
me, only the police and firemen are more important to the maintenance of
society. But we're a very materialistic society, and when people look at
$30,000 a year, $15,000 the first year, they think — "not important."*

*And teachers get to thinking that way too. Imagine that none of the
overtime that you put in is going to get you anything monetary or even a
promotion. If I worked two extra hours every school day and every
weekend day, I wasn't going to be given time and a half; there was no
bonus coming at Christmas. How many jobs are there where you don't get
paid for overtime? Business executives get promotions for extra hours of
work. What promotion is there for a teacher? You can't move up; you can
only move out.*

*My brother would get a $2,000 Christmas bonus; I would get a
stapler . . . .*

And teachers reach the peak of their pay scale after twelve to fifteen years, and then usually there are no more raises until something like year twenty-two. What motivation to work? What stimulus to put in those extra hours! What a great way to run a company . . . .

And don't believe people who tell you that more money isn't needed for materials and supplies in the schools. If they're teachers and they say this, they teach in a nice suburban school district and they're too ignorant to look around. There are two school districts in this nation, the suburban-rural ones that are usually getting by with just enough money and the city ones that aren't. What could be bought with more money? Smaller class size so that more children would succeed, books for every child (no, there are not in every district); better facilities (in some schools plaster falling off the ceiling is a daily occurrence; I've seen it); better equipment — the most advanced technological society in the history of the world and teachers are still using ditto machines!

But don't just listen to me.

Tape #172

Mr. F. had started out in retail management, but felt that there was just something missing when he started getting upset that people were buying toiletry articles and ruining his display. He got into teaching and at the time I interviewed him had been teaching sixth-eighth grade social studies for fourteen years.

Currently in the Southwest, he hailed originally from New York City, and there was still something of New York about him, especially in his voice. He was dark and fleshy at thirty-eight, married to another teacher and father of three children. I interviewed him in his office as for this year he was out of the classroom and functioning as his local association president. It was a large local with many hundreds of members, and his comments were greatly about money and politics.

(Why did you go into teaching?)

"Stupidity! (Laughter) No, I went to college mainly because it was expected of me by my parents and I figured that if I had to go, I might as well go into something where I would make money . . . so I went into retail. After graduation I spent about a year and a half with the K-Mart Company. I was very successful, but I didn't feel like I was impacting on anything in any way, on anybody. I remember feeling like there were just some things that were in conflict. Case in point, I remember one night when I was the manager in charge, my staff left at 9:30 and then I stripped to the waist and totally took apart the toiletry articles department. I redid the shelves as pictured in the merchandise display book, put the merchandise back on the shelves from the basement, finished about 5:00 in the morning, went home, showered, came back to work — showed it to my boss. The store opened . . . somebody came and bought something and ruined my display. I was mortified, and I found myself for two days standing at the end of the toiletry department, and if somebody bought something I would run and get one and replace it. And I thought — is my life going to be replacing hair spray? I had been successful — I had had three promotions in fifteen months. But I just made the decision that that wasn't what I wanted to do. I got no intrinsic satisfaction out of that.

"It took me a year to get my teaching certification — I think I always wanted to teach. I think there were two reasons why I didn't go into it in the first place: number one, you can't make any money at it; and number two, my mother always thought I wanted to teach. Our income level went down by thirty percent when I quit my job, and my wife started teaching to support us while I went back to school. So money was always a consideration, I guess."

(What do you get out of teaching that you didn't get in the business world?)

"A good feeling — I remember a girl I had seven years ago who came to me in the sixth grade not knowing how to divide. We went through the process. I said, 'Kathleen, has anyone ever taught you how to divide?' 'Oh, yes, Mr. So and So taught me in the fifth grade and Miss So and So in the fourth' — she said, 'I guess I'm stupid, Mr. F. I just can't get it.' I said, 'You're not stupid; you'll get it.' And so we did it in a group, and we did it — the full class, and she and I worked one to one. And I'll never forget one day I was sitting at the same table with her and I started doing it again with her, probably the sixth different way. Then she looked at the book and she looked at me and her eyes lit up, and she said, 'That's not so hard.' And I said — 'Oh, thank God!' (Laughter) And now she's a math major in college, a *happy* math major. And it's that look in her eyes that keeps teachers teaching. Because, no matter how good that hair spray display was — so what? And yet frankly, I could go back to that game now. . . ."

(Because?)

"Money. I grew up in an ability grouped school district in New York. My best friend and I were never in the same classes because he was always in the bottom of his class and I was always near the top. Of course, now I'm driving an '81 station wagon and he's driving a Mercedes — he sells. He's offered me a job — traveling in sales for him. He said, 'I don't know what you're making, but whatever it is — double it and that's where we'll start.' And he said, 'You'll probably double it again.' My wife, of course, when she heard about it, asked me — 'Are you out of your f____ mind?" She didn't like the three out of four weeks away. She wanted [us] to raise our kids together. I pointed out that she could stay at home and quit teaching. That made her more mad; she *wanted* to teach . . . so I turned the job down, but the money was a temptation."

(Does it make you feel any less not to be in business like that?)

"No, I don't think so — I had to think that one through. But I think it does to a lot of teachers. How many times have you heard — 'I'm *just* a teacher'? I think it's mainly a money thing. Why do they consider it moving up to become a principal? That's not moving up; that's moving out. That's moving from being an educator to being a manager. I have no problem with people who want to do that; I have a problem with people who say they are moving *up* to be an administrator because they want to benefit more kids — what a crock! I stay in the classroom because I like kids; I like seeing the explosion of knowledge going on in their heads. Principals — that's a management position, not an education position. So why do administrators make more than teachers? I deal with the future of America; administrators shuffle papers and go to meetings. I would say they make more money because it's another administrator making that decision. My figure is that an administrator should get whatever they would get on the teacher pay scale and prorate whatever extra weeks they have to serve during the summer. That's reasonable. You have about one hundred schools in this district . . . as association president I've been in seventy to seventy-five of them. I can't find you five excellent principals. I know one guy that from the beginning of his teaching career was in the central office emptying superintendent's garbage cans if he could — just to get known. His main objective was to be an administrator from day one on . . . and my understanding is that he was the youngest administrator in the district — at twenty-nine.

"In the future, I see dramatic increases in teachers' salaries . . . or massive strikes. We need to increase salaries to get better teachers. My brother is younger than I am with only a bachelor's degree and he makes twenty thousand more than I do — as an accountant. I'm teaching the future of America . . . he's putting numbers down in columns . . . The first step is to convince teachers that they're worth a whole hell of a lot more — to get out of this mindset that — yes, I went into teaching and I knew I wouldn't make much money . . . That's a crock! You're doing a meaningful and probably the most important job in the nation. And yeah! I believe in internal gratification, but I still contend that when my doctor cures somebody he gets internal gratification while he makes 120,000 dollars a year.

"Part of society's lack of respect for teachers may be due to teachers not *demanding* that respect . . . *demanding* those salaries. I guess I see strikes because the NEA is the only union-type organization that is increasing in membership — we've already picked up an additional 20,000 members this year. And that's the only union that has. Teachers are finally realizing that there's nothing wrong with making some money. I have a friend who took a job in this district teaching — a wife and three kids — and his kids are eligible for a free hot lunch. That's not right! That's not right!

"All states are hurting for teachers except one — Alaska. They average around 41,000 dollars a year for teachers there. It may have a higher cost of living, but they're paying to get teachers. There's no teacher shortage there. I see teachers leaving daily. I had a teacher sitting in that chair over there last week — a good teacher, an association activist, past president, teaching fifteen years — just an outstanding teacher — and we were talking about how I was offered a job with an insurance company recently. And she said — can you please set me up for an interview . . . I've got to get out.

"That's not right! I don't think people realize the stress or the frustration. I read an article where teachers, especially elementary teachers, have the highest incidence of kidney and bladder ailments — that makes sense because I can go to the bathroom just before my kids come in at five till 8:00 and then I can go again at noon, and heaven help you if you've got to go in-between. They don't understand that on the outside . . . and those are the same people that are saying — they only work nine months a year. That's a crock. We've done research in this district that shows that yeah, you're only working a forty week year . . . but you're working fifty-four hours a week. And when you work that out, you've found you've worked a fifty week year but you've done it compressed — in a nine month period of time. And you're not on vacation anyway; you're on a forced leave of absence without pay. In the business world, you go on vacation, the boss hands you money and says — go on vacation; have a good time. They keep paying you. You don't have to go to work — that's a vacation. And to people who say — my teachers taught thirty-five kids in a class, why are teachers complaining? Well, just because you went to a backwards school when you were a kid doesn't mean we have to maintain that ignorance. They did a study with kindergartners 15-1 ratio and 30-1 ratio. The kids who went 15-1 half a day came out more knowledgeable than the kids who went 30-1 full day. So . . ."

(What percentage do you think are good teachers nationwide?)

"Ninety-seven percent.

"Our association has a real strong commitment to professional and instructional development, but that's because our school district doesn't. And I think *we're* turning the school district around. For example, we have a workshop starting tomorrow for first, second, and third year teachers only. It will deal with things like drawing up a discipline plan that they can use, how to get the proper forms filled out to get materials, how to refer a child for special placement, where do you go to get materials — the special resource center, and a whole raft of things. It's being done by the association although we did get the district to co-sponsor it so they are providing some money but that's all. This has all been done by teachers — for teachers. A few weeks ago we had a teacher do a workshop on right brain, left brain. In fact, we had a restriction of thirty people to sign up . . . we took sixty and turned another forty away. The one tomorrow was to cut off at thirty — two full Saturdays and one Tuesday night. We're going to repeat it on Tuesday and Thursday nights. We had close to two hundred people show up for a workshop from four to six on a Tuesday afternoon. And our association does an excellent job on contract maintenance — protection of our members.

"Examples? You interviewed a lady yesterday who is an excellent teacher working with emotionally handicapped children — has had a kid for three years and handled him the same way. Last night his parents said they were going to file a suit against her for child abuse. Just out of the blue — she called me and I turned that over to our professional staff. Without the association, parents pull on a string, the administrator dangles and the parent gets what the parent wants. Without the association, parent says — child abuse, teacher gets terminated. The association will make sure that the teacher knows all the due process, that she goes through the due process, and has all the rights therein. Without an association, you've got nothing. My own building principal, when he found out I was running for association president, said, 'Mr. F., as far as I'm concerned you can take your contract and throw it right out the window and you can follow it.' And he didn't talk to me for a year and a half. Those are wonderful working conditions. And if he had the opportunity — he would have fired me. We had one lady call us and tell us — I'm going from one school to another and my administrator is going through all of my boxes. He's claiming that I'm stealing things from him. We called personnel; get that man out of those boxes or we're going to file a grievance and then we'll sue. Lo and behold, it stops. Class size! We have class size maximums in our contract — with set provisions. At thirty-four we don't care where that kid goes, he can sit in the principal's office — we don't see it happen. So a teacher calls up and says I've got thirty-five kids in my class. That administrator should never have put that thirty-fifth kid in there. Our contract is board policy. I try to rectify the situations without a grievance and most we can. But in this one the regional superintendent just sat on it so I called back my teacher and said, 'File the grievance.' We filed the grievance and within two days, the kid was moved. It shouldn't be like that. And most of the time it isn't. But it shows we need the association."

(Would you go into teaching again?)

"Certainly not. Too stressful and not enough money — you're probably doing this book because you like writing, but I'd guess you were feeling stress in the classroom too. My wife — out of the blue one year took a leave of absence. Stress. My family doesn't talk to me for two weeks after school lets out — time to unstress. Highly stressful, highly emotional — I'll never forget my first year of teaching. I got a call from a mother during the school day. She said, 'Mr. F., will you please tell Alex his father just died.' I said, 'Don't you want me to send him home for you to do that?' 'Nope.' 'Can he come home?' 'Nope.' She said, 'He was sort of expecting it as he's been ill.' I said — 'That's not my job!' She said, 'I'm making it your job.' That was part of my indoctrination into education . . . and for the salary I make . . . ."

Tape #123

Mr. and Ms. W. were married teachers, each working on a second marriage and two children. I interviewed them in their living room after a very suburban lunch of something over toast. The two pre-school aged children colored on plastic mats at the table as we sat. Then the younger was off to take his nap and the older to watch an educational video. Even

though the house had been seriously picked up for my arrival, there still
was a sprinkling of toys about — almost all seemed new and the majority
looked like the "right kind" of toy.

Mr. W. was thirty-six and taught instrumental music in the same
suburban school district that thirty-five year old Ms. W. was in charge of
one elementary grade level of a pull-out magnet program. They were very
sincere, good people.

What was it like to be a teacher couple? What was it like to live on those
salaries?

(Have you ever considered not teaching, getting out and doing some-
thing else, especially in the music field?)

Mr.: "Yes. But I've stayed I think because of the security of the job. It's
a gamble. And I don't dislike teaching, for one thing. If I didn't have a
working wife, I would probably have to find something additional to do if
I stayed in teaching."

Ms.: "It would depend on the lifestyle you wanted. We don't live that
great! We did it [only husband working] for short periods of time. We did
it for six months after each kid was born and we had to make tough
decisions. Plus, we planned for a year each time. And we always paid our
mortgage ahead of time too. It's difficult. I don't know how people do it."

Mr.: "Now in our mid-thirties, some of our friends are starting to make
the big bucks and buying 100 - 150 thousand dollar homes. It has nothing
to do with education or how well they do their job; they're just starting to
make the big money. But we're reaching the top of our salary schedule.
We won't be making any more than we do now."

(What's wrong with public education?)

Ms.: "I think that the status of the teacher isn't as high as I'd like to see
it. I guess paying them more is the way to get it higher, at least in our
society. I don't know if this has changed over the years or not. I've always
been very satisfied with my role, and my family has always reinforced that
— to value teachers — but now I'm beginning to wonder if we are valued.
But now I don't even want to know what my non-teacher friends make in
salaries ... I don't want to know. I used to think that society respected
teachers a lot, but I'm beginning to waver on that."

Mr.: "I hear students say mainly things like — I would never teach
because you don't make any money. That's the biggest lack of respect that
I see. Of course we teach in a very affluent area and I think maybe their

expectations are a little higher. They drive better cars than we do and they wear better clothes and they go home to better homes. At times I guess I feel like they're spoiled and it probably does affect my reaction to them. I mean — not in a great way, but I probably have less patience for kids complaining or things like that. If that's the environment they're coming from, then they're just used to getting their way."

Ms.: "On the positive side, it's real important to see that we don't turn anybody away. So many of our teacher friends, who teach in public schools, send their kids to private schools, but I figure that these are the people you live with and you should show some loyalty. We haven't even considered a private school for our kids."

Mr.: "And I think public education gives the kids at least a little better perspective on the world in most cases. And I think we do a good job; I think the kids and the taxpayers really get their money's worth. I would say sixty to seventy-five percent of our kids get what they should out of high school. It doesn't sound like a whole lot perhaps . . ."

Ms.: "But it's not bad when you're considering everybody."

Mr.: "And when you consider that we often have a president elected by fifty percent of a quarter of the voters. That's twelve percent, and a top baseball player who can hit 300 percent is considered a marvel. I mean if we had somebody batting 750 . . . percentages are very relative. But sixty to seventy-five percent is pretty darn good."

(What's it like being a teaching couple?)

Ms.: "I think for the most part it's great, though it reduces the money a lot. (Laughter) For one thing, it reinforces the job a lot. You can understand a lot of the environment and I think it helps in a couple to understand the other person's job. And the scheduling is wonderful. We are both free at the same time; we purposely don't work other jobs; you know, the money would be nice but to us our family is real important. That would be the major thing against going into another job: free time together. Because then we'd have to work all year long, so that scheduling is great. And the understanding is just one thing more in its favor. In a way it closes your environment a little bit because the people who are your friends tend to be teachers too."

Mr.: "I think there are some plus and minuses. You go the big route and we certainly are understanding of each other and what we're going through on a day-to-day basis. When it comes down to specifics, sometimes we can be supportive and sometimes we — at least I feel that way — I don't want to hear any more of it. I know sometimes I'll come home and she'll say — how was it? And I don't want to talk about it again. I know she'd be more understanding than anybody . . . but I think we live on a little bit more narrow scope because of that. I think it's good when we have to listen . . ."

Ms.: "There are a lot of teaching couples; I don't know if that's the same in other professions. I'd say there are a lot of male teachers who marry female teachers."

Mr.: "I think it would be very difficult for a man who taught to live with a woman who worked in the business world, the discrepancies in salary and that traditional male dominance role that are breaking down. On the other hand, we know a lot of couples where the female is a teacher and the male works in business, and it's almost like the women is dabbling for extra money. But I think it would be difficult to go the other way."

(What do the other couples that you socialize with who aren't teachers think of your being teachers?)

Ms.: "Well, there aren't very many of them."

Mr.: "I think they look on us respectfully. And they appreciate what we're doing kind of like you appreciate the person who comes and cleans your house."

Ms.: "Oh, my god! I don't think it's that bad! (Laughter) I think it's respectful and yet — we live in the real world. I feel a little bit that the way that we dress for work — you know, we don't dress up."

Mr.: "Yeah — I set my ties at a different length to be a teacher." (Laughter)

Ms.: "And yet, when asked if they would like to do it — they say no way!"

(Do you think that they would want their children to go into teaching?)

Mr.: " No."

Ms.: "No. My parents all along thought that was really wonderful for me; they were never real cheerleaders; they never pushed me that way. I guess because they felt I had to make up my own mind for something like that. But there weren't that many people who went to college in my family."

Mr.: "Our backgrounds were really pretty similar. We were the first ones to go to college in our family, and I guess we slipped from a blue collar world into a white collar world. And my parents thought that was great. There's no doubt that our parents are very proud and respectful of what we're doing."

Ms.: "Although I don't think that means much outside the classroom. It doesn't impress much at parties to be a teacher. It doesn't get any kind of respect except at parties where you don't know people and you tell them you're a teacher and they say — 'Oh, let me tell you about my child!'"

Mr.: "I don't mind telling people I'm a teacher."

Ms.: "Usually it gives everybody something they can talk to you about, either about when they were in school or about their kids now. I think that's one thing about teaching; everybody feels that they've got some familiarity about it. I've never really been in an executive's office. But everybody's been in a classroom. Everybody kind of feels like they know what school is like and therefore, that kind of lowers the job. I think that's really sad because that's not really fair."

(Do you think public education works?)

Mr.: "Sure."

Ms.: "Sure. I do. I really think it's great. I think most of the people in our country were educated publicly. I think that public education is the backbone of America. I do! And I feel like I'm doing a real good job, sometimes an ok job and only occasionally a poor job. It's not unusual at all in our school to have these long conferences about one kid. And there's usually a group of six to ten people sitting around for a minimum of forty-five minutes talking about this one kid. I don't think ten people have ever sat around and talked about me for forty-five minutes in my whole life. (Laughter) And I've said before that I'm amazed at the attention we're giving this one kid who's having a minor sort of problem. And we're sitting there — the staff psychologist, the social studies teacher, the district teacher, the principal, the parents. That's really good and that can happen to almost any kid. And it does happen for all kinds of students, not just my gifted students but for LD students and for average students too. All of that's free counseling and that's available."

Mr.: "It hasn't reached the baby on board status for a sign, but I like the one for teachers that says — We have done so much for so little for so long that we can now do anything with nothing." (Laughter)

Tape #251

Mr. P. had taught for seventeen years at the high school level in a very suburban school district. He was the department chairman and as he noted, the only social studies teacher in his department who didn't coach. That caused him some consternation.

Mr. P. was married with two young children of his own and forty. He had met his wife at the high school where they both had taught.
Money was an educational problem.

(Would you say you found it hard to raise a family on a teacher's salary — one salary?)

"Yeah — to some degree. It's a little different since I've already basically paid for most of this house . . . for reasons we don't have to go into. But I think if I were a typical teacher with a wife and two kids and my salary were the primary salary, it would be extremely difficult for me to live in this house, which is a very, very modest house, because I bought it seven years ago and the interest rates were thirteen percent, and if I had not put down more on the house than I did, it would have taken like half of my salary to pay for the house. When I originally went into teaching — all I knew was that I was not going to make a lot of money . . . and I knew that. So money wasn't too much of a thought. I was very lucky as I had a master's degree when I first started teaching, which got me a little bit more — not a whole lot. And I lived with my parents the first couple of years I taught. I live very modestly — I mean, I had [the same] car for fifteen years. So I saved some money. I just don't spend a lot of money; but — I guess more than anything that it bothers me that there are other people around who make much more than I do with less education . . . and they don't work any harder . . . and they're making forty and fifty grand a year . . . easily . . . and I'm at the top of the scale almost and I'm making about thirty-two a year, so —

"I think finances is one of the major problems of education. To people who are competent people and want to have families and don't want to have two incomes in the family — don't want to have to have their wife work — I think they're just going to have to pay [teachers] more, which I don't think is ever going to happen. Because public education for the most part is based on the local school districts and the public perception of teachers, I don't think it's going to change that dramatically. I hate to stereotype this, but a lot of the perception of the public is — the man has a job; the woman teaches elementary school. She's off in the summer; she's off for breaks and so forth . . . And I don't know whether the public has a high image of teachers or not, but they look at teachers as social workers and they do not associate it with business jobs; they do not associate it with high paying jobs. They may see us as professionals to some degree . . . but certainly not like a lawyer, certainly not like a doctor — I guess somewhere along the lines of somebody who would see a —

nurse as a professional — a teacher is a professional. But the public pays for the teacher, and basically through the whim of the public — that is one area that the public can control — education. They can't control so many other things that they pay taxes on; they can't control federal government or state government. The one thing they can control is local government — education primarily. You know, I have heard this for seventeen years — stay in teaching, the pay is going to get better. Every report in the country has come out that they need better pay. But — you're still going to get your two or three percent raise a year. And that's it.

"One of the things that really frustrates me is that some teachers work very hard at their jobs and they will get the same pay as the teachers who do virtually nothing. And I feel particularly frustrated in this because I'm in social studies and from 1969 when I was hired, I can only think of one other teacher in our district at high school social studies that was not hired to coach. So out of all the people that we've had in the last eighteen years, I was probably next to the last person ever hired not to coach. I have a department of eleven people and ten of them coach and they were *hired* to coach . . . and their day starts at 2:15 when schools lets out. They were hired to coach and they're very good at coaching, but their primary interest is not what's going on in the classroom. I think teachers should be hired to teach. I told someone in the English department the other day — I'm envious of your department because you've got ten or twelve teachers in your department, and the weakest of your teachers could teach circles around anybody in my department. And they were hired to teach English.

"I heard the principal one time say, 'Well, we've got a vacancy in social studies; let's go pull the coaching files.' And he tells me this, and I'm chairman of the department. So I'm working with people who are in athletics and I'm not in athletics. I'm somewhat of an outsider in my own department in the sense that I don't coach. You know, I hear about English department meetings lasting an hour; ours last ten minutes, fifteen minutes, because they get up and walk out. And I work hard at teaching; I spend a lot of time grading papers; and I work at my subject matter and I read and so forth and I know that most of the other teachers in my department do not do that. And you know, it seems like nobody cares. Some districts are getting into hiring coaches outside the school . . . and I see problems there too — they don't understand kids; they don't know school rules. Ideally it would be nice to have coaches from a cross-section of departments. I think one of the problems is that we get people who are hired to coach and in three years they quit coaching and they keep their jobs — we have an ex-coach who was hired to coach and now all he's doing is teaching. He wasn't hired to do that really in the first place . . . it's a difficult problem; there's no question about it. But you have to decide what your priority is. And some schools have decided that athletics is important; you've got to have a good coach.

"And another problem is that I just don't have the time to prepare some lessons that I think would be exciting and interesting. I have so many papers to grade and so much to do that when I get done with all that, I'm just tired. And here again you have a problem in social studies, because these people are coaching from two to six o'clock or seven; there is no way they even remotely have the time to do the job in the classroom. I do not know of any teacher in our department that makes kids write essay tests. I don't think the principal has realized this problem. They've gotten involved in the district in this mastery learning thing which I think may be a way to help the weaker teacher. It may be one of those subtle things that they're doing to work with some of those less good teachers. But I've never seen him directly do anything about those teachers who are not teaching very well."

(Would you go into teaching again?)

". . . yeah, I think so. I think I still would. I'm going to retire the very first minute I'm capable of retiring. I don't think you're going to see any more teachers going thirty-five to forty years. I think it's physically too hard; it *is* a stressful job, no matter what people say. There are unique qualities of stress in teaching. So when I'm fifty-three years old and I've got thirty years in . . . I'm quitting. There's no way I'm not, because I can tell that at age forty there are physical demands on this job . . . I've been in school districts where there have always been a couple of teachers who are sixty years old . . . and I just don't think you're going to see that anymore."

Tape #223

Ms. T. was in a hurry. She had been a part of her association's bargaining unit for the last several years and was very active in association work. At the time of her interview she had just gone back to classroom teaching at the first grade level after nine years as a district grade level supervisor. She was teaching at an inner city grade school and was glad to be back to the challenge of the classroom.

Ms. T's soft voice and warm manner made for camaraderie. She spoke honestly and with a sense of humor. Her years in education had worn her down, but not worn her out.

"I got into bargaining for my local association because I find it fascinating. You start to get into the law and the legal parts of it and teacher rights and what kind of grievances you can file. My thing was taking a team and getting them trained and getting them together to bargain — and it can be hell, just hell. And there is no — thank you from the teachers. And there's no income from it, so it was almost like you had to be a family and keep them together. And that was hard; this year was very difficult. We had things that we wanted that we were not able to get, like agency fees. I mean, the [bargaining] team was absolutely committed; would have fought to the wall, stayed out forever. The teachers, on the other hand, weren't. But it's fascinating; it's a blend of the legal aspects and the emotional things that keep people going."

(Did you feel real conflict between administration and employee?)

"Yeah. We've had three superintendents in the past couple of years. The first one had been here for ten years and the board got rid of him; the second one lasted less than a year — he was a real idiot. And this new one seems real dynamic and energetic and I think he lied to this board four times that I know about. To me, that's the ultimate. The first one was real political and got out, but to my knowledge, he never lied to me. This guy, he's already lied to me. We had settled on a salary and after the next day he said it wasn't what he meant . . . after we had called off a strike."

(Why do you suppose administrators look at it as us versus them?)

"Well, they don't — at least to hear them tell it. They say we didn't mean this and we don't have the money . . . and that's what I mean about the language — we need to be able to catch that and make it stand up in court. We're down there in good faith; a lot of our team has been giving up their summers year after year . . . and these idiots are lying to us. Then you start to wonder if these are really terrible people . . . or stupid or devious . . . ."

(Why are they not trying to help teachers get the best deal they can?)

"Well, they could — they'll say they are; it's money from the state being cut. But then our financial people don't agree with their financial people. The past history from the twelve years I've been around is that they hide money, and then later they find money. Whatever the board wants to hear is what the accountants tell them. Now we have people who are sophisticated in reading their budgets to know exactly where it is."

(Do you think it's legitimate when they say there isn't money there?)

"No. We have the facts this time; we've had it from the beginning and they had to do a lot of dances to cover them. They just keep dancing around and never give you a straight answer. In our state they must spend fifty-five percent or more on teacher salaries and they're at 55.7 or something like that, and they can't afford to cut more. Even when we got our ten percent raise a year ago, they came out ahead the next year due to retirement. So when you come at them with things like that —"

(Why do they do that?)

"They want to settle for less. The board's very political and we haven't until recently supported the majority. Also we have only a third of the teachers as members and everyone gets the same raises. Even a lot of my friends aren't members . . . I give my life and summers, and that kind of grates."

(Do you think teachers leave for higher salaries?)

"Oh, yes. The woman that teaches next to me just resigned two weeks ago for a job; she starts at $40,000. She just got her MBA; she's thirty-four years old. Now our highest salary — after twenty-two years and sixty units extra — will go over 40,000 dollars.

". . .Yes, I think we have bad teachers — I don't know — maybe ten percent. But I think you have bad people in any profession and maybe especially in teaching, because you're isolated, and if you don't get any support — not just resource people, but a lot of materials and administrative support — you're really out there alone. You throw in big classes and you throw in bilingual issues we have in this city, and you're really fighting a lot of battles."

(But if you say there are ninety percent good teachers and more money will bring in better teachers — that doesn't jibe.)

"Well, a lot or them are old — the average age here for teachers is like fifty-one. And I don't think new young ones will come in. There are a lot of people who won't even look at it as a profession because of the pay, I think.

"I don't know why people become teachers . . . I think in the old days it was to have a vacation. I don't have a vacation. It doesn't stop. And working here at the local association I have less time during the year — I haven't graded papers in a month. Soon that'll hit the fan. Without good salaries I don't know how people will continue to go into it. But there are some things you get from the kids that you don't get in other places. I could do research for ten years, but the nicest report in the world doesn't measure what you get in the classroom."

(Do you think you'll be on the bargaining team again?)

"Yeah . . . I said goodbye with a lot of fanfare and two weeks later we needed to bargain again and there I was. I know a lot; I know where the bodies are buried now. It still bothers me, though, to give this much time."

Tape #168

"I don't think we can defend a stupid country."

She was wearing a black t-shirt that had written on it "love of reading" — in Spanish. And yes, she taught in a Chapter I bilingual program in a fairly large Southwestern city. I observed the last five minutes of her class and listened to a record about touching your nose, etc., while the kids and Ms. H. danced around doing what the singer told them to do — bilingual education. Ms. H. was a great proponent of this. With her dark hair, bushy eyebrows, and brooding face, she looked a great deal too serious. But her words had deep thought and sincerity, a combination hard to beat. She had two children of her own, and at one time her son had qualified for free lunch because her teaching salary was so low. Both of her parents had been college professors.

"I taught for three years in a rural setting, commuting from the city until I could get a contract here in the barrio. But I would prefer to be in this setting — I think we need qualified teachers here. Ninety percent of our kindergartners qualify for Chapter I — the majority of the students in our school qualify for federal funds. In this city that has one hundred schools, I just heard that we rank sixth for the percentage of children who qualify for free lunch. So it's a very low socio-economic background, a very high-density community. Most of our children walk from less than a mile away and we have over 650 kids. But there's an attitude here among parents and the kids — maybe because there's nowhere to go but up — but I find an attitude that they want their children to be here and they want their kids to learn and the kids apply themselves . . . I really think that the majority of them do. We have a very strong bilingual component and I do have bilingual certification. So two-thirds of our program is bilingual."

Chapter I kids? Well, for instance the Chapter I kids come into kindergarten probably not able to write their name, probably not counting up to ten, probably have not been to preschool . . . maybe had Head Start. Chapter I children are low socio-economic background, probably one or both parents did not graduate from high school, and a lot of the indicators are that these children are going to be the ones who drop out before the end of high school. So what we're trying to do here is an intervention program. It isn't that these kids are failures like in the pullout programs of the upper grades, but at the kindergarten level it's that we have the indicators that they may not do well . . . and there is strong teacher evaluation and input — our district, luckily, still values teacher input. And we then work with the parents, doing parent education, and we try to find the kids a broader base of experience from which to learn. We do use a picture vocabulary test to help place them too . . . which if you've never gone fishing, you don't do very well on, and that speaks poorly since we're in the desert! (Laughter) But now we use a new one which was developed here . . . it tests basic concepts like little versus big. They're not intelligence tests. We're looking at the conceptual development and generally these children are a little developmentally behind the others and they can catch up.

"And they're not learning disability kids because they have to have a certain amount of strengths and weaknesses so if you're all weaknesses, then you're not learning disability so you don't qualify . . . and that's where the Chapter I funds come in. We work with these 'grey area' kids. Now it's all federal funding, but there's a school a half a mile away that says the Chapter I kindergarten can't serve the Spanish speaking kids!

"But the program has been in existence now so that we have kids who have graduated from high school. We've lost a lot of kids who have moved, etc., but the kids that they followed [had] a much higher percentage of high school graduation than anybody could have ever predicted from that population. And the qualifications for the program were one or more parents not graduating from high school, another language spoken in the home other than English, qualifying for free breakfast, and another sibling who qualified for the services. And it's far less costly to establish those kinds of programs and far more easy to work with four year olds than it is to establish something to reform sixteen year olds. It's a very successful program."

(What would you say to people in Washington who are tying to cut these education dollars?)

"I don't think we can defend a stupid country. What's the point of building up a defense for a country that has no education? We're the only country in the world that offers an education to everybody, and we're about to eliminate it. We're having kids who don't go to school because their parents can't afford it. And the teachers can't afford to stay as teachers. So we'll have inadequate people teaching in an inadequate system. And then all of our money's going to defense . . . and what's there to defend? And they complain even in the military that they're getting people who can't read the manuals. Education is freedom and our country was built with the [idea] that we all have the right to be free. And if we all have the right to be free, then we all have the right to education. If we have educated, critically thinking people, then we don't have to worry about our people knowing what's happening. Because if it's right, they will make those decisions; and if it's wrong, they'll make those decisions and do something about it. And so the freedom and the defense of our country is based on a good public education.

". . . So I think teachers need more money. My husband and my two kids and I were on the front page of the paper. My husband is also teacher-certified but hasn't got a job; as a fourth year teacher, I'm supporting a family of four. My five year old son qualifies for free lunch — I make $21,000. We were on the front page because of my income and the fact that I couldn't afford to keep sending my son to day care where he had gone because of increases due to new state regulations. But people need to know that as a public school teacher, I can't afford the day care — a fourth of my salary goes to child care. And that doesn't include the diapers! And that's pretty common.

"A lot of our teachers are going out of teaching — they're burnt out and can't afford to stay. We're losing a lot of good teachers . . . and we're getting a lot of bad ones. And think of on the university level. My father is a full professor in the education department, and he gets half of what a lot of the professors in other colleges make. I'm not saying the others don't deserve it, but I think their priorities are skewed. I think he should get as much as the football coach. And I know what they're offering a football coach because they just had that opening, and it's a lot more than what most of the professors are making."

Tape #255

Ms. B. was a special ed. teacher in a run-down inner city grade school.
She was a very tired special ed. teacher of emotionally disturbed children.
Her room, though decorated with posters and games and students' work,
was dingy and poorly lit. It was directly across the hall from one of the
noisiest cafeterias I've ever heard in my life. She said she had lots of
problems with her students and no help from her principal in dealing with
them.

What kinds of problems, I asked . . . and she told me about the boy who
exposed himself in class, the boy who threw a pencil — through another
boy's cheek, and the girl who couldn't stop cussing, and on and on. It was
obvious that Ms. B. was on the verge of burn-out . . . after only seven years
of teaching. She was thirty years old, pretty, with lovely dark hair. What
would it take to help her teaching become more effective? — money.

When leaving the building, I saw a girl crying to a hall security man
that someone had called her a name . . . and stolen her purse.

"I graduated with a degree in working with mental retardation, but when I graduated there weren't any jobs in that field. And the way it works in this state, you have a blanket certification and that means you can teach any grade, any field in special ed., so I've been teaching here, grade school special ed., for about seven years. Maybe someday in the future I probably would like to go back to the mental retardation field. This has been a very difficult field, and yes, I'm very, very tired now.

"I think the biggest reason for burnout in this field is lack of support. People in the state departments of education make up these rules and regulations, and they don't see these children as very disturbed, maladjusted children . . . and I'm all by myself. And when there's a problem in the room, there's not a lot of support from the administrators; it's a part of this school, unfortunately, but it happens all over the city. I know several colleagues that are in the same boat I'm in. They're all frustrated. If they gave me six of these children with a full-time aide, I'd probably be successful and could stay in this field for the rest of my life. But it's money; I think what it comes down to is money. I work with twelve kids now . . . and it's different here than in the suburbs. We are the inner city. I don't care where you go, what city, if you're in the inner city, it's different. The children in the suburbs that are emotionally disturbed — are different."

(Give me an idea of some of the problems that you have to deal with here.)

"People wouldn't believe what goes on in this room. I've had a child expose himself to the class; I've had a child steal my wallet; I had to go into the ghetto to get it back — alone. It's a really dangerous area and if you're white and a white woman, you really don't want to be in the area. But I wanted my wallet back; I knew this kid had it — he took my wallet and he pawned it off to a fencing operation . . . and he was only twelve years old.

"The foul language is unbelievable. My children know everything about sex; they know every type of position, every type of word, noun . . . I mean, they know more about sex as grade schoolers than I did as an eighteen year old. It's unbelievable . . . their mouths, their foul language, it's disgusting. I don't know where they're getting all this language. They're very disturbed; they show a lot of problem behaviors. They're problem children in their own neighborhoods; a lot of them have probation officers, and they're only twelve years old. A lot have tried to kill themselves. Many of them have used drugs and are on drugs. They've seen it all. One child, Morris, witnessed his father go off on cocaine and shoot the mother in the stomach with a .38 caliber gun; he witnessed the whole thing. This is just the tip of the iceberg.

"I could sit here all day and tell you all of the stories, but I don't think people really know what goes on in these schools. And I don't think they really empathize with the teachers. You know, I think they think we're overpaid; we have it made — we get about a day off a month. There's — 'Oh, what are you complaining about? You get your whole summer off.' I'd love for them to walk in my shoes and deal with what I have to deal with. Who wants to go to their job and be verbally abused? Who wants to go to their job and be physically assaulted, which I have been by these children. Who wants to see them — you know — physically assaulting each other? I had a boy last week throw a pencil and puncture a child's face, blood pouring out of it. The kid left a very noticeable mark; he may be scarred for the rest of his life. It's just a very difficult situation and when I have a problem and I take it to our principal, it's like — [it's] my fault all the time.

"She doesn't take into consideration the severity of these children, that there's twelve of them. She feels that there shouldn't be any problem! There shouldn't be any problem — twelve emotionally disturbed children! You look at each and every one of these children and not one of them has a father at home. Most of them don't know who their father is. They've had numerous problems with the law; their parents have put them up for petition — a person needing supervision because the parents can't control them so they go to the courts to try to get help, and they may institutionalize them or they put them in foster care or something like that. Half of my children have been put in one of these petitions. We, of course, have to take them; my class [has] problem kids but not the worst — there you get into a class with one teacher, one aide, and six children and you have very, very abusive children, very, very violent kids."

(Do you feel that you accomplish anything in the classroom?)

"Very little; my day is basically dealing with behaviors. I feel like I'm a policewoman all day long. They want you to teach; they want you do the three R's — reading, writing, and arithmetic, yet they don't take into consideration all the difficulties that you're going to have during the day. I stop doing a science lesson or a reading lesson — I can barely get through my reading groups every day because there's always a problem. Someone gets out of their seat and wants to start with this one or someone can't be quiet. Someone's having a bad day and he just can't settle down. I have to take that time to deal with it. If I just had six kids — with an aide — oh . . . I'd just accomplish so much more. I think they'd progress better both academically and emotionally . . . we don't give them enough — we don't. And — no one seems to care.

"All the state people care about, all that the principal cares about, all that my supervisor cares about —is that there aren't any problems. 'As long as there aren't any problems, we don't care.' We don't care if you're spending your whole day disciplining your kids and keeping them in line! Most of my children will go to a junior high disturbed situation like this. And then it's a high school setting like this and then out into society . . . with very little hope of amounting to anything. I think we should do more; I know we *could* do more . . . but — I don't know where to begin; I don't know what would have to be done. You know, special ed. teachers are crying all over the place . . . but they don't want to listen to us. Or at least that's what it seems. If I could have six kids, plus give me the money and the materials that I need to give them what they truly deserve and need, yes — I could make progress.

"This is not exactly a beautiful place and there aren't a lot of materials. I have ten science books and twelve children. You want to know what it's like for those two children who don't have a book to try and share with someone? It's like — 'You ain't using my book! Get outa here! I ain't sharing this book!' I mean — silly little problems like that. I don't have enough language books to go around. And really, by rights, they all should have their own books. You know — pencils, paper — they won't even give us white construction paper, because they say they don't have it. It surely is a crime . . . .

"I can't see myself being a teacher for the rest of my life; I've already looked into other careers. I think I'd really like to go into child psychology. I really love working with children. It really breaks me up inside when I think of leaving it, because I love all my children. As difficult as they are, I'm devoted to them; I love them; I'd stand up for them no matter what. But, there are just too many other factors; there are just too many other variables coming into play that are just overwhelming; it's wearing, like taking more and more pieces away every year. But recently the pieces seem to be bigger. These city schools here went through a whole new change in their special ed. I used to have only ten children and I thought that was a lot, but now we're under these new state regulations and I'm up to twelve. And I'm just overwhelmed. And I've squawked to my supervisor and she's squawked to the people higher up and no one seems to care. No one seems to want to do anything. So eventually I will probably get out of this field. I think there will probably be a lot of other people going with me. I can't speak for the normal classroom teacher, but I can't see many of the special ed. teachers sticking with this . . . I really can't.

"Look at today. We were having a very nice lesson and a child made a comment. Another child took it to heart so he got out of his seat and he went over and smacked him right in the side of his face. It left a very noticeable mark. Those kinds of things upset me . . . you know, things are going along beautifully and one of them has to be a hit . . . and they lose it. That's how it is all day long. There just is never a good day in here. What makes them the way they are? Their environment. I really believe it's their environment; I really believe it's their home life. And we get no cooperation in this area from the parents.

"I contact parents all the time, all the time. And their parents are as frustrated as I am. Some of these are mothers with ten kids and no father. They're on welfare, public assistance. They can't control their child any more than I can. It's a no-win situation. I have a mother in here . . . actually it's a grandmother. She's been raising this boy since he was eight months old. The mother couldn't raise this child so she's been doing it. And I would call her on the phone when this boy would have a problem and she's like — 'Listen, I thought by putting my son in this special ed. class

I wouldn't hear from you anymore, now would you leave me alone!' And I would say, 'Mrs. _____, I need your support here; we have to work together.' 'No! Uh-uh — school problems — you deal with it in school. When I have a problem at home, I don't bother you; I don't call you!' — on and on and on. She's terrible. I hate it when I have to call her. It's always the 'school's fault.' Her son gets into a fight; she can't understand why he's getting suspended. 'He's only eleven years old; I can't believe you're suspending a boy who's eleven years old. I mean, for fighting? — how trivial!' — you know, even though he almost knocked a kid's eye out. She doesn't see that. So — no, there isn't any support from home.

"You know, I think I have two kids in here whose parents seem to care and their behavior is fairly good. You know, they take home weekly report cards at the end of the week and the parents have to sign — half the children don't take them home; the other half that do, their parents sign it but they could care less. There are about maybe two children in here whose parents really take the time and sit down and talk with their kid and they really care about their progress. I have some of these kids now — well, some of them have been with me for three years since I've been here and they have made progress. They've learned to deal with their feelings in a more appropriate manner. They have had some gains in their academic ability, but I know it could be better. I know they could learn more and they could get more.

"The big problem that I see — when you put twelve of these children in one class, twelve children with severe emotional problems — they feed on one another. There's no positive role model except for myself. And it's sad; they eat each other up. It's a vicious cycle and they feed into each other's problems. I don't know if this is the answer, putting all these kids in one of these classes . . . I just got a boy from another class, who came from a 'normal' sixth grade class, and he's not that bad . . . he's been with me now for three weeks. All of a sudden, I started noticing. He's picking up the foul language, the aggressive behaviors — and when he came from his school, he was having problems but nothing aggressive, no verbal language abuse to speak of. He was just having some problems relating to his peers. And that scares me.

"I think one of the biggest things to help make things work would be to have enough materials to go around. There are just so many neat educational things available on the market today that I could get for this class — like a computer. I would love to be able to work with them on a computer . . . I think my children would get a lot out of a computer. That's the big thing now; that's the way we're growing. You know, really! I feel like a little pack rat. Whenever I go to the store, whenever I go anywhere, I always feel like I'm looking for things for my class. Class, first; me, second. . . ."

Section 12:

IDEAS

Imagine this scene: You're rushed into a hospital for some emergency surgery. When you get there, they present you with — "We have two doctors here who can do this surgery for you. One is a guy who has been teaching people how to do this surgery for the last ten years, but he hasn't actually performed the operation since he left the operating room ten years ago. The other is a guy who has worked as a doctor for ten years and has performed this surgery on an almost daily basis . . . Now which doctor do you want to operate on you?" Add to this scene the elements of the hospital administrator walking into the operating room and telling the doctor how to operate and the doctor first reading through a list of policies recently mandated by legislation in his state, and you have a perfect analogy for the lack of teacher control in public education today.

Working teachers are rarely listened to or even asked about usable solutions for dealing with the problems of public education. And face it, who would know best? It's principals (administrators) and central administrators like superintendents and curriculum specialists and college professors — none of whom have been in the "operating room" in years — who are making the decisions. Go back and look at interview #254, short as it was; would any doctor be told by a hospital administrator that he or she couldn't speak with someone during his or her lunch break — in that hospital? Would a doctor be told he or she isn't allowed to leave the hospital until a certain time?

In one district where I felt teachers had a lot of control over the curriculum, I found some very happy teachers; it was also a district with quite a good academic reputation. But curriculum specialists and college professors in their sterile academic utopias have helped to get us into the mess we're in. And they change their minds every seven years anyhow.

Why not start listening to the teachers who are trained and have the experience to work with these things?

State legislatures also want control of the curriculum. They have started mandating tests for all students, merit pay plans, and other things they know nothing about. Would they mandate certain operational procedures for a doctor? They want to prove all students have learned by asking them to pass little memorization tests. Yet, not all students learn that way, and memorization doesn't mean much anyhow. A chimp can memorize. Most legislators know nothing about teaching.

Teachers need to be given the leeway to handle each student in a different way, the different way that that student can learn from. We're dealing with human beings, young ones at that, and you simply can't legislate tests that will make each of them learn. We need a variety of teachers, methods, and tests so we're more likely to hit what each kid needs to learn and progress. Restrictive district and state policies are counterproductive, and they're rarely teacher initiated.

It's no wonder teachers had no trouble finding things wrong with public education and hemmed and hawed when I asked them what was good about it; teachers have no say in the policies. Indeed, lack of teacher control was one of the most mentioned reasons for leaving the profession. And, most other teaching ideas somehow seem to relate to this problem.

If a hospital is ineffective, the hospital administrators are blamed, not the doctors; if the schools aren't run effectively, blame the school administrators, not the teachers, who unlike doctors, have no say at all. One inexpensive way to improve education is to give the teachers a lot more control of it.

Tape #112

"People aren't leaving education because of children but because of other adults: incompetent principals, supervisors, and board members."

Ms. D. was a large black woman in plain clothes, teaching in a Southern inner city school. I observed her teach for an hour and interviewed her in front of her fifty-fifty black and white fourth grade class while they worked on a social studies and coloring project. She maintained control very well and did, indeed, seem to be a power in their lives. She had taught for twenty-three years and had one child of her own. At the end, she referred to some notes she had written for the interview. She felt, like all teachers, that we no longer control the profession. She went so far as to compare teachers to slaves.

"The major problem of education is that we're trying to pattern education off of something different than education is. I think education is really meeting the needs of each child, which means that it cannot be prefaced in a lesson plan. Trying to make a business out of education takes away from the personalization that's needed. One child might need one thing and another kid something different. I disapprove of management by objectives. I don't believe you can create objectives for living beings because you really do not know what any child brings to the classroom. They all bring something new to the classroom. And they all have deficits, even the bright ones. And I think when you try to pull something down the middle of the road, you miss out on a lot of bright kids and a lot of slow kids. So I don't think you should take business principles and superimpose them on a human structure. And a school should be a human structure. That means that if I as a teacher decide that walking across the street to see something that is happening over there would be more beneficial than working on a time schedule, then I should be able to do it.

"For example, I really don't think that lesson plans are beneficial to anybody but the principal and the supervisor. You simply can't know the amount of time it's going to take to administer a lesson, to know what kids will know and what they'll need you to go back and do again or to do something else to help explain the new material so that they can master the skill. Today, I've been working on quotation marks. We've been working on them for about two weeks. But I still have some people in here who may not understand them. And if I'm tied to a lesson plan, in two weeks I probably should have moved to something else.

"I also think accumulative attendance is something a teacher shouldn't have to do. Once you tell who is absent in a day, you shouldn't have to add them up at the end of the month. They will ask you fifty times how old the children are, what color they are — and surely those things don't change much during the year. But on the first day of school, you're asked how many whites, how many blacks, how many others and two weeks later, you're asked the same question. The kids don't change colors so I have problems with that and I don't even answer that. It goes into the garbage. I put in ten or twelve hour days. I believe in individualized instruction, and when you believe in that kind of system you do a lot of testing to see what they can master. And then you work on whatever the problems are individually or in a group. So I'm probably doing more than what most folks would do, but I think it's important.

"I think the school just has to let me do what I'm capable of doing. I read up on curriculum and in the educational field. I read about an hour a night and I've been doing that for twenty years. And I think I am more equipped to deal with the problems of this classroom than the principal or anybody else. In fact, I feel hindered by my principal. I've had what I consider valuable field trips turned down by her. Also grade levels — I think I do a fantastic job with fifth graders getting ready for middle school. I think that I'm probably the best upper math teacher in the building. And yet I'm moved to the fourth grade. I do a good job here, but children in that fifth grade should have the best in math they can get. I was moved because the principal was trying to get rid of me. It was harassment by her. I think she fears me. I think I'm pretty popular and she just hasn't had the experience that I have.

"I think our state does a disservice by allowing people with only three years or so of teaching to become principal, and the master teachers are in the classroom. At one time we used to have only the older teachers become principal. And we had better schools then. I think by pulling in the younger teachers and making them principals, a lot of times you set up problems. They are not knowledgeable; they are jealous or envious of people who know more about teaching than they do. I think then that, nationwide, principals are incompetent. They are not masters of their areas that they supervise before they go into it. They should have to have taught at least — twelve years. At that point, you've seen many changes in curriculum and many new innovations and you know, hey — it can be done many different ways. After many years of experience, you learn that there are many ways to do things. But the principals in the building should be going in and helping those people who do need help, whether it's subject content or structure of the classroom, and you won't find many people who can do both of those.

"And principals vacillate. Today calling a teacher a — MF is bad and the student gets punished. Tomorrow — 'Oh, he had a bad day; let's just let Johnny go.' And we can't be like that. We have to come up with a firm standard every day. And a lot of superintendents lean with the parents. I know people who contrast teaching to other professions because in any other profession, no matter what the profession is, they *are* the ones who make the decisions. Take the medical profession. If a doctor said, 'A group of us think your knee needs to be cut off,' if they don't' agree, they're not going to let the public know they don't agree. And think who is going to walk up there who is not in the profession and say, 'No — cut off his toe.' That's what happens in the education arena. We let people who have had no education back us up against the wall and tell us what we ought to be doing.

"You know, I compare teaching with slavery. It is no worse and it is no better. Think about coming into this building in the morning. You are restricted; you cannot leave this building. Even at lunch time, which is supposed to be a free time, you cannot walk over to the grocery. You could not leave the slave plantation either. You do not have a scheduled time when you can go to the restroom. If you were a slave working in the fields, you did not leave to go to the restroom. You make no decisions here; you do what somebody else has told you to do, even when you know it's wrong. So teaching . . . is slavery. And unless we free teachers to teach, we can't expect much."

(How would you describe this school as far as philosophy goes?)

"A limbo philosophy. The rest of the school is in a breeze. Today if the breeze blows this way, it's this. Tomorrow if the breeze blows that way, it's that. You see, I have a strategy to get my kids to do their homework. They do it ten times if it isn't done. And most folks would rather go ahead and do it than do it ten times. I make them do it in the classroom; I monitor it myself. And once parents begin to see the progress from this, then they support the homework. I sent a letter home the first day of school saying these are the kinds of things I'd like for you to do. Just make sure they have a quiet place to study, the TV, radio, stereo is turned off, and the folks who talk a lot — somewhere else. And I require conferences with each parent during the first month of school. That's not district policy but I will raise all kind of hell; I will stay late so I can have it. I believe that a parent and a teacher should know where they're coming from from the very beginning, so I like to look at the parents' eyeballs and tell them that [their children] have homework every night.

"I also deal with discipline at this first meeting. I say to each parent, have you had discipline problems in the past. And if the answer is yes, I ask them what they did about it. And if they didn't do anything, I ask them, well, what can we do to deal with this problem. And if they don't know, I ask them if I'm free to handle it. And that means — am I free to paddle? I ask them to fill out a form that says they give me permission when needed and I do paddle. Most kids only need to be paddled once or twice.

. . . It's funny but once kids see what they can learn if they do not cut up, they realize the importance . . .

"I like to feel that I am helping some people who have come from families who have had no success in education become successful. I think you have to break the chain of poverty through education, and I believe that once a family sees some progress, that it will cause the next generation to move farther. I firmly believe that if each child in this class finishes tenth grade or twelfth grade, then that is progress. And if they do finish twelfth grade, then they will have children that they demand go to college. I think you do it gradually. And for that reason . . . I stay in education."

Tape #43

I was met in the elementary school office early in the morning by Ms. L. She had arranged the interviews for me. First, she asked if I would be buying lunch because that would have to be ordered for me. Then she showed me where the restrooms were. Then she escorted me to the room I would be interviewing in. She was dressed in shorts and looked the role of the elementary phys. ed. teacher that she was. She was single and had taught for eighteen years, now in a poor suburban school.

She pointed out how lack of control by teachers can combine with another problem — no advancement, no rewards for staying in the classroom — to explain why fewer people are going into teaching.

"A lot is done as far as decision making without ever asking the teachers whether they want to do it or whether they think it's a good idea. And a lot of things come down from the top, and sometimes they don't work. In this county, they do have teachers on their curriculum committee. But they have a majority of administrators and even higher than that, supervisors and assistant superintendents and that type of thing. And what they do is, they have fifteen upper echelon people and three teachers. But we are the ones that have to deal with the children all day, every day, and we know things that work and things that don't. Sometimes they come out with these great big books that are like this, and that's their curriculum, and you're supposed to teach that. Most teachers will tell you, I think, that they have found that no human being could ever teach it in the time frame that they have set up. And also, some of the things in there just don't work. If you have a bottom class, those things aren't going to work for that bottom class. If you have a top class, they're not enough. I think that's why you need teachers on those kinds of committees. Because administrators have curriculums pretty well set up like in a time frame. In other words, it should take you three weeks to do this social studies unit; it should take you two weeks to do this social studies unit. And — the kids just don't fall into that time frame, I don't think, and I don't think the classroom teachers feel that they do, either. Why such uniformity? We had a meeting — I'm on the board of directors of the teachers association, and we had a meeting with the central staff just on that issue. Because we called it cloning. Basically what they're trying to do is to clone people and not leave room for any kind of differentiation and teaching style. Of course, they vehemently deny that. But we see it, as teachers. Because everybody has to do everything just the same.

Then there are competency tests that were sent down by the state. We had no choice on that whatsoever. The state mandated that. The local board of education has been very helpful to get some changes made in some of the testing, because some of the testing, nobody could pass. I don't care who you were. [Only] ten percent of the seniors were passing it. [The tests] came from the state. I have no idea who wrote them. But it was all state mandated. If kids don't pass, then they don't graduate. They start taking them toward graduation, I think, in tenth grade. So they have tenth, eleventh, and twelfth to try to pass it. Let's say they fail the math test in tenth grade. They might pass the other ones, but they fail math. Then when those results come back, the next year they are put in a remediation type class so that they'll be able to pass it. In some respects, I think it's good. But there are some children who are never going to pass those tests. Never. They're very low as far as learning ability, and they are just never going to pass those tests. I think they should have more than one test to administer. You can't expect children who are that low to take the same test as somebody over here, who's — you know, gifted and talented. It's just impossible. But it's one test that we didn't write."

(Why do administrators seem to forget what it's like to be a classroom teacher?)

"I don't think they do it to begin with. I've been here long enough and I've been through a lot of principals and assistant principals in this building. And the ones that are very new at being an assistant principal haven't forgotten for the first year or so. And then, they have. Because they have been away from it enough, they don't deal with those thirty bodies all day, every day. I think maybe they should spend more time as an administrator working with kids, because very few administrators ever work with kids. Once they get up in those offices, that's it, and you know, they never come back out.

"A lot of them want that advancement — what other incentives do teachers get? The teachers' association put out a pin last year that said — I forget what it says — 'something together,' and then it says twenty-five. And it was for any teacher who had put in twenty-five years, in the system. And you would not believe how the teachers died over that pin. You would have thought that was the best thing anyone had ever given them — because they spend twenty-five years and no one had ever given them a thing. . . .

"We have discussed incentives to keep teachers in teaching as opposed to going into administration. Basically, our goal was to find qualified teachers, keep them in teaching, do something to pat them on the back at the same time. And of course salary was the number one thing we came up with. Really, that was our basic one. We threw out master teachers; we threw out career ladders, and we did extensive study on all this. We've been doing this for, what, three years. Basically, we thought the master teacher idea creates more problems than it solves. Because you end up in a building, instead of working together as a team, you're all against each other. Because I'm going to get that money, and you're not, is what it boils down to.

"And it's the same reason against merit pay. We threw out all of those types of plans because we just felt that it was more divisive than it was anything else. And we needed something we thought that what we needed was something to keep us together, not to split us apart. So the things that we came up with were things that we thought would help keep us together. Now we plotted out two of our twenty-five recommendations. One was the recognition type buffet for the people, and the other one was — and this is an expensive one — people to do non-teaching duties, clerical and other things. Teachers have to collect money. Teachers have to — do so many non-teaching duties.

"See, we went out and interviewed hundreds of teachers all over the county. And then we studied every source that we could find on any kind of teacher incentive. We spent three years doing this. Delegating duties — that was one of the biggest things that teachers said to us: bus duty, hall duty, cafeteria duty, collecting money. Just things like that — that sound maybe picayune. But when you add that on top of all the rest of the things that you have to do during your day, it's monstrous.

"And it's demeaning to have restroom patrol — absolutely! It is! I remember when I did my student teaching in high school, and I had to go and sit outside of a bathroom, you know, and what did I spend all this time and money in college for? To go and sit outside a bathroom?! And even sitting in a cafeteria and watching kids eat. I mean, why? You know, I really don't want to see children eat. And so that was the biggest thing, and that was one of the ones we plotted out, because that was such a big interest with the teachers. And we have the other twenty-three recommendations that we came up with. Oh, pats on the back were cheap, but some of them were expensive. The one, hiring of people, that's very expensive. But we felt, if they're really interested in doing this, if they really want to do it, then that's probably the biggest thing on the teachers' minds, is not having to do those demeaning duties."

Tape #159

The interview was fascinating as Ms. D. was one of those teachers who not only knew her stuff, but had researched it and kept up on all the names and jargon. And she could articulate it. I, however, would have been much happier listening to her if I hadn't been trying to constantly balance myself in a first grader's chair . . . for over an hour. Still, it was good to talk to an elementary teacher about how to teach reading and writing and feel like you'd really heard something practical and fun.

Ms. D. was fifty-two and had been teaching in a suburban district for seventeen years. She was married with two kids of her own. She wore strict clothes and she looked somewhat severe but when she smiled, you saw the love that kept her in education.

She was working experimentally in her district on what was called whole language, another program that seemed to work and was teacher instituted, at least in this district.

"My goal is to be a first grade teacher and here I am. I don't really need the doctorate to teach the first grade. You see, first grade is so important because this is the time when you really get down to business on using what you want to teach. And I think, done right, it sets kids' sails for the rest of their time in academics. And I'm really interested in how to do it right, and how to be successful and how the kids can be successful. There's a whole new area of research coming out — not that stuff from the lab. And it's saying that it needs to be natural curriculum and it needs to — well, what has happened since the behaviorists took over in the 20s is that somebody decided that all skills need to be sequentially ordered. And that person ignored the fact that kids have been learning language since they were in the utero. And when they come to school, nothing about what they knew about languages was being used.

"It was as if teachers were teaching English to kids as if it were a foreign language. And, like in an inner city school where a kid needs as much language as they can get, they're not getting it — they're getting phonics and all this garbage that words are just isolated parts of sentences. When in fact, language is learned as you use it and you use it every day. And we know words predict things like if you hear a word like *lots,* the next word is probably going to be *of.* We have a sense of how a sentence ought to go. It's already firmly in place when kids come to first grade. All you have to do is show them how these words mean those things and get them to see how to predict and relate how things will turn out. It sounds like what we're doing is voodoo here, but really it isn't magic. They're reading if we give them a lot of experience with language and show them a lot of things. We do point to words as we read them and if the kids see that, then they learn to match up. They start noticing words that they've just heard before and they start learning what they are. Adults rarely analyze words; we just don't do that. You and I don't do that. Now parents just shudder when we say this so we don't tell the parents, we just tell the kids — when you see a word you don't know, just skip over it . . . because that's what adult readers do. When you read a French phrase and you didn't take a French class when you went to college, you just skip it. And you can learn through the context of the paragraph or page or section — you can figure out what it means usually. And go on. And what happens later is that they'll go back because they're curious about what it really means. And they usually know pretty well from the letters what it ought to say or sound like, but we don't teach them to sound it out.

"I even wrote a proposal for the school board to get permission not to use those darn basal readers. You know, the ones that say, 'See Spot run.' And now I'm using good old plain English language with kids — the kind they hear. It's really interesting that New Zealand and Australia and England have it all over us in this as they've been doing this for years. Even in the '50s people were teaching a thing like this called language experience. But we get our books now from Australia and England. Of course, the problem with that is we get words like *Mum.* (Laughter) Now, part of the proposal said that I would drag out the basals and test them on them several times a year to see how they were doing in comparison. So about mid-November I pulled them out and they just breezed right through them.

"Another area we do all this in is writing. We let the kids write. We call it process writing. We divide the writing into pre-writing activities, sharing, and writing, editing activities, rewriting, and on to publishing . . . and not everything is written to be published. So what we do — on the first day of school — we spend some time on pre-writing, which means talking about something like buying school supplies or something they can relate to. And I'll give them an experience of mine and tell them about it and then ask them, did anything like that ever happen to you? Well, with six year olds, they all want to talk. Then we give them these books that we've put together by folding two pieces of paper together. And we staple them to look like a book and we put each child's name on one. And we say now you write in it what you want — about this experience if you want —but anything they want. And I'm going to be writing too. And they'll say, 'You want me to do what?!' But a writing activity is beneficial to them. It doesn't matter what they're writing. Some of them write what they talked about. Some just write what it says on their school bag or their box of crayons. And if I'm writing too — they can't ask me how to spell things. And I tell them, I'm going to need real quiet time so they and I can write. And they learn about all sorts of things in the writing experience, including about quiet time to do it in.

"To deal with spelling, we don't let them take any papers home until we've had a chance to talk to their parents at an open house where we explain that they shouldn't correct anything or get upset about the spelling. There are papers at the beginning that I can't read. I tell the parents to have their child read it to them. If they want the spelling done right, they have to write it down and ask us so we can point out how close they were. There is no way to expect first graders to know all of those spelling rules . . . which don't so often apply. But we give them a dictionary . . . that has many blank pages so they can add their own words. And I have kids who are writing wonderful things. And we get into other types of writing.

"I think one of the big problems of education is legislators who don't know anything about education or anything about research that tells how kids learn, deciding how I should teach and how I should evaluate how I'm doing. And I think a lot of it is based on this behaviorist business again that everything is sequential and linear and that you can quantitatively evaluate how a kid is doing by somebody's version of a standardized test. And all the research now is talking about qualitatively evaluating kids today. And the big problem that we're up against is how can we say to the district we don't want to do this competency test because they really don't evaluate how kids read. And then the district turns around and says, well, yes. But the state says we have to do it.

"Educational Testing Services has put out a book on how you can qualitatively evaluate students. You can put it in black and white so that some supervisor, some school board, some state education department person can say, yeah, the kid is all right. At our level, kids can fly through these competency tests and not be very good readers. Or the tests don't evaluate what we think is important. Legislators started all this because so many kids weren't reading properly. And I think kids weren't learning to read because of all we just talked about — what the behaviorists did to the basal readers manufacturers. And the bad thing about those basal readers is that they do not represent any language pattern that the kid has ever encountered. There are verbal language patterns that we all know from when we converse and then there are the written language patterns they know from all the books that have been read to them and those basal books are the most peculiar kind of prose that's ever been invented by man. I mean, they're terrible. They aren't predictable, they don't use language patterns kids know, and they can't read them . . . because they're supposed to use phonics and apply those skills. And more kids can't do that than can. And there are several people in the first [grade level] who are saying that why Johnny can't read is what we're giving him to read.

"Legislators who know nothing about education just know they want something done. But the blessing is that people like the International Reading Association are saying that in their declaration from 1986, that the choice of reading materials and the decision of whether or whether not to use basal readers should be made by the practitioner . . . the person who is closest to the learner — the teacher. And I think that's going to be real good news.

"I am also bothered by decisions that come down from administrators when those decisions don't always make any sense. This happened more several years ago. Say, ten years ago there was a large number of children who were not learning well . . . here. And so there has to be accountability. There has to be somebody to pin the tail on. So — it's the teacher. We didn't teach them. So administrators are feeling a great responsibility to give the public the dollar's worth of the stuff they're buying. But administrators are taught how to administer, how to keep large groups of people busy and happy — that sort of thing. But as far as how learners learn and what are the optimum opportunities that learners should have, I think they have no idea. I was in a class at the university a few years ago — a class on learning principles. And there was an elementary principal who was unbelievably ignorant about how kids learn, especially how they learn to read and write. I think to get an elementary principalship certificate you have to have taught, but that doesn't mean anything. You could have taught PE as many of them did. . . .

"It's a real important thing we do here. We're really helping kids set notions about how they're living their lives and what they're going to do with their lives, and how they're going to do it. And it's mostly attitudinal, mostly affect, I think. Yeah, we're teaching them academics but we're also teaching them how they feel about themselves. And when you look into a prison, it's usually people who didn't feel very good about themselves who get in there in the first place. And I see my mission as making twenty-two kids feel pretty good about themselves every day. And I really enjoy watching that happen."

Tape #237

Ms. M. had been a nun at one time and was now in her twenty-ninth year of teaching. She had been teaching math for a long time at an inner city California high school with a large ethnic population. At one point several years before she and three other teachers there had run an alternative school that still brought a blissful smile to her eyes when she talked about it.

Ms. M. was a liberal though she didn't realize the labels. She was now fifty-two, single, and had gray hair and glasses. Her face was warm and smiling.

Several students sat around her room working on this and that as she spoke to me during her free period. She had taught first and fourth grade at one time and seventh and ninth, as well as summers at the college level. Her hobbies were history, horses, and hiking.

Here's a program that worked and then was stopped by administration. How many efficient teacher ideas has that happened to, I wonder?

"What's changed here? Well, the principal we have right now is interested in a *teaching* faculty, and those who weren't pulling their weight are gone and new teachers that he hired — work. They do their job; they're in their classroom, they're here. They're doing what they need to do. They're not reading the newspaper and having the kids do paperwork. That's one. The other one is the atmosphere on campus here is much more academically oriented because of the programs — that teachers are involved in doing and setting up. We had an alternative school going here in the past that we thought was wonderful. The principal thought it was crappola — a different principal. And he gave us nothing but problems with it the whole eight years we ran it. We took the kids that were dropping out — and were basically dropping out because they weren't being challenged. The first year we interviewed students and the parents, and what we ended up with were sophomores and juniors — cream of the crop — that were getting Fs because they weren't coming to school but were very, very intelligent. And our school was absolutely fabulous, which made that principal upset because those smart kids were not taking the classes in the regular section of the school. Well, the next year they made us take kids out of juvenile hall and all. They signed up the kids for our school. The principal and the vice principal did that, which was all right because we could still work with them. But our scores were so high that they figured that we were probably not teaching . . . they figured the scores were so high that it probably couldn't be true. The reason that the scores were so high was that we had four teachers and we had 150 students and they loved what they were doing. So when they took a school-wide test, they loved what they were doing and they did well on it. (Laughter) And yet they weren't supposed to do that well because they were not — regimented. They were off campus a lot and they weren't sitting in a regular classroom all the time. It was all these outside things going on for them — intellectually they advanced. What we found out in our final survey at the end of eight years is that most of our kids went into forming their own businesses when they got out of high school — making three times as much as we were."

(Why did it end?)

"The principal and the vice principal of that time had just decided that they were not going to allow us to schedule kids into our programs, and so the next year came and — we had no kids. They felt we were taking away from the regular school by having sections of the school that they wanted to use for I don't know what and that these students should be in regular class, sitting in regular rows, and I think they felt that they were not being educated. They all graduated and they all had higher grades and they all got into colleges or, as I said, formed their own businesses. Their statistics were all bundled up. They were very annoyed because the district came down to find out why our alternative school had the highest reading and math scores — how did that happen? And these two who were running the regular school were more concerned about not being bothered than they were about upgrading the education of the kids — and they were being bothered by us. One of our teachers quit; he went into being a ranger. He was really the founder of this particular school, but he was so discouraged by what happened that he quit teaching. But I suppose mentally we still do a lot of what we did then in our regular classrooms. Being able to program what we were going to do every week made it easier to get off of campus and — go to the bank for your consumer math class, to find out what happens to your check and all. We could do things like that — spend the whole day on your consumer math class. Or they might go to the court and spend the whole day on their civics class. But in the regular school when you do things like that — well, they're missing their English and their math or whatever.

"Now our current principal has PR'd the school. He put his vice-principal in charge of curriculum and working with the teachers, and he's gone out and gotten us publicity. I mean we've won this award and that award and it's published. He's put it on television. I think people see it differently now. People support us now. They never did before because they were never allowed on the campus. But he's gotten a core to come. In the past they were encouraged not to set foot on campus. Now they're encouraged to be here all the time. I demand parents to be involved — they should, definitely. The principal went to every kid's home during the summer months and met with each of their parents . . . that's incredible. I had a couple of fathers who needed an algebra class to advance them in their masonry careers so they came right into the classroom. Well, I'd like to see more of that — I'd like to see more parents in my classroom. It makes a big difference."

(Did you feel disappointed to come back to the regular classroom?)

"Oh God! That's when I almost really quit. When I came back and the first year I was back in the regular school, I almost died. I took two months off, and almost stayed off. I was devastated. I couldn't handle it. It was just too outrageous. It was like — how can I get to them?! There were just too many of them in the room and they're all lined up row by row, and I wanted to turn the rows around and I couldn't. Yeah, I was absolutely devastated. But I gave it some heavy, heavy thinking — came back in and decided to — conform, I guess. In my mind I thought — maybe what I could do was use that structure and teach the way I would like to teach using that structure — get my brain to work that way again. It took me the rest of that year and all of that summer to make me put myself back into that static category . . . and I liked the kids here. I've taught in Washington and Watts and Salinas but this is where I liked. They're very real kids, no affectation about them at all. They just call it as they see it. They don't put on airs; their parents don't put on airs; they're just real down to earth. You can go home and have a cup of coffee with them. They're just very sincere . . . and struggling . . . struggling for survival. And I like working with that type of kid."

(Would you go into teaching again?)

"At this time today I would say yes — note that date! (Laughter) And probably most of this year I would say yes. Now if you would have asked me maybe six years ago, I would have said absolutely not. It's better now, though — more support.

"But two weeks ago our governor said why should we give the teachers more money when they're doing a terrible job? Why should we encourage that? The test scores of California went way up. They came out last week. This week he said — why should we give the teachers more money for supplies and all? They've done a terrific job with what they have. . . . Now — there's the catch-22. If you do a lousy job, then you don't get compensated for it. If you do a terrific job — well, look what a good job you did with how little you had. . . .

Tape #24

Ms. S. was working for the first year in a school that had just started in Mortimer Adler's paedeia school set-up. Like alternative schools were yesteryear's "good idea," paedeia is one of today's. She was thirty, had long hair, and wore a large, oversize sweater when I interviewed her in her antiquey dining room. She had taught six years in Catholic schools (elementary) and one in an inner city junior high known for its unpleasantness. She had been assaulted while there. Now she was in an alternative inner city school. The Catholic schools had bored her. She taught math and science. Her hobby was running.

"Why did I go into teaching? I guess I sort of decided that if you want to work, if you want to make social change, you've got to do it through the kids. I looked at social work and teaching and those are two professions that don't pay a whole lot. So obviously I had some sort of goal beyond making money. I figured that I could make some change and make a difference."

(Why did you go into the paedeia program?)

"A couple of things — last year I was at a city junior high; that's good enough reason. This one had the reputation of being the worst school in the district. It was on "That's Incredible" a few years ago . . . the kids are the poorest that I've ever seen, all ways — monetarily, socially, maturity. They were as poor as you'd ever want to believe. And it was rough.

The day after Martin Luther King Day . . . I was assaulted. A kid came into my room; he had been suspended for behavior he had done in my class. He had been put out twice and wasn't supposed to be back there. The first times he was in, there were just threats, and I reported that he was in the building. The third period I was alone. My door was shut but it wasn't locked . . . what does that tell you? Do I have to lock my door? And he came in and said, 'Why did you get me suspended?' And I said, 'Get out of here.' He was just a little guy, a seventh grader, but he was a repeater. Over half the kids I had were repeaters of one or two grades. And anyway, he said it again and I was sitting with him behind me so I just turned back to my desk and told him to leave. And when I did that, he popped me — a fist to the cheek.

"Afterwards, I didn't feel a whole lot of support from my principal. All year I'd felt that she'd slapped their hands and sent them back to class. Anyway, when he did that, I just thought — it figures. Then he went downstairs and the assistant principal saw him in the building and asked him why he was there, and he said he was going to the principal's office because he had just hit Ms. _____. I mean, he admitted it; he didn't care. By that time, I was in tears. But I fully recovered and went back and taught classes for the rest of the day.

"They said I could go home . . . and I filed a police report and they pressed charges. If they hadn't, I would have. I just wasn't going to let him get away with that. And by the time I had even got down to the main office, recovered and composed enough — I had run into another teacher's classroom the kids in the hall already knew. So I figured that if I went home, they'd say, 'We got her.' So I stayed out about a period and a half and went back and didn't take any s___ out of them the rest of the day. And they were really good after that. It was very difficult."

(How difficult was keeping discipline in that school . . . in your class-room?)

"We always had the option of sending them to the office so that if you had to get them out, you could get them out. All it took was a call to get the security guard and fill out a form . . . which took a lot of time, but — it wasn't so bad in my classroom after the first day. The very first day, in one of my classes, I didn't get anything done. I had to go around to each kid because I couldn't call roll. As soon as I called a name, somebody else was yelling and they were all off. I had to call a security guard on the first day to get them quiet and as soon as he left, they went wild again. That night I called over half of their parents. It was better the next day either because I did call some of their parents or because I sent some of them out or because they didn't show up . . . and that was the biggest thing. My supervisor who evaluated me always put on my forms that the administration had to do something about the attendance problem because Ms. ____ can't be expected to teach when students aren't there. That's the biggest problem. My first class, I was lucky if I had ten out of twenty-five. It was sad. It was all general math; we didn't get past two digit division . . . which isn't really that big a deal. But they learned something. My test scores went up. I felt I soon had a controlled classroom, but I just sent out the kids who were trouble. I cried a lot. . . ."

(But by the end of the year you would have been willing to stay and teach there again?)

"Yes . . . but my math supervisor had told me about this new paedeia program. She told me that this would be a program that I would be interested in and I would be good at just because of the way that I teach. So she got me the copies of the books — the paedeia proposals. And I read them and they sounded good so I went for the interview. I did a lot of calling even before the interview and talked to the guy who was bringing the program into the city. And it fit exactly what I do anyway — my role; my job there is to coach. And the coach works with skills and doesn't just teach. And in math anyway it's real easy to coach because you give the kids the information and then you spend ninety percent of your time drilling it. Except with paedeia, their coaching said 6-1 [student-teacher ratio] is the max. Now ours is 15-1. But part of that is public school money. So I figured — this is what I do anyway. And I'll be paid to do it; I'll have the resources to do it — since it was an alternative school program, there was funding for it. And it was something new . . . I got a chance to team teach. It worked with one of the people I'm teaming with and not with the other.

"Compared to the city junior high it *is* that much more effective. A lot of that is the teachers. The only reason the kids were accepted for the program is fifty percent white, fifty percent black. So we have a range of kids from the very brightest to kids who can't multiply . . . at the junior high level. The science teacher — a new teacher — keeps complaining that she can't teach because the kids don't do their homework and they can't read. Well, it's my philosophy that if the kids can't read, then you teach them to read it. Or you at least give them the concept, which is also the paedeia philosophy. Also it teaches that there is the philosophy that there is one curriculum for everybody. Everybody learns the same thing. There is no grouping. Adler equates it to containers. You know, your container may be this big and mine may be this big but they can both be filled to capacity. This one shouldn't get a substandard education. I should get as much as I can just like everybody else. And it works very well. My schedule now is that I have the kids one day a week for science and one day a week for math. That takes up four days as I have two of each so my fifth day of the week I don't do anything — right! The math teacher takes kids or asks for who needs extra help — and I'll work with one at a time or up to five and work on what they need. And sure, they're losing the content of the classroom that they're out of, but they're getting one on one.

"The best way to describe the program is it's the way teachers want to teach if they had the time, the money, the support. We have the advantage that we can pretty well write our own curriculum as long as it sticks to state standards. For example, the English teacher is using all the paperbacks and he's developing concepts. And he also team teaches writing. So he basically has a 15-1 [student to teacher ratio]. But he's got his curriculum so it's all intergrated with the social studies program. The kids who are studying American history are reading all American novels, etc. Unfortunately the science teacher didn't cooperate, but he started out with creationism stories for ninth graders — including *Genesis* — and comparing. And the assistant principal goes into his classroom once a week and works with small groups on concepts.

"My big thing is that every teacher knows every child's name in the building . . . due to the small numbers in the program this year. That makes a big difference. You're walking down the hall and this one's talking to this one . . . and I have everybody's phone number and everybody has everybody's phone number. Yes, that makes all the difference in the world — pupil to teacher ratio. Go into my junior high last year; there were 600 kids. I didn't know these kids at the end of the year. I didn't know who they were. How can you have control in that situation? We accepted 200 and wanted about 180. We have 160 and are getting the numbers up. We have a long waiting list. . . . I think kids want to learn if they're not lectured to constantly.

"And I think public education can work . . . I wouldn't be in it if I didn't. It slays me the number of administrators who send their kids to Catholic schools. Our assistant superintendent sent his kid to Catholic schools the first six years of their education. It just slays me. But I think public education has the resources, the money and the staff to work . . . it *has* to work."

Tape #242

Mr. K. seemed like a citizen teacher, a real civics teacher, and he taught social studies in a way that showed he was dedicated to public education and expanding his students' knowledge of the world around them and their own country in particular. He had been a soldier in Viet Nam and had come home to teach high school social studies, which he had for the last fifteen years. Dressed in a tie and coat with patches on the sleeves, he spoke to me in his classroom in one of the largest high schools in the nation. Mr. K. was thirty-nine and married to a teacher, with three children of their own.

He proposed the logical idea of two levels of graduation, something directly opposed to paedeia, but also a program that could work.

"When I got into teaching at the beginning of the '70s, the end of the Viet Nam Era, the educational system that I walked into was very much into —'Let's make the students feel good about what they're taking.' And I think that led to some very watered-down curriculum. Now we have the political situation — the Japanese and the Russians and the Serbo-Croatians are going to beat us and we're going to come out in twelfth place. And I think there's some room for concern in that; I think there's something important in that. I also think you need to look at the nature of your society. Our society has made a decision, at least altruistically, that a basic, sound education is what we want for everybody. Not all societies make that decision and follow through.

"Secondly, we are a very heterogeneous society . . . at least out here in California. So I have a big concern about things like homework. Why do ten hours a week when twenty hours is better? And there's a place for that if you're preparing people for college because college is exceedingly demanding. My concern is — when I look at the custodian doing his job, and when I go to the grocery store and when I go to the gas station — we don't know what percentage of jobs really require a college education. But I think for a democracy to work, everybody needs to have a *basic* education. If raising the homework has the result that everybody is going to have more knowledge and have more understanding of the world around them and have more comprehension and be able to perform better, then absolutely it's one hundred percent successful.

"My early guess is, and I think it's being proved out statistically, is that a great number of people are just going to say — I quit; I can't compete on that level. What does that mean for democracy? We've got one of the lower voting rates as it is. If people quit the education system, if they start quitting the participation in the electoral system, if we have a great financial difference between the haves and the have-nots —those are things that I see as real threats to the meaning of what democracy is. If you see democracy as just a bunch of words on a piece of paper, then ok, but I don't see it that way; I wouldn't be teaching government if I did. And I just get more and more frustrated with the back to basics, the ability grouping, the more homework — what we haven't done is put in the support here for that large group that isn't going to be going to college but *is* going to be functioning in our society. If they're not functioning because they gave up, then they're a liability to all of us. There's a schism between us.

"There does need to be a different layer and level of graduation. You can walk out with dignity with something like a certificate of completion and this would say — you completed high school and high school is the end for you. And you have this much comprehension in English, this much in your math, this much in your science, social studies, etc. And then there is another level, and that is the diploma. The diploma says you have qualified for the four year university. In effect, we do more and more of that anyway; let's not bandy with terms. Let's have it. Let's have the certificate of completion and it's good for most jobs if the employer wants to know — can this person read and write. Have they followed through and stuck to a pattern that shows that they perservered? The high school diploma would designate a person on the four year college track. The completion certificate should get you into a two year college and from that you can get back into the four year college plan so you're not completely shut out. But because the standards in so many high schools are set for what the universities want, the scores are set so high that it discourages so many people. Our dropout rate here is approaching fifty percent. If you want to be a functioning citizen, then the certificate is fine and then let's make the diploma a diploma.

"Functioning citizen? Oh, I believe there should be at least three years of English, to be able to read and write. There should be basic math skills so they can do ciphering and figure out your income taxes and your income receipts. There should be U.S. history in both levels; there should be government in both levels. And there should be options in psychology, sociology, and social problems for the second group of kids — the skills where they're going to be able to go out in society and get a job and perform. Maybe you'd do a little more of living exercises if you will: how to do a checkbook, how to balance a checking account . . . those kinds of things. They're out there now but — there's a work center and a vocational center that can only handle a handful of kids. And that's become almost an elite in the de facto second track. Why make it just a handful of kids who have an option? Make it important — those are important jobs! Somebody is driving those trucks; somebody is working in those stores; somebody is doing all those kinds of things. And they will be. I'd be willing to bet my house that in my lifetime we're never going to see an entire society run by computers, everybody at their little consoles. It's not going to happen. I like ice cream; I want to go to a ball park; I want to see a play. Those are all valid, valid to all of us.

"The upper level of people tend to vote . . . the upper middle class — we vote. You look at the voting patterns. We cover our fannies. We have vested interests. So let's slow the pace down; let's make civics a whole year course instead of a semester like it is here. Make it a year course, and include a lot of participatory democracy. One of the things that I have my students do is write a letter to an elected official . . . on some problem or issue. And it's a pain in the bucket . . . because a lot of them have never ever written a letter. They don't know how to do a return address; this sort of thing. And how do you write to a high mucky-muck and this sort of thing, with a real title? But they go through it, and it's neat. They get the responses; there's a real person at the other end of that address. They never have seen that; they never have thought that — there is a senator — Whoever. And they'll write back to you.

I can envision having students involved with local government. That's where the real power is; that's where so many things that affect your daily life are. But in a semester you can't touch it — I spend two weeks! And I feel like I've cheated everything else. It alone should be a quarter and in that time, slow down the pace. And then if they can see that there is a reality, that it's not just a handful of people — 'I can have impact — I can have meaning; I can be counted.' That's why most people don't vote; they don't think their vote counts for anything. And the lower you go down the scale, at least on any chart I've ever read, the lower the participation rate is. Now some people will argue — well, good; they're stupid people and they shouldn't vote. I don't believe that way. I believe it's their country as much as it is any millionaire's. It's their country as much as it's any college graduate's. And if it doesn't work for all of us, the vast majority of us, then I think we're in trouble.

I can see some ability grouping within the two groups. In social studies we don't have ability grouping. So I have to have my work so that most of the time someone who reads fourth grade can do it and have an involvement in the class, and most of the time people who are reading at the college level can do it and have an involvement in the class. The textbook runs at about eleventh or tenth grade, [and] the homework can be paced at their own [rate], but that doesn't mean the comprehension's there. That's a real frustration. Yet, if I were dealing with two groups of kids, U.S. history diploma and U.S. history completion, then I could pace and I could develop things differently. Then it's two sets of ability groups. The frustration we have now with the non-ability grouping is that if I don't challenge the top kids, we're going to look bad on the state tests — but on the other hand, you leave behind the lower group and they just drop out. They don't bug you much, but they're sure not helping our society much.

"I would say about public education that our intentions as a society are good; I would say that puts us somewhere between good and bad. We've never developed to my perceptions a clear, overall, unified direction we're willing to go and follow through on. And I believe we have never yet addressed the needs of all of the people. But I think public education symbolizes the sense that we all have some value; it's an option for us all to be equal. It is a vital part of our democracy. People from all socio-economic classes, all races, all religions have a shot at it; now some opt out, for whatever the reason. But I think that it is there and it has value. And a tremendous amount of our people who succeed in industry and in government and in sports and in entertainment come through public education . . . it must be doing something right. Think how many good everyday people it's helped to just build a life of quality, a life of meaning —I think there's something to be said for that."

Tape #114

Ms. B. was in an old, long winter coat when I interviewed her at her association office. She was fifty-five and looked every year of it. She said she'd been having health problems recently and after twenty-eight years of teaching, she may have to get out. She taught third graders at the same school she had gone to as a child. It was now an inner city school.

"I remember I had this one group of children for three years — third, fourth, and fifth grades. Fifteen of them were advanced children and the other eight were LD students, learning disabled. And they achieved with those children beautifully. But I had the support of the parents, the support of the teachers, the support of the principal, and the children loved it. I had some help from the university in student teachers and a paid student aide, which is not usually done. And we got the children through four to five years of work in three years. Some of them had not even been ready to go into the third grade when I got them in the third grade. When they left me, they were already two-thirds done with the sixth grade work and only entering fifth grade. Even later in the middle school they kept them together as a group, and they went on to achieve 4.0 standings, perfect attendance, and won all the honors and so on. It was the first time that I ever did it and I'll probably never do it again, and it would probably never turn out that way even if I did. It was the 'Marva Collins approach' to working with the children and as I said, the other teachers were so supportive. I think somebody could do it again . . . but I don't know if I could do it again. It took a lot of work. Never was sick once, though — felt great. Never wanted to go home. We were all working just flat out. Nobody wanted to go home. The children didn't want to go home when the bell rang."

Tape #29

She met me in the hall and walked me to her classroom through well-kept hallways of her middle school. The kids walked around us. In her classroom Ms. A. sat in a sixth grader's desk and couldn't quite get comfortable. She was very large, and I had to smile when she told me she worried because so many of her children couldn't even touch their toes. And yet, after her initial nervousness wore off, she came through as so very sincere and so very effective as a teacher. She put her heart and soul into it. There was ample love in her ample body.

Her answers had been well thought out. She wasn't letting herself be interviewed because she thought it would be fun or would give her a small call to fame. She was being interviewed because she thought it was the right thing to do — she had things that should be said. Her classroom bespoke efficiency; there were lists everywhere. When she finally smiled, you could understand a sixth grader loving her by Christmas.

It was her discipline program that interested me the most. She did it for thirty students and thought any high school teacher could do it for two hundred.

"It really gets you in your gut when you see someone struggling, finally understand and their eyes light up, and it just gets me — it makes me feel good to know that if no one else cares about them, I do, and they can come to me with their problems and I can help them. I feel that as a teacher, I touch the future and I want to be part of that and make a difference for tomorrow, because these kids are going to grow up one day, and when I'm old, these are the kids who are going to be the people we are now. I want to make sure that we have as successful a future as we possibly can, because I've helped and made a difference.

"But it's a lack of public support that is public education's biggest problem today. It has improved slightly in the last couple of years. But we don't have support, even from parents. They don't care what's going on at school, unless their kid is in some kind of serious trouble that they have to come to school and straighten out. They are too busy with their own lives.

"But parental support would give their children some worth. If they have someone paying attention to them, then they must be doing something of value. And if no one pays any attention to them, they aren't worth more than that trash can. This is the time when they are going through all that hormone stuff — and who am I? What am I doing here? And with no self-worth anyway, no self-esteem, and no one paying any particular attention to them — then that just shoots it right down again. That's the number one most important thing. If we focus on developing the self and on developing the kid to the point where he accepts himself, he can do anything. But if he is sitting in the back of the room, hating himself and hating everything around him, then he can't do anything. And if we can get past that barrier, and that's one of my number one goals, they can accomplish tremendous things.

"What do I do? I call every parent before school starts, spending at least fifteen minutes talking about what their kid has done in the past and what we're going to do this year, and try to develop a caring attitude toward their kid before I've even seen the kids. I do this the first week before school starts. I go through their permanent records before I do that so I have a feel for their past problems which I can zero in on and say, 'Why do you think your child is having problems in this area?' I try to figure out home life without prying. I tell them how happy I am to have their child in my class, etc. Then I have my rules posted. Then, for the first day or so, if a child breaks a rule, I restate the rule, have the child restate the rule, then the class restate it. Not in a negative way, but . . . it's hard to learn a new routine and remember the rules. We practice that for the first week. Then I have a folder system. I was blessed with a computer and I keep all my grades on the computer. Every paper I grade goes in this folder. Every Wednesday I send home the folder with the graded papers and a copy of their report card, complete with what their average is, off the computer. Also, a note to the parent about what is in the folder, what they should look for, and then I handwrite how the child's behavior has been, how their attitude has been, and good things they have done, problems they've had. That goes home every week. The parent signs it and sends it back.

"Yes, the parents cooperate in sending it back. If they don't, I keep the kid at lunch and we go down the hall and call the parent and I very diplomatically explain to them how important it is for their child to be learning this, and how important it is for all of us to have a close working relationship; what better way can we serve their kids? Once I make those phone calls, they've 'seen the light' and I need not call them again. I also give the kids passes at the end of the week if they've had all of their homework done, which entitles them to a 'free A' on any homework assignment or to be excused from a homework assignment. I also have a homework log and every day I write the homework on the board while they write it in their log. We have an organized notebook — I've set everything out and their parents have to sign the homework log every day. The school supplies the notebook. And they get a 'smelly sticker' if they have their homework done and they have it signed. I am also into student team learning which is out of California, and the kids are broken down into heterogeneous groups by their average in one subject; so there is a high kid, a super high kid, and super low kid on every team and they are study partners and they work together on given assignments. Their goal is to get everybody on the team to understand the concept. If someone still doesn't understand or the whole team is lost, they come to me and we work it out. Then we have a team test and they are scored so the lower kids are able to get all the points the higher kids can. The scores are posted on the wall and at the end of the contest the team with the highest score gets to go to McDonald's. This method of teaching has been very successful for me. Another program I would recommend to people is teacher expectation and student achievement. That's also from California. If you develop a relationship with kids first, they know you care about them, and there won't be quite as many problems. I believe in teaching success while others teach failure. You catch more flies with honey than you do with vinegar.

"Of course, I put a lot of time into this, especially at the beginning. But as the year goes on it doesn't require a lot of time. I spend all my free time working on it but I don't take a lot of stuff home. You must be organized. I don't think you need to do everything. Parent phone calls and sending home the averages are the most important parts, and would not be that difficult. Despite having to go against some tough odds, we're turning out some well-educated people and topnotch people. We are publicly educating people, which many countries are unable to do. And we're doing this with a lot of success. About seventy-five percent of our kids are successful and are doing what they want.

"We'll talk about Tina because she's a good one. She came in to me last year with no skills at all, no self-concept, no anything. Her parents abused her. She was just ready to quit. And I worked out a contract with her . . . 'Be successful at what I give you, that's all I ask.' And I never asked them to do more than they can be successful at, because you have to learn a pattern of success . . . what I said before . . . If I give you fifty algebraic problems to solve, and you aren't an algebraic equation person . . . you're going to be frustrated. But if I give you two algebraic equations that we've just talked about, then you're going to feel successful. Well, that's what I did with her. Individually, we worked. And everybody else maybe had ten math problems to do and all she had to do was get three right. That's all we had to do. And I kept a score card for her. And we went out to the ice cream parlor when she had so many things accomplished. And so many tasks down. You've got to teach them to be successful . . . a very gross generalization here, every unmotivated child is unmotivated because they failed so many times that they don't want to try any more, because why try if you're going to fail? My experience . . . that's why they are unmotivated . . . you've got to teach them to succeed. You've got to teach them that pattern."

(Can public education work?)

"Yes."

(And do you think it is working?)

"No. I think it's working in selected areas, but as a whole generally no, I don't think it's working successfully."

Tape #4

There is one thing we can do, which almost every teacher I talked to recommended, to reduce the majority of the problems in public education and accomplish a lot, lot more: reduce class size. Period.

Mr. L. wore his white science smock. He was single and had taught for seventeen years at an integrated middle school. Currently he had things to say but not the security to say them. After the interview he told me he knew science teachers who don't know their subject, and a math teacher who didn't know how to divide. But he seemed an uncomfortable man until he said, "Teachers are used to not being rewarded so they aren't like superintendents who want feathers in their caps." He was thirty-eight.

"Speaking as a science teacher, I do not have a lab equipped to handle thirty-two or thirty-three. Many superintendents argue the opposite, but they aren't in the building. They're not the ones who have to go in there hour after hour and try to teach while at the same time overcoming all the other difficulties that, I perceive, have been created somewhat by masses of human beings in the hallways and conflicts that they get into before they get to class. Just the idea of the buses, for example. These kids are packed on those buses. They get off those buses and they charge to the door. There's a horde that comes through the doorway. There's bumping and jostling. There's a panic, almost, that starts the day, and it carries with them all through the day, and any problems that they have in the hallway or in another classroom or on the bus or on the way in the morning follow them right on through the day. To me it's just not a healthy environment."

(Why would a superintendent see it differently?)

"I think it's a monetary thing. It's definitely easier to finance and pass millages and so on if you can concentrate your flow into fewer areas of the city. You don't have the buildings to take care of, staffing, and so on. Some superintendents quote studies that say school size doesn't affect performance, but there have been studies recently done in New York that show that the smaller buildings did make a difference. But you see, I don't know about studies — I can only go by my observations and how I feel. I know that if I have a class of twenty-one to twenty-four students in a lab, we do far more activity; there's a great deal more time in the class for interaction between myself and the students for discussion and one on one, whereas if I have a class of thirty-two, I almost don't want to do the lab. As a matter of fact, there are times when I don't do [the labs] because it's just too much of a hassle — I'm bouncing like a yo-yo from one side to the other trying to help that many people and they get frustrated because they don't get the help. They'll complain because they had their hand up and 'you didn't see me' and that kind of thing, and I just don't have that with a class or twenty-three or twenty-four. So from my own perspective, I *know* size is hindering my ability."

Tape #53

Superintendent: "What *is* drama anyhow?"

Ms. O. had strong answers for almost all of my questions. She was a very forceful young woman, age thirty-six. She had one and a half kids, as she said — one due in a few months. She taught English and drama and was currently working half-time as only a drama teacher. She put on all the high school plays, etc. At one time, she had left teaching and managed a farm, clerked and sold insurance, but she came back. Now she had taught for fourteen years at grades six to twelve.

There was no doubt that she was successful. She had started a program in her first district in drama for eighteen kids and four years later she had 120 . . . unfortunately, with the same amount of equipment and space. She had felt her hands were tied; she even had to ask for the key to the closet that contained the drama equipment when she wanted it. That was when she quit teaching. Now back in it, she had lots of things to say, including the pluses of smaller classes.

". . . Actually, student teaching is what made me realize that I didn't want to do professional theater, that I wanted to teach. I had such a special bunch of kids when I student taught. I got to teach them Shakespeare, and they actually understood it and liked it . . . I had had a professor who said that you can't force a rose to bloom. But when you teach theater and get to have kids for two, three or four years, you get to see all the roses bloom . . . .

I teach twelve kids in my one class this year. It's clearly a privilege to have a class with twelve students in it. It is amazing. I have done a year's curriculum with these kids in eight weeks. That's the difference class size makes."

(What would you say to superintendents who say class size is not important?)

"I would look them right in the eye and tell them they were full of s___. Pardon my French. I think they're working within the constraints of a budget, and they all have their personal priorities and their personal pet projects. And as long as they can squeeze a satisfactory performance out of us with forty kids in the classroom, they continue to do so. And then they're surprised when nobody passes the writing test. We all know why the kids didn't pass the writing test. And yet they were all teachers once. That's one of the things that really amazes me.

"But it's so political at that point, and it is so dollars and cents. And that, rather than having a philosophy of what's best for the kids, guides where the dollars and cents go; the dollars and cents guide what's best for the kids. You could lengthen the school day and that would reduce class size. Wouldn't cost a penny to keep the kids in the building another hour. I mean, shoot, you have to pay for labor anyway, the heating bill and all that stuff. The bus runs would all be the same. It wouldn't cost a penny. Our director of curriculum came in and taught a non-grade English class for three weeks last year. And it provided him with tremendous insight which has since manifested itself in policy and curriculum. If I could do anything, I'd bring the whole central office back, back in the classroom for a month. You know, it's one thing to look at forty kids on paper. Forty kids in a theater class is dangerous. You've got a circular saw over there, and you've got scene paint over here (that happens to have lead in it). You've got to make sure it doesn't get on anything. And you've got a kid over here, playing with the makeup, and he's got the wrong brushes. He can easily poke an eye out. We got another kid up in the catwalk, with crescent wrenches that can fall down and bang a kid on the head. Forty kids in that kind of setting is dangerous. I won't tell you how many times I've tried to tell those people it's dangerous. And you know what? There's still forty kids in the drama class.

"I'd like to have the superintendent teach theater arts classes for a month. I'd love to. He asked me one day what was drama anyway.

Yeah! I sat on an arts advisory committee for five years. And he came into several meetings, to check the progress and so on and so forth. It was at one of those meetings when he looked at me and said, 'What is drama anyway; what do you teach in that?' I just sat there with my mouth open. I didn't know what to say."

Tape #50

At a younger age, Ms. H. had joined the Peace Corps. After that she had taught inner city junior and senior high in a large Eastern city. Then she had taught voluntarily in a reading program she created, to prove it could be done successfully if left to her own devices. She wrote a small book on that. Now she was graying a bit at forty-three after having taught for fourteen years, currently in a suburban/rural surrounding not far from that same Eastern city. She was very soft-spoken, and she talked with her arms folded protectively over her chest.

While we talked, we were interrupted several times by students that she had coming in on their lunch break to make up work they hadn't done for class. She seemed almost too gentle with them, and they didn't seem to care about much more than missing their lunch. Her patience was praise-worthy.

Her hobbies were reading, gardening, bicycling, and cooking. She was currently teaching high school English.

"Why the Peace Corps? I feel very strongly that the way to peace is by understanding other people, that it doesn't happen through the governments but it happens on an individual basis. I felt I could be a part of that process so I joined the Peace Corps, and I taught English as a second language in Tunisia. It was very different from what we do here. They were on the French system and everything was very strict. Discipline was enforced through physical punishment. The teacher was also much more respected, one of the most respected people in the community. For example, the students all stand when the teacher walks in the room. And the students value education so much. On the one hand, I see that as a good thing because they see education as their way out . . . to do something better with their lives. The kids in Tunisia took their education then a lot more seriously than Americans today.

"Some Americans do take it serously and some don't. I don't think American kids realize what life is going to be like when they get out of school. I've taught lower level kids for years and those kids are constantly waiting for the day they get out of high school so they can go and get jobs. And so often, fifty percent of the time, kids will come back a year later or three months later and say, 'I'd give anything to be able to be back in school.' They don't like going to work every day; it isn't a bowl full of cherries out there. And they wished they had learned more while they were here . . . but then it's too late.

"I do think one of the problems we have in our school is the large class sizes. I taught in a large inner city school for three years. After becoming very frustrated with a class that was forty-two strong and kids who went home and didn't take a book home and didn't do any homework, having a terrible attendance rate — no continuity existed from one day to the next — after three years of that, I quit. I wrote a letter to the board of education and told them that I thought it was really silly that they were putting that many students into that kind of class. They couldn't read and they couldn't learn. So I went back after I resigned and I wanted to prove my point that if there were fewer kids in the class they could learn — in a small group basis or one-to-one situation. I volunteered and taught for half a year — took kids who didn't know their alphabet, couldn't read anything, and taught them to read. I taught sometimes one to one, sometimes two and three. And this proved to me that those kids were not hopeless, sitting in the back row. They needed special identification and special help and then they could learn too. I did then use this sort of experiment as a basis for my master's degree . . . (I probably should have re-written the board of education!) And I started a volunteer tutoring program on the high school level.

"I really feel that kids can learn if given the right instruction and the right class size. School boards and superintendents say they can't lower class sizes because of money. I think maybe like they say, you could have forty or so in a class if they were highly motivated academic students, but other than that . . . If they argued the point, I'd say — come and teach my classes. (Laughter) Last year I had thirty-three in a ninth grade reading class . . . and . . . the kids were bouncing all over the place. You can see that this isn't the largest room in the school. Their attention span was about ten to fifteen minutes long; it was very difficult to constantly be watching every corner to make sure that no one was writing notes or — off task. And to make it exciting and involving for all of them — that was quite a challenge."

(Would you go into teaching again?)

"Yes, no doubts. I read somewhere recently something about teachers. It said something like how teaching was such a fine job, how teachers were constantly working to better themselves, to be better at what they do in serving students. They were not backbiting; they were not competing with each other in any way. Whereas, this person wrote, it was totally different in the business world. When I read that, I thought that is what I really value in being a teacher. So it will be interesting, as you do your interviews, to see how many Peace Corps members you get because a lot of them went into service related jobs and many of them became teachers. I think most people expect that of teachers, but I don't think they give teachers the respect that that kind of person is due."

Section 13:

OTHER PROGRAMS

"... I knew I wanted to be a coach before I wanted to
be a teacher."

It was Coach R., not Mr. He did football and track and taught social studies and American history. He felt he did both jobs well so there should be no complaints from anyone. When I interviewed him, he was eager to talk, had volunteered willingly to do so. He had taught for thirteen years in several high schools, moving up to larger and larger schools and more and more prestigious football programs. At thirty-five, he was big and balding and talked a lot about sports. He wore a tie under his argyle sweater. I ended up liking him, even when we disagreed.

Mr. R. was married with no children. His hobbies included skiing, windsurfing, and reading. He taught in a large suburban high school in the West.

Athletics is one of many *extracurricular programs that public education offers to help students succeed.*

"I always wanted to teach. I was fascinated by the subject matter when I was a kid. And I still think kids keep me young. My father was a teacher; it was a good profession for him, and I seem to have an aptitude for it. I've always heard people say that history is boring, and I know it isn't boring so I thought I could be a good history teacher and change some attitudes. I approach it with enthusiasm and a program of interesting stories. It's not just anecdotes, but you try to show some causes and some effects and some reasons that history occurs. And you try to translate it to your lives today. But I think it should be interesting. I know a lot of people find out how interesting history is after they graduate and they start reading like mad. Well, maybe if they had a good teacher, they'd have that spark beforehand.

". . . I grew up in a college town, and my father was involved with sports so I was always around sports. And I got fascinated. I figure I knew I wanted to be a coach before I knew I wanted to be a teacher, but both occurred about the fifth or sixth grade. I just decided I was always fascinated with coaching, and especially football. I programmed my education to qualify for that.

"I think the sports program fits into the secondary education fine — I like the term co-curricular. I know that there are things that I can teach on the football field — in that milieu — that cannot be taught in the classroom. And, whether we like it or not, many of our athletes are much more affected by what happens on the field or on the court than they are by the classroom. They can see the relevancy much more there. There are some things that you learn out on the athletic field that you don't learn in school. And I also think it's one of the few places where we still reward excellence, where excellence is what makes it go. And being the head coach, it all reflects on me. I don't know any other situation in education where you're evaluated publicly in the papers of the state for ten weeks. And to me, that keeps you improving. You've got to work on improving . . . you can never let up. It doesn't bother me; it comes with the territory. You expect it, I think. I mean, I know why I coach. Personally, there's nothing I can find that matches the excitement of those ten afternoons or evenings in the fall. There just isn't.

"And it's interesting that last summer I got together with five or six of my college friends — all of them earning much more money than I am — and all of them fairly successful in the areas that they went into. And I thought it was very interesting that when we got to talking — this was a summer barbecue type of thing with our families — we talked about high school football. I mean, there's got to be something that everybody likes about it.

I think students immediately see the results of their efforts on the football field. I mean, they work on a play or a defense all week long and then on Friday they find out what happens with it. And it isn't just that — they work the whole summer to get ready for football season. And they see immediately how [successful that can be]. You know, even in math or science — which are sort of sacred cows right now — well, even in those skills, they're learning things that won't be readily apparent to them for several years. So that's why I think we teach football; that's why as much as anything — that it's immediately relevant and they get a quantitative evaluation . . . you know what I mean?"

(Do you see yourself as a coach-teacher or a teacher-coach? Which do you think comes first?)

"I've been asked that a lot of times, and I probably think . . . that I can't make the decision. I enjoy aspects of both. I know this — I would not want to be a coach in the way of the Texas coaches; they're just the head coach and that's all they do. I wouldn't want that; that doesn't appeal to me. I was a good student. I was an academic all-American. So I've always felt the importance of academics. So I really couldn't say. I've run into a bit of other teachers thinking less of coaches who teach. But once people get to know me, I've been considered a good enough teacher so that it's never been a problem. And I go out of my way to try to recognize what other people do as well as what I do. They spend a lot of money on football; well, I think I can justify it. The largest crowds, whether we like it or not, the largest gatherings of people in which we see people connected with this high school is a football game. And I don't think it's wrong that people are hired just to coach; in fact, I think it's a valuable thing. Hey, we hire people *just* to teach chemistry, and we hire people *just* to teach drama. And we hire people *just* to type, so I don't see anything wrong in it . . . yeah, that's my specialty. As long as I'm doing the job, I don't see what it — yeah, I got this job because I could coach, but I've earned my keep, I think, in the classroom.

"Now, no pass/no play I think is a result of the over-emphasis. It came out of Texas where they hire people who *just* coach. And those guys get so fired-up that they force the kids through their time demands to neglect their academic pursuits. I think it's a result of over-zealous coaches and boosters and that kind of thing. But I think it's an over-reaction. I don't think you can overlook the fact that there are a lot of kids who are involved in athletics who wouldn't be in schools if it wasn't for athletics. And it's our job that while we have them here, to show them that there are other things. That's something that we try to do in our football program, that we want them to take something out of football that they can use in later life besides football. I mean, I haven't ever coached a professional player so there's nobody that I've had that's making their living by playing football. So I *hope* that they've gotten some of these other things out of it. In our state you can't play if you're not passing five classes, and I think that's a good rule. I don't think it has to be any more strict. And I don't think, as they have in Texas, that if you flunk one, you can't play anything. Because a lot of time it has the possibility for a personal dislike for the football program . . . the kid, the coach — you know, being used as something to punish the kid because he doesn't stay in line . . . and that's not fair. I think people are mistaken if they think that's going to get the kids in line."

(Do you think public education works?)

"(Laugh) I've got a running battle with my dad. I sometimes play devil's advocate . . . yes, it does. I think it's generally compared with something that it isn't . . . what I'm talking about is the foreign schools. I mean the English don't try to do what we do . . . even the Canadians don't. So there's really no way that you can compare it. You can talk about the Soviets and the Japanese but they — weed the bad kids out. They're trying to develop specific things; we're tying to give kids an education, a general education. Now whether or not that's going to continue to work in the future is a question. But at this point I think it's better than saying, yes, some of you can learn and some of you can't learn. I *would* like to see the courts butt out of education. They have put more restrictions on us than I think is reasonable, and I don't think they have any real feeling for how people learn. I've seen attendance policies that were really effective that were thrown out because they supposedly violated somebody's rights. And I guess what is really frustrating about it is that the courts are never cited as one of the problems facing education. And I think that they're among the biggest [problems] because we're afraid to do what we know is right because we'll get sued. And you don't win a suit . . . I've been sued, by the way. I mean, there's no way you win. Even if you win, you lost money. I had a kid who alleged that I didn't treat him right when he got hurt. It was simply a matter of he didn't have the money to pay and he wanted somebody to pay, and I was the one he went after. It was settled out of court. And we could have won it; I know we would have won it. Our lawyer in depositions destroyed the kid's case. He said, 'No, it wasn't Coach's fault.' But the school board said that from an economic standpoint it would cost more to win it than to settle out of court and that's stupid, but that's the way it is. But it's been three years and I haven't had any repercussions. I guess what it really comes down to is that it really bothered me the first night and then I went back and looked at [the situation] — did I do anything wrong? Did I do anything that I wouldn't do again? No. And after that, it was kind of a bothersome thing but I didn't feel guilty about it."

(Would you still become a teacher?)

"Yes, no question about it. I've been in two situations that were very good teaching situations — one that wasn't, but I still enjoyed the teaching. I wouldn't trade it. I don't really have a lot of frustrations. You have to have some challenge. But there's nothing that grates on me . . . now I've been in schools where I've had problems with administrators . . . one in particular whom I didn't get along with. Interestingly enough, when I had a problem like that, I actually enjoyed the classroom experiences more than ever. I think I used it as kind of an escape. If I can't deal with the politics of the head office, at least I can do a good job in the classroom. Kids keep me thinking. I'm thirty-five years old but I really don't feel a whole lot different than when I was twenty-five years old. And I'm still learning; I don't mind teaching new things because it allows me to do some research. And every year, even when I teach a course twice, I think it should improve."

Tape #163 Special Education

Special education programs have grown by leaps and bounds in the last fifteen years, proof that education either effects or is affected by societal changes, but proof we care. Following are brief descriptions of three of these programs.

Ms. K. was a very pretty lady of thirty-four with one child of her own. She was now a slightly burnt-out teacher working in the area of emotionally handicapped children. Her enthusiasm was still there — she just knew that the candle was burning down and she would have to, sometime in the near future, take a year off and work as a regular elementary classroom teacher for a while to recharge. She was very sweet, but I discerned an inner toughness. Her face was the symbol of that toughness, weathered as it was by her years in the Southwest.

I ended up eating dinner with her teacher-husband and her that night and found that they were into trunk restoring . . . and other arts and crafts. She was also expecting her second child that June. What was it like to deal with emotionally handicapped grade schoolers all day?

"I've wanted to be a teacher since I was little. In fact, I would gather the neighborhood kids together when I was little, and I think that was my need to want to help others. I enjoy working with emotionally handicapped children. I was kind of asked to do this and the reason I was asked was that

I was told I was very patient and I was always very calm. I could handle conflicts in a very calm way. I objected, though; I didn't think I'd be happy doing it, but they asked me to try it for a year. And it was the first year I really enjoyed teaching. I wasn't certified in this so I had to promise that I would get my certification in emotionally handicapped. It only meant getting one other course. I had taken courses in this before and had thought, 'Well, I'll never go into that. I know enough about it now to know I'd never pursue it.' (Laughter)

"You see, special ed. covers a wide spectrum of classes. There are learning disabled kids, emotionally handicapped, physically handicapped — blind and deaf — mentally retarded, educable mentally retarded — all are a part of special education. Emotionally handicapped kids are children who cannot control their emotions, their anger, their sadness, and dwell on those things so that it affects their ability to do academic work. It could be caused by physiologic conditions that are sometimes controlled by medication. And I have children who have been abused mentally, physically, sexually. So they've learned these habits over a period of six or seven years. We try to gain appropriate behaviors in a matter of two or three years, so it's hard to fix those sometimes. Our goal is to get these grade school children back into a regular classroom. The program that I'm working on here is designed to get kids into a regular classroom. That is our goal. We had about a twenty-five percent success rate. And that's grown to maybe thirty to forty percent in the last two years. The kids who do not go back to the regular classroom would go to other emotionally handicapped classrooms at the junior high level. But they may not necessarily go to another program like this one. This program is specifically designed to get kids back into the mainstream. Other programs, I feel, are simply holding tanks to keep emotionally handicapped in a specific area. Other programs are designed to simply keep them under control.

"We have kids recommended for this class through regular classrooms when the child has been 'acting out.' He hasn't been able to do his work due to his behavior. So they go through a child-study program and finally get permission from parents to put them into here. Most parents usually cause no problem. Typical behavior to get them considered for this program? Let's say a child overreacts to another child hitting him or they get horribly frustrated with an assignment — they're not on task — a lot of hitting, you know, a lot of physical aggression. We have kids who are noncompliant; they don't work, they don't respond; they defy authority. We also have kids that are mainstreamed into this program from hospitals, uh — mental hospitals. So they can come from regular classrooms or the other end of the spectrum. Sometimes if a child doesn't make it, this is a last resort. If they don't make it here, they have to go to some sort of residential treatment center. Sometimes they have psychiatric treatment, if it's recommended. But a lot of the time, I do it myself. I have to work with parents sometimes because [the children] need really intense training which — sometimes is just not available. It costs too much money. So parents on their own often have gone out to seek professional help since the school district can't afford that.

"When these kids get up to the high school level, it's very difficult to mainstream them into regular classrooms. Because, after the age of nine, if the problem hasn't been identified and there hasn't been some work to try to remedy the situation, then it's hard to change. But I don't see what I do being done in most [emotionally disturbed] primary programs — trying to get the kids back into the regular classroom. There hasn't been a lot of study done on it. I've seen lots of programs where there isn't a specific goal designed to get the children out. That's why I like this one, and that's why I chose to work here.

"I think in the past teachers ended up with these kids in their classrooms, and they may have sent them to the principal's office or they may have gotten them suspended. With my kids — they never get suspended from school. They rarely see the principal unless they've been good. We go there for good behavior . . . We are different than a regular classroom (smile). The discipline philosophy is the same, but the frequency of rewards is greater. Lots of positive feedback is given . . . more frequently than they do in a regular classroom. There are, of course, fewer students in here. If there were more students, I wouldn't be able to do what I'm doing. Right now we have nine, that's one more than what I feel comfortable with. If it were any larger than that, I wouldn't be able to do the things that we're doing. Large discipline problems still exist even with this small number. (Laughter) They don't go away once the child is in here . . . and we work on showing them the appropriate thing to do. We reward only the good behaviors. We try to intervene with the bad behaviors that are consistent. For example, a mild discipline problem would be a child not complying, not doing his work. I would go up to the child and say, 'You need to be on task.' Here we have a point system. We give points for getting work done, following the rules, getting along with others — it all depends on what the task is. At the end of the day we use the points to determine what their adaptive behavior is — [the children] use the points to buy things. They can buy activity time — their own crayons, to sharpen their pencil, free time; they rent equipment for PE. They rent trucks to play with. So it's based on a real life situation, almost.

"Now if a child is [doing] what we consider the three D's —doing something dangerous, disruptive, or destructive — we have what we call detours. And we assign them to a detour — which is a non-student status. If they're just doing minor bad things, they're still considered students and we give them four opportunities to earn their points. Every time they go through a level of intervention it gets easier to earn their way back to their desks. But to get a detour is pretty serious. And they are only allowed three of those a day. After three, they're not considered students for the remainder of the day. And what happens? Oh, the worst thing in the world — boredom. They're placed over by that sign marked detour and when boredom sets in, it's really a very good motivator to get them to be interested in what students do. If they're in detour, they have nothing they're allowed to do. The first one is five minutes. The second one is ten, and the third is fifteen. If they earn any more than that, then they're a non-student for the rest of the day. The whole idea is that they're completely ignored and completely away from the class. They're looking at the class and seeing how these kids are being rewarded and it's highly motivating for them to want to be with the rest of the kids, because the teacher is rewarding the rest for being students and completely ignoring them. And that's hard to take, for a little child!

"Now, if they misbehave while in detour — we remove them from class. We have time-out facilities — a locked room with an aide. Usually we don't remove them unless they are highly disruptive or dangerous. And even then it's done in a positive way. We take them over there and we say, as soon as you calm down and you're able to do your work, we'll bring you right back. And usually it only takes ten to fifteen minutes.

"You know, doing this really was the first year I enjoyed teaching because with this program you can see immediate results. And, my biggest thrill is seeing a child smile. If they have so much anger inside of them and so much hurt, and all the years they've been going to school everyone else has turned them away and said, 'We don't want you here — you misbehave; you're a bad boy' — and they come here and we'll say to them that they can do it, 'We believe in you' — by the end of the day usually — the first day — they walk out of here smiling and loving coming to school. And I get a big charge out of that. (Laughter) It doesn't disturb me what our rate of return is because I know that eventually they will [return]. Our longest case was six years. There are very few kids who don't make it.

There are some kids that this program simply won't work for. And I know which ones they're going to be because they're the ones where parents won't support the program. And we have a few of them — right now. I can almost tell them from the very start — 'If you help me, I can guarantee success with your child. But if you're not, I can almost guarantee failure.'

"If it's a case of [child] abuse, we have kids who are then with foster families and we deal then with the foster parents. It is very common to have these abuse problems. I believe abused kids become abusive parents. I've been in special ed. for ten years and I see a lot of abuse, some of it reported and some of it not. I've reported several cases in my ten years. A lot of [the children] will come up to you and say, 'Something hurts.' 'I have an injury, an *owee* on my knee.' And they want you to look at it. I'll look at it and say, 'How did this happen?' And a lot of them will say, 'I don't know.' 'Well, that looks like a pretty serious injury — it's not something you can forget about.' And still — 'I don't remember.' That kind of clues me in that maybe there's something more to this, and I take them to the nurse and she asks questions and then follows the procedure. But you know if the child hems and haws or changes the story several times as to how that injury occurred, then we get suspicious."

(How do you deal with this kind of stress?)

"Well, the way the program is designed . . . I guess it's all based on a certain philosophy. You do not get yourself involved emotionally. The children deal with the consequences of their own behavior, not you. 'It's no skin off my back, honey. If you're going to do that, then *you* deal with the consequences, not me.' And I love this — because it works. It's great! It's difficult to do; it took me a long time. I didn't learn it automatically. There's a lot of good positive reinforcement along with this philosophy, and it's a good combination to get children to start taking responsibility for their own behavior."

(Let me play devil's advocate a moment and ask about what you said a minute ago about enjoying their smiles. Isn't that sort of allowing yourself to enjoy with them while at the same time you don't have to suffer with them? — laughter —)

"(Laughter) Well, yeah — I can. I can enjoy them as people. We get down to a human level and we joke around sometimes. And if they're having a tough time, if they're having a tough day, I say, 'Ok, I won't bother you.' You know, I tell them. I'm just as human as they are and I can take a detour too. And I do. I'll say, 'I've had it. I'm going over there and that means I don't want anybody to bother me and I won't have anything to do with you?' They get tickled; they get real tickled."

(Have you ever considered getting out of teaching?)

"No. But I have thought of doing something different in education. This can be a real burnout job. It's supposed to be designed so that other teachers can change with you frequently, but I'm the only one who's been in this program for any length of time. I would love to teach normal kids again, I think. At least for a period of time to recharge. Then I'd come back to this. . . ."

(Do you think education works?)

"Yes."

(Would you become a teacher again?)

"Yes. I really got turned on to teaching more when I started working in this program. Because, I was ready to quit . . . I really was. In the learning disabilities field, the resource programs, I didn't feel like I was helping kids. And I didn't think the program was helping kids; it was just a lot of paperwork. And it was just not what I felt education was all about — here we were just filling out paperwork and diagnosing problems. You could only see students on a thirty minute basis every day. That isn't going to do. And I didn't feel like I was helping. So I was kind of glad to get this opportunity of working in a self-contained classroom with these kids, even though I was kind of apprehensive about it. I knew I would be up against some struggles with kids, some physical struggles — getting hit and stuff, and I was worried about that because I didn't want to hurt any children either. I wanted to protect myself, but I've learned how to do that and restrain a child without them getting hurt. We had some people that came in and trained us how to hold children without hurting them. And also without getting hurt — how to protect yourself against the biting and the slugs. It used to happen more often than it does now. Originally they put kids in here from juvenile detention and mental hospitals, and those kids were streetwise and — well, we couldn't help those children. I know that for a fact. Those kids are wise to everything you say or try. They're beyond public education. They require something different, a little more rough and tough. But with those kinds of kids we did have a lot of physical aggression. I wish we had gotten combat pay at that time. . . ."

(Two days after I interviewed Ms. K., she was sued by a parent for child abuse . . . one of the hazards of the job.)

Tape #79

We talked in the library workroom at her junior high school. She had taught LD (learning disabled) for fourteen years. Before that she had been a social worker and a secretary. She also wrote in her spare time. She was married with three children. She spoke with a slight Southern accent and peered seriously at me from behind her glasses.

(What does an LD resource person do?)

"An LD resource teacher tries to find out by testing and screening what the problems are for each child. Everything is individualized. Most of the deficits are in language arts and math. And what we try to do is just come up with a plan, a program that will remediate the deficits that we find in the testing. We also act as a resource for the outside classes or the regular ed. classes that our kids take. Most of our kids are scheduled for more mainstream classes than they are LD classes. That's the concept of resource. We try to help them with those outside classes, so they can maintain themselves, and hopefully go for a high school diploma.

"On Wednesday and Thursday we do math and they have workbooks. And each student has his own folder and his own lesson plan. And he would go to his folder and get his workbook and his folder and find out what pages he had to do, and then I would come by and help him or her individually as needed, check their work.

"The largest class I have is seven and the smallest is four. I think seven is too many. Four of five is about right. If you have been a regular classroom teacher — that probably sounds like a dream made in heaven. However, when you talk about seven kids, you're talking about seven different lesson plans and seven different things going on in the room at one time. They get their lesson plans from me. However, I will drop the lesson plan that I have made if they come to me with problems from the other teachers, from classes: a project, or they need to study for a test, or they need to take a test. We do a lot of oral tests. If a student has a health test, he can't read the questions but he can listen in class. He can pass the test if I read the questions and sometimes write the answers down for him.

"I would say that there are a lot of kids who, with some extra help, can get to high school and get a diploma; especially those who are average or above in intelligence, who should be working at grade level but who may have a third or fourth grade or fifth grade reading level when they're in junior high. They need some extra help. But a lot of them are good listeners. So if they are good listeners and they care about what they do, then they can do all right. But they need someone to help them with tests, someone to talk with their other teachers, to make the teachers aware of the problems and how to maybe give them shorter work units, strategies for working with them in a regular classroom."

(How many kids is this program successful with?)

"Well, it's hard for me to answer, because I don't see the end of it. If I were a high school teacher, I might. I might see more. Now I recommend probably at least a third of my students a year to an all-regular program, out of LD altogether."

(What would happen to these kids if there weren't an LD program?)

"Well, I think they would be dropouts. Some of them are anyway. Some of them, I can't help. They're from other school systems that have not identified them early enough. They're the kids who sat in the back of the room, that everybody called names. They were either 'dumb' or 'goofy,' or dropped out of school; nobody liked them because they didn't do their work. These are the — not just the LD kids, but any special ed. kid of the past. Maybe they were mentally retarded; maybe they were learning disabled; maybe they were emotionally disturbed. These were the kids that basically nobody cared about, that everybody just wanted to be rid of. I remember. I was in a small Georgia town. We didn't have anything. And you can imagine how long ago it was when I was in school (smile). We had no special ed. And these were the kids that everybody called 'dumb.' I was just as ugly and mean as all the rest of the kids, and we called them names, and they sat in the back of the class. And they sat back there because they called less attention to themselves and the teachers didn't want them.

"So LD programs represent a positive progression. We have made attempts to reach more people.

". . . I started LD teaching in Kentucky. The principal told me on the first day that he didn't want the class there; he had fought against the idea. If there was trouble with my kids, he would just call their parents and tell them to come and pick them up. He wasn't going to deal with it in any way. I could do whatever I wanted to, as long as I kept them out of the hall. I just kind of — said ok. Yes, it is awful. It really is. The first two schools

I taught at were that way. And then in '73 I was put in a pilot project, which was an LD class. [It was for two] large high schools. Both principals did not want me in the school; not me personally, but did not want the program, didn't want to have to deal with the kids. I think they didn't know — it was a foreign thing for them. And they'd probably heard a lot of scary stories about special ed. kids, and — we're all afraid of the unknown. That's a human kind of a thing. And they probably felt they had hard jobs anyway and they just didn't want this. This was extra aggravation and they just didn't want to deal with it.

". . . I think the most positive thing about the program is that it gives kids help when they need it, and it gives them support. It gives them more of a personal relationship with a teacher than they would normally get in a regular classroom. And I think kids need this. There are some kids that come to us that are just starved for adult attention, that either they don't get at home or they have kind of been lost in the shuffle. So [this program] is probably the best thing.

Tape #224 Special Education III

After thirty-four years of teaching special ed., Mr. A. still "loved it . . . loved it." He seemed to me to be a special man. He was fifty-three, married with two children of his own, and he taught in an urban area in a large northern California city. His special school was located inside a regular high school. It was California beautiful with a large and lovely courtyard running down the middle of it.

Mr. A. taught mentally retarded students in a room that was like a small apartment, as he explained, so they could learn how to do basic survival things. He also had a work lab next door. I walked in while his class was still there and saw two girls in wheelchairs, one who looked like she was just barely there. One boy instantly wanted to know if I was there for Mr. A. and kept repeating his question in that typical way of retarded youngsters until Mr. A. answered him with a smile.

When the students left, we sat on a couch in his "living room" and talked for an hour. I watched his angular face register excitement and contentment about his work. It wasn't utopia, plants and all, but it was cheering. People don't realize that this is public education too.

"Yes, there is a high burnout rate for special ed. teachers and yes, I have been at it for thirty-four years. I went to a conference a few years ago and there was a seminar session on teacher burnout. And the seminar leader asked how long people had been in it and my hand stayed up from two years, three, to anyone longer than, you know. At that time I'd been teaching twenty-nine years. And after about six years, mine was the only hand left up. The statement I made at that time is that I strongly feel that, yes, special ed. does have a strong burnout rate; you are under a lot of pressure. But I feel that people who would burn out in a year or two would probably have burned out in anything, in any profession that they chose. And as I said a moment ago — I have too much fun. I enjoy what I do and there's not an awful lot of people that I know who can truly say that. I've been teaching long enough that when the fun stops . . . I'll get out. But it hasn't stopped yet, after thirty-four years. Every day is different. Every day is interesting. Some days are really rotten, but that's . . . what do I get out of it?

"After working and working and working on a minuscule little concept — to see the light that finally shines — you know, the bright light bulb that comes when a concept is finally internalized and generalized and the student realizes themselves that they know it — that light is so much brighter to me than with any normal child. Yeah, I have a couple of bright youngsters at home of my own, but with these youngsters — young adults, actually — when they finally see that bright light — it's exciting to me. I look at the best of my students who are living in the community to the best of their abilities, even if it is a protected living situation, but going to some sort of work daily. Having some sort of social and recreational life, they are living a *quality* life. And that to me is exciting because it not only is positive for them, it's less of a drain on you and me as taxpayers because they are productive members of society, and they have a right to that.

"There are various trends in education; there are buzzwords. To me, I've always been extremely practical in what I've attempted to teach. People need to be able to function productively. I like to remove barriers. If, for example, a student is never going to learn to tie their shoes, then you buy them loafers. Why beat your head against the wall? Velcro is marvelous! (Laughter) These kinds of things . . . and I would much rather teach a student how to fix themselves a simple meal than to worry if I know they're never going to be able to balance a checkbook because my students won't — they're that low. They're not going to be able to read for pleasure. Well, there are a lot of other things you can do for recreation. There are a lot of people in this country who lead full, productive lives that are functionally illiterate. They can't read a newspaper. But they can understand an awful lot of things. So I tend to deal with very practical things. My room is set up as an independent living center. This is a training situation. It's a place where they learn to make choices, more often than not for the first time in their lives.

"Our program is mixed. We have community-based instruction; we have students in training in offices. We have students in training in garden programs, garden maintenance. I have a food service training program. And these kinds of things we do out in the community. We also do basic training here at the school site. We are fully departmentalized as any regular high school would be. And our students move as they do in any regular high school from class to class, which is unusual in a center. I teach independent living in this particular room which is set up as an apartment, living room, dining room, kitchen, bath. And although the furniture is a little old, it functions. We do food service training here; we run a lunch program for the staff. We do not make lunches every day, but once a week they are preparing — doing the counting for the food that we have to buy. And next door I have a workshop and that is vocational training. I do office skills and packaging skills and the jobs that we do over there are based on real jobs; they come from the electronics industry, from various packaging firms . . . and it's a production workshop. And they move from me to transition into agency workshops, supported work environments in private industry. And — this is very positive! It would be a job for them once they're out of this setting. I'm quite strongly in favor of instruction in the local community environment. But there are certain things that must be learned in a more controlled environment prior to going out and transferring those [skills] to the community. Because, no matter what the so-called experts say, there is a community out there that is not ready for this. It's going to take a lot more money, a lot more in-service training and PR before the community is ready for it. There are parts of the community that are interested in involving themselves with the handicapped; there are a lot of wonderful employers out there, but generally the man on the street isn't ready to see some of our students. They don't want to see . . . they would . . . rather not."

(Do you ever find it depressing to you to have to deal with these kids day after day?)

"Oh no. Not at all. They're some of the most wonderful people I know. I was told very early on — to not get emotionally involved. But you cannot be objective. And I truly don't, because I do leave it here when I leave. But when I'm here, in the particular environment that I've set up — we have to live together — you do become emotionally involved with people that you live with. And they're friends too . . . as well as my students.

". . . Yes, we have two students in wheelchairs in that class, and the one young lady is really quite capable. She's in a motorized chair; she is being trained in independent community mobility. She can ride public transportation; she's quite verbal, but she will never read. She will never be able to balance a checkbook. But she will ultimately be able to know that she's not being cheated at the grocery store, this kind of functional handle on things. She has conceptual understanding of a broad vocabulary. She will not be able to transfer that from the printed page, but she will be able to function quite well; she will always need support; she will always need care — she cannot transfer herself from a wheelchair to a bed, to a restroom, but there are a lot of things that she can do. And as I said — she's quite verbal, good clear articulate speech. And she will function very well. The other young woman — we are quite frankly surprised that she has lived as long as she has. She is here for social reasons. She does respond to music; she does respond to voices. She has little or no movement. There's a small amount of mobility in one arm. We're attempting to train her to use her responses and her like of certain kinds of music to turn on and turn off a switch for a radio so that she can have it when she wants it — limited abilities but — she responds. She moves with all the other students to all the classrooms. She's being exposed to various kinds of people, voices, and she is reacting. She has likes and dislikes and they are known to us. And she needs to be made comfortable. And she is gaining from this; she is not just lying in a bed in a hospital somewhere."

(What would you say to people that would argue that some of this money spent here might be better spent on "normal" students?)

"The money that is spent I think is well spent, because in the main, these students, if they can become to a degree functionally independent, they are less of a drain on society. For example, the young woman that we were just speaking of — if she were placed in a state facility, the costs would be astronomical. It's much less expensive to have her here. Her parents are not putting any drain on the public; they accept nothing other than the free and appropriate education that she is given by law. She's entitled to it. Public Law 142. We know these things . . . the public doesn't. Everyone, no matter what their level of abilities, is entitled to a free and appropriate education in the least restricted environment — but she does well; she's happy! There's a smile on her face most of the time. And when she's not happy, we know it. So it's not as though she just always has a smile on her face. But she is much less of a drain when she's with me than if she were in an institution all the time.

"... Oh, having more money in a program like this would be nice; it certainly would. For example, in our community-based program, if I want to teach something like — how to use a vending machine, vending machines do not give receipts. And without a receipt, I cannot be reimbursed. (Laughter from me) And people need to know how to use vending machines. They're all over the world . . . and that's just one little item.

Our funding is state and federal . . . but not to the degree that I think it should be. I wrote a grant a number of years ago to set this program up; it was a one-time grant and since then, it still functions without any additional funding than what every other class gets. A lot of things, though, could be done if I had some more money here. I would like to be out in the community in restaurants; I'd like to be out in the community in stores, not just out buying, but buying groceries. We buy groceries for a purpose, because I've established a food service program . . . that is subsidized by this school staff. It's kind of ironic . . . I mean they're perfectly willing, because [the teachers] don't have to bring a sandwich from home once a week, and the cost is minimal. We put out a very nice lunch for a very small amount. And it does allow us minuscule amounts of cash. But in a way, we're being subsidized by teachers — who else has subsidized education in this country? Oh, I suppose I subsidize this class personally — oh, it varies — but to a tune of six to eight hundred dollars to a thousand a year."

(Do you have any discipline problems with these students?)

"Oh sure, I have stabilized teeth — where they were knocked out. I have a broken nose; I have knife scars . . . We all have had our share. You learn various methods [to deal with these problems]. I don't believe in all the negative behavior modifications; there are very positive behavior modifications that I use. As I said before — if something works, I'll try it; and all things will not work with all students. I have an extremely violent young man who managed to pick up . . . a piano the other day. He threw it and broke it into — lots of pieces. Oh, but he's a *good* kid — he's a good guy, a really good guy, and he's come a long way. But he had a short period of aggression there."

(What does one do in that situation?)

"Well, if all else fails, we call the police and they put him in a lockdown or a seventy-two hour observation because he was severely emotionally disturbed. And we work very closely with the parents and everyone else because this is a young man who is totally capable of productive employment, and we want to see that he gets there . . . and that he gets the counseling and the psychological help that he needs.

"I think public education in general is vital to the survival and success of this country. And yes, I do think it's working. I think we get a lot of bad press because negative press sells papers. You don't see articles about — a food service training program for severely and profoundly handicapped students being selected over others to — for example, cater a reception for three to four hundred people. And that would make a great story. It's what we're doing! We have an outstanding teacher ceremony in this county coming up in April. And my students were selected to cater the affair! And they'll, of course, be paid for their services, but they're in the process now of planning, in the process now of going to wholesale suppliers for various things. You know — just as any caterer would. They're figuring all the ramifications of an affair like that."

(And a lot of work for you, I would imagine?)

"Oh yeah, but that's what I'm here for — to guide them through something like that."

Tape #93

Integration has been used as a "method" to improve education, and it's hard to argue that it hasn't in many ways improved education from the all-black schools of the past. However, it may have its negative results as well. But what might be the most important thing to learn from the court ordered integration of the schools is that this is a perfect example of how society expects the school system to correct society's mistakes.

Mr. B. was a very large black man who had taught high school math in a Southern school district for twenty years. He was wearing a t-shirt with his school's mascot on the front. At forty-one, he's been through the whole spectrum of integration and teaching in general, but he hadn't lost an ounce of his friendliness and charm.

". . . We went into an integration situation here in 1969. Now about thirty percent of the teachers are black. There's a lot of bussing, but it hasn't completely integrated the schools. We have a middle school —

about 1,500 students, and it's only about eight to nine percent black. There's a lot of gerrymandering of the lines. We have to keep looking at this. But as far as the blacks go, they have to gerrymander to try to get the numbers right. So I think bussing serves its purpose. I don't have any problem with it. I think it's necessary as a tool for integration and just transporting the kids. I mean we're going to have a problem next year when we start trying to integrate that middle school, but bussing is a reality here the way this county is spread out. And the way the schools are located, there would be bussing whether it was for integration or not. There's probably not a whole lot more bussing than there was before we integrated. It's just that the busses are going different places. One of our high schools is right downtown and everyone has moved out from there so we'd have to bus kids into there anyway. I don't really have any problems to mention with white students. Even before the major push for integration, I taught summer school in a school with two blacks and about thirty whites as teachers. As a matter of fact, a couple of students at that school recommended to the principal that he hire me full time! (Laughter) When I started teaching in '66, I was in an all-black situation."

(Do you think the integration has produced any changes?)

"Yes, it has . . . not all positive. (Laughter) When I was in high school in an all-black situation, in my high school we had two physics classes; we had three or four algebra II classes and several algebra I classes in my high school. So that's a large number of black kids in physics and those kinds of math classes. If you look at the total number of blacks who were in those classes back then and the number who are in them now, it's very out of kilter. It's gone way down. That's my other motive for working in the entry level of mathematics, because what is happening is that you have a lot of people who are Puritans in mathematics. In other words, there are plenty of kids who are plenty capable but just not ready yet so you have to get them ready and be careful not to discourage them. Now I do the same thing for a black or a white, but I just think that at that level, at the gate — to higher mathematics — if I can encourage a black to move on, then I'll really try to encourage rather than discourage them. I'll say, 'So you got a C, so you didn't do that well this time, you're better off in this class than you would be in a general math class.'

"But there are positive effects too. We know more about white people and white people know more about us. We bleed, we hurt, we have feelings, we have the same emotions, the same problems. Not all white people are rich; not all black people are poor. And shoot, yes, I see a difference in the interactions of the kids! I went to a 'white' high school under force back then. HEW came in and said we had too many black kids in basic courses and we needed to transfer these students and these numbers of teachers and you know — so I went to another high school — mid-year. And at this school, they said, oh, we want an average of five blacks in every class. It didn't matter if they were basic or what, they said — you're going to integrate this school. And teachers were swapped due to their skin color — whatever was needed to balance the numbers decreed.

"Now the reason that HEW was involved and the reason they were expanding all these things was that before at this high school, they had had major problems — rioting and those kinds of things. They had had to bring in highway patrols — I mean, it was really under siege out there. It was just like a police state. I mean, the hatred was so bad that you could just see it . . . you could just cut it with a knife. And I saw that back in '73-'74 and I experienced it. It really was bad. Blacks and whites were not talking to each other, and that was, to put it nicely, a part of the whole city here. We had our good ol' boys — you know, that section of town. And they weren't even speaking to each other. Now — they're buddies. Oh, we see traces of the old, but you know — they get along with about a third black. Now they fight about normal things; they don't fight about black-white stuff. I've seen a change; I've seen it happen at my high school. So I see the positives of integration. You do have people who dwell on the negatives, but I like to see the positives. Oh, we have our troubles — but basically it's just the regular things that kids will fight about, which is nice in comparison to what it used to be. The only time I hear *nigger* is when blacks call — you know — in just conversational stuff. But you don't hear all that stuff. I used to hear it all the time."

(What do you see as the largest problem in public education?)

"Funding. We need to bring education into the modern age. This is the high tech era and I'm still sitting up there with thirty-two kids in my basic class. Give me a room and give me fifteen students and I'll bet I could do more. I'm just thinking facilities in general and just plain old bringing it into the twentieth century. And then the salaries, of course. Citizens will back that sort of tax support for schools when they are forced to. When citizens are made aware and start to trust, they'll put the money up. Now, I think one of the things that's happened is that people in administration have not been exactly truthful in presenting the situation as it really exists to the public. They've tried to make the public think that everything is ok to save their own jobs. They'll say — everything is ok, but I'm sitting there. And I know that I could do a better job if I had my own classroom. I need to be in my classroom for my planning periods because that's where all my materials are. There's just so much I can put in my briefcase and take with me, and I need an adequate place to go."

(What will it take to wake the people up to see that the schools need more money? Will it be falling test scores, lack of teachers . . . ?)

"When the Russians do it. If they see Russians have fifteen kids in every class, then they'll say, 'Well, by god, so will we!' (Laughter)

Tape #127

Ms. S. was very young looking for her thirty-five years. She had taught for twelve years, the last nine at the grade school level in the suburban part of a small Southern city. She had one child of her own. She came to the night time interview in a pink sweatshirt, jeans, and gym shoes; she was from my generation.

But, Ms. S had grown up in Georgia in segregated schools. She had moved to the West and taught children from the Hispanic minority there. She had seen two different kinds of integration and she knew whereof she spoke when she dealt with the change of the '60s . . . in education and society in general. She was a very thoughtful, young woman.

(What's wrong with public education?)

"It's so easy to give a real quick answer, and I don't think that it's one particular answer. You almost have to go into what's wrong with society or what's wrong with the United States to answer that question. Because I think it has to do with the line between right and wrong being a little bit more blurred than it was, say, back in the '50s. I'm not saying that people didn't do the same things they're doing now. But — I don't know, there were certain things you did and certain things you didn't do. And if you did them, you were ostracized as a child. I'm talking about in the classroom. So once you've lowered the lines, then no one is quite sure exactly what to do — I'm not saying that it's wrong. You know, I think when you went through the '60s and '70s and questioned those things . . . it's good to question. But by the same token, now you have to redefine everything again. When I first started teaching, it was still like [the old days] a little bit. When you said something, it was because you were the teacher, and that was all that was necessary. If you said it, it was so. Or if you told them to do something, they did it. But it's more difficult today because of the lines being blurred. I think it's not only difficult for the children, but it's difficult for the parents. But I think you come up with children who can be more creative and who will be able, I think, to solve the problems that are going to come up as the world gets more complicated. At least that's what I think with my own child. But it's a lot harder. You almost have to think every day, in everything you do. Where I think before, with my parents, you know, it was always done a certain way. This is right, that's wrong, and that's the way it is. And now, something will come up, and I'll have the impulse to do it the way they did. And then I'll think, well, that's not really exactly the way it should have been done. It also makes it more difficult to be a teacher nowadays. But it makes it more interesting, too.

"But I think it helps children to be more comfortable if they know that someone in the classroom is setting the guidelines. I don't think they want — not right now, anyway, at the first grade level — I don't think they want to think no one is in control. They want to know that if somebody gets out of line, there will be somebody there that will take care of it. They're just — babies still.

"Of course it was hard in New Mexico — you know, they only spoke English to me in the classroom. This was a Spanish-speaking community. And on the playground and in the lunchroom and the plays at Christmastime, it was all in Spanish. I speak some Spanish. But when the parents would come in, I would have to have an interpreter. Plus, coming from the South, you know, they probably thought my English was a little strange!"

(What do your think the kids thought of you?)

"Growing up in the South there was the minority that I was familiar with, the blacks. And when I was growing up there was a real separation. The water fountains were men, women, and colored. And the restrooms were men, women, and colored. And the shows, the blacks sat upstairs and we sat downstairs. So I grew up in that. And then when I went away to college, you know, it was just this real awakening.

"And when I went out to teach in New Mexico, I really was not as aware of the Mexican-Anglo thing. I mean I would have probably been aware of it, had they been black and white. To me, it wasn't there. But I think the children still felt it, because they had grown up in that. Well, I was a minority there.

"What's good about public education in the United States I guess is the fact that we try — we offer it to everybody, you know, no matter what your financial background is, or what your parents did. You have the opportunity to go as far as you want to go."

(Have you taught here before integration?)

"No. Only after. It seems to be, just from the time I've spent here, it seems to be a real upheaval all the time, even now. Every time they get what they think is a balance, parents move around and then they have to do it all over again. And I think it's real hard on the children. I think they need to have stability, or a sense of a continuum. That was real important when I was in school. You know, in kindergarten through the sixth grade, you knew all the boys and girls. You went to a school pretty close to you. And I think that is important, and I think that they forget about that whenever they're moving everybody around. I say that [for both] the black and white children. I think that [the children] feel that also, having to be bussed way across town into a neighborhood that they are not familiar with, houses that they don't know. I don't know what the solution would be, really. I'm just saying what I feel."

(Any societal benefit to integration?)

"I know that going to school like I did and never even seeing a black child was not good. And you were afraid of what you didn't know. And so when I — in '69, when they had the first black students come to the high school, you know, we were afraid of them, like they were from another planet or something. What would they be like, and were they going to be real rough, which is what we had been told. [With] my ten year old son, Josh, we have always been real careful not to say that there is any difference. Although by this age, he has formed his own opinions."

(Would you say he's different from you in that area?)

"At that age, yes. He's been to an integrated school from the beginning. And he knows a lot more. But I don't know that it is just integration. That may be the times. Still, I think he deals with each person now as an individual. I don't think he notices color, as such. Although I do — I'm being honest with you. If there is a group of children like from a project area and they're black, he will say, they're always fighting, or they're always this, they're always that. Even though we try not — I mean he's formed that opinion because that happens to be the way it is. There are a lot of the kids that are rough, you know. And that's not necessarily because they're black. It's probably their — financial status. But for him, those are the black students that he sees. So in a way, that's hurt him, that those are the only ones that he sees. And he doesn't necessarily look at color. You know, like when he sees a child, like at a park or something like that, he'll easily go up to one or the other."

(Would you have done that when you were ten?)

"No. Oh, no."

(Do you see that as progress?)

Yeah, yeah. I would, definitely. Yeah. I hope he would look at everybody individually now, where I wouldn't have at that age. Yeah, that's a benefit, for sure."

(Do you think public education works?)

"Yes. I think that as a teacher, if you can take hold of the passion that a child feels naturally at a real young age and get that turned on to something that has to do with them as part of the human race. They're already passionate about just about everything. If you can give them something to hold on to, like getting involved with saving the whales, or the hunger in Africa — if you get that burning inside of them, and if you give them something to hold on to, I hope that that will be something they'll carry on as adults."

Section 14:

FINAL THOUGHTS

"They don't clean up children's desks here every day and first graders do a lot of cutting and pasting as it goes along with development of their manual dexterity. [So] we just mop up; it's just assumed that we'd do it. Of course, I'm sure my dentist doesn't clean up after the messes his patients make . . . a hygienist comes, but I don't have a hygienist. I don't even have an aide. Well, I do not have to scrub the commode. I do not have to mop the floor. Of course, sometimes you do have to mop the floor in the cafeteria if it's your child that dropped something. There's not enough staff to take care of all that. So you either leave this mess for kids to slide around in or — you know, you mop it up. Can you imagine a new teacher coming out and thinking they're going to go out there and affect eternity and all that . . . and you hand them a mop?"

a North Carolina first grade teacher

What do I think? I think this is what I think.

Tape #181

Ms. R. was working on her doctorate in education while still teaching full-time — two jobs at the price of one. She had been teaching high school English and speech for twelve years at the time I interviewed her in an upper-middle class school district outside a big Western city. Her answers were articulate and just slightly strident — I had known her for several years and couldn't keep from entering into the dialogue more often than usual during these interviews. I found myself playing devil's advocate by asking the impossible questions about teaching I asked myself. I felt both reassured by hearing basically what I usually answered myself and disappointed that she couldn't' find any better answers either.

Ms. R. was married with no children. Her hobbies were reading, cooking, photography, and calligraphy.

(Why did you become a teacher?)

"Well, it hasn't changed since I told you that day in the park so many years ago — I went into teaching because I like to talk to kids. And I like helping them find out things that they don't know. And after twelve years of it, I still like it . . . at least more than anything else I've ever done. Why English? Because I think the very basic need is to be able to communicate clearly, and English teaches all those skills of speaking, and listening and reading and writing."

(Tell me why you think you can teach teachers to teach.)

"I don't think it's some mystical skill; I think part of learning to teach is the modeling that good teachers do. I think a lot of good things that I do when I teach are a reflection of good teachers that I had, some of them might be a reflection of bad teachers that I had — not doing what they did or even doing what they did badly! But part of it is seeing other people do it well. And I think part of learning to teach is seeing yourself do it. I'm really pleased that so many teacher training programs now ask for videotaping. And I guess I think that you can teach a teacher to think if you define *teach* as — help them figure it out. Because I don't think you can say — this - is - how - you - teach . . ."

(Can you take an average teacher and help them become a good teacher?)

"Some — if it's that they're doing an average job but they have an above average potential, then sure. If it's just that they're an average person with average intelligence and average motivation to teach and average performance, then I don't think you can do it."

(Do you think there are unteachable students?)

"I think there are students who don't work in the system that we subject them to. Somebody today, while we were walking at lunch, was talking about this kid who was very dramatic. He's a senior and he's probably going to fail this year because he won't do the stuff that he sees as busywork. We had a student just like that when we were working together — Tim. He was just like that; he was as smart as anything, but he thought all of this was piddly stuff and wouldn't do it. And probably he will have a happy life and be a fine person. But I don't think the school did anything for him. I had a kid in junior high who kept failing English classes, mine was the third one he'd failed. They passed him around from honors on down to average, and finally his parents had him tested and they found out he was gifted, and I don't think we do anything for gifted kids."

(Do you think we're successful at all with any kids?)

"Yeah."

(Let's take secondary schools. What do secondary schools give or teach a kid? I mean, usually by that time they know the basics in math and reading and writing — with exceptions of course . . .)

"Well, I think that we can give them the basics in other situations, like we can teach them the kinds of writing that they need to know to apply in college. And we can teach them the kinds of social group skills that they need to know in order to get along with a group of people. I think we can teach them — or expose them to things they wouldn't' find otherwise. For example, I don't think that we should just teach adolescent literature; I think that we should have them read things that they wouldn't read outside of school. So there are those things. And I think they all add up to that we can make them feel more competent and confident if we do it right."

(So non-academic things are more important than academic things in a secondary school?)

"I think that doing the academic things well adds up to a better self-concept."

(Do you think it's important for students to know geological formulas and chemical formulas, parts of speech, and who won the Civil War?)

"Well, I don't think it's the only thing they should know, and I don't think it should be the majority of what we teach. But I do think that there are certain — like historical facts and common knowledge things that other people expect them to know; therefore, if they know it, then they are more self-confident and competent members of society. I don't think we need to spend whole long periods of time on it because I don't think that's all there is."

(Do you agree with me that that's what the majority of high school is now?)

"Umm — I don't know; it's so hard to know what everybody else does. You only know what you teach and maybe what your friends teach. My impression is — that there's still a lot of garbage out there. What I hear about what kids do in other classes and the writing across the curriculum . . . I don't know if [memorization] is all it is anymore."

(What percentage of kids do you think get out of high school what they need to get?)

"I don't know; percentages are really hard. I think there are many who don't get what they ultimately need because they didn't know at the time what they needed. And I don't think you can teach them unless they're ready to learn. You can make little bits of ready-to-learn with those anticipatory sets, but I'm not sure you can make major differences in things they really don't want to learn. Since I never knew much about algebra and geometry . . . I never had to do anything with it. So I don't know — maybe sixty or seventy percent".

(What do you think should be the majority of what's taught?)

"I think they need to learn — it sounds real cliché — but they need to learn how to learn; they need to learn the process of investigating things, of being curious, of asking questions."

(Do you think that's what boards of education and administrators are looking for when they evaluate a teacher?)

"Huh-uh — they want to see good results on a test; they don't want to see any sort of exploratory information . . . if the district aims towards any kind of competency test or any kind of district test . . . and our district doesn't. We give a writing sample in English and those are graded holistically. If a kid doesn't do well in grammar or punctuation, it matters; but it's not the total grade like a test which asks you to put the commas and the periods in the right place."

(What do you think is one of the major problems in public education?)

"I think it's that we have to institutionalize kids, and when we get overcrowded we have to institutionalize more, and there is no time or space to teach processes; all you can do is just that objective stuff. Everything else is just too much trouble and impossible with a class of thirty-five or forty."

(Turn it around then, what would you say to a parent who doesn't want to support a school levy? What would you say in defense of public education?)

"I think that people get a really good deal for their money. I think kids become socialized; they learn how to work in large groups; they learn how to work under incredible distractions. I think they learn those social grouping skills. I think that we teach them a lot of academic stuff that seems to be good for them when they go on to college if they do. I think that public schools offer vocational programs; I think sometimes we offer too many things. We offer everything: they get free drivers ed.; they get quality, in our district anyway, concerned teachers who care about that kid's education; and they get people who are willing to take over part of the job of parents."

(Do you think most teachers are good teachers, bad teachers, in-between teachers?)

"Most of the teachers I know are good teachers if by good you mean concerned, caring about kids . . ."

(How about effective?)

"Well, how are you going to measure effective?"

(Whether they get across what they propose to get across?)

"Which is?"

(Well, it depends upon the circumstances.)

"If affective things are important to get across, then they're good if they're caring. If intellectual things are what you want to get across, then it doesn't matter if they're caring."

(How would you evaluate a teacher if you had to?)

". . . on things like rapport with the classroom, on professional activities, on intelligence."

(And does that include whether they've communicated their subject matter?)

"Yeah, I think that's rapport and intelligence combined. That's a pretty good communicator.

". . . I think that teenagers today have a really hard problem deciding how they fit or where they fit as a group. I think that they have a difficult time choosing not to do the things that their friends do. And there are a lot of kids who find problems too hard for them to handle. They don't know what to do and so they escape them by partying and drugs and that kind of stuff. They have probably adopted the values shown on television soap operas."

(Do you think the schools can do anything about those problems?)

"I don't think the school as an institution can have a great influence. If we identify kids and try to deal with their problems that may be affecting their classroom performance, then that would make a difference. But I don't think the school can do more than they already do, I mean — we're not society. We're a small part of it. We can't take the place of those kids' parents."

(What about individual teachers? Do you think teachers who are not "certified" as psychiatrists are doing that sort of job with students?)

"Parents aren't certified as psychiatrists either."

(Does the thought of a lawsuit stop you from doing that sort of thing with a student?)

"No, because the threat doesn't seem very real. I can't think of a situation where I have been asked to help a student that would be in conflict with the law. I've never taken a kid to get birth control pills. I've never recommended a dirty book, although I let some kids read some! (Laugh) I can't think of a thing that I would do that would leave me open to a lawsuit."

(What can you do for an unmotivated student?)

"Well, I think you can try and motivate them. Sometimes you can motivate them, and this is a bad reason but at least they're doing things — they'll do things because they know you care about them, which is probably better than their liking you. Maybe it's the same thing ... but I'm not sure that I'm comfortable with the idea that we need to get students to do things. I think that what we need to do is remember that they are people with the right to choose. And I think they need to be made aware of the consequences of their choices, but I think we ought to let them choose."

(So if a parent would come in and say, "Why isn't Billy working?" You would say to him, "Well, he chose not to"?)

"I'd say — look, I did this, and I did this, and I did this. He knows what's going to happen if he doesn't do the work. I don't give any escape clauses at the last minute. And that's what he chose to do. And besides that — I notified you forty-two times on interim reports."

(But if they asked — what can we do? What can we do? What can we do? What would you tell them?)

"I think I'd tell them to be sure that he knows that they care about him and that they care about what he's doing and that they won't hate him if he's a failure, you know, if he fails in classes, but that they are just concerned that he do the best he can and then — leave him alone."

(And do you think all kids will come around?)

"No, but I don't think they would have any other way either."

(What will happen to those kids who don't ever succeed in school?)

"They'll go into the army. (Laughter) They'll play pro baseball. (Laughter)"

(Do you think that's ok that we just let these kids —)

"Well, I think it's realistic. I mean, even God can't take care of everybody. Some people fall away."

(But if we've got kids who are sitting in our class and- not working — would you really feel satisfied with yourself to say, well, he made that choice? I can't believe that.)

"No, but I'd want to be absolutely sure that he knew what the consequences were. I'm not going to give up entirely all semester or anything. But I'm not going to stress myself out spending time on kids who don't care and who don't care even after you've done everything you possibly can."

(But is it their fault they don't care or is it because of their background?)

"I don't care about the — I mean, it may be because of their background but what am I going to do? It's got to be what I do with that kid."

(But that isn't fair. Those kids are not getting something not because of their own devices but because of what happened to them from other people, and you're just adding on to it.)

"No, I am giving them every opportunity possible."

(But they need different opportunities or they wouldn't be in that position to begin with.)

"Then put them in somebody else's class. What do you mean, different opportunities?"

(Well, they need something different than a normal person with a normal background.)

"So what am I going to do in a class of twenty-five? It's not possible to deal with every single person's individual problem. Classes are too big for that. I have 130 students. I have huge amounts of patience and caring and love for my students. But I'm not going to kill myself over the ones that don't respond."

(What's the worst discipline problem you've ever had?)

"You want students in my class or students in the hall?! (Laughter) The kid masturbating in the hall outside my classroom was quite a discipline problem. It wasn't disruptive or anything . . . It wasn't in class either. I've had defiant students in class. I had a boy in junior high who when I asked him to leave the class because he was being disruptive, refused to leave. And they sent up the vice-principal who told the kid to leave and the kid wouldn't leave. And finally, this went on for like twenty minutes — the longest twenty minutes of my life — I was just standing there with the rest of my class. They were all in shocked silence. Finally they brought the sheriff down, and it was the end of class, and the sheriff took the kid away. That's the worst [case]. I think he was suspended for three days. And I don't think he did come back to my class. What had happened was that he had had a fight with his girlfriend on the bus that morning and he was angry at the world. And that's happened once in twelve years of teaching."

(What's a sweet memory of teaching?)

"I kind of like going to these bars with two kids to pick out a prom band when I was junior class advisor. (Laughter) It was kind of fun. (Laughter) I don't know if that's one of my sweetest, but that's a real nice memory."

(Was that better than being voted teacher of the year?)

"I don't think I'll ever be that . . ."

(But you were back when we taught together —)

"Oh, yeah, I forgot about that — by the seniors . . . that was kind of neat! I forgot that happened. But I think individual things with students provide some nice memories. Like the bar thing was kind of showing them something they didn't know . . . and probably didn't need to know! (Laughter) And taking a group of freshman girls into the inner city to pick something up and the fact that they'd never seen the inner city. And one of them noticed that these people didn't have any yards . . . (Laughter) That's kind of a nice memory. And things that kids have done when I've left. The first few years of teaching they gave me real nice — sweet gifts when they knew I was leaving."

(Do you think public education works?)

"Yeah, for the most part. I think it's like a democracy — it works for the majority."

(Do you think there's any way it can work better?)

"I think that — if we could keep the institution away there are many nice things about public education — like opportunities for all and that kind of stuff . . . but if we could make classes smaller, I think it would work better."

(And yet you don't think we can reach all students?)

"I think *all* is immediately dooming yourself to failure. There are lots of reasons that teachers can't affect all students, like their family background, the fact that some kids just don't want to be there and won't learn no matter what you do. You can spend a lot of effort, but at some point you've got to say — these other people are more important . . ."

Tape #101

"Every time they start reforming education, they start reforming the teachers."

Ms. B. was fifty-two and looked the role of the mother-grandmotherly grade school teacher she had been for the last twenty-two years. She didn't particularly want to be interviewed, but was very pleasant about it — she wanted to help out if she could. We talked for the full hour. At the end, she looked at me and said, "You know, this interview has made me think about my career and my career choice for the first time in ages . . . Thank you. I really enjoyed this. It really stimulated me." It was the normal reaction from a lot of teachers.

"One of the problems is legislative people deciding what the education reforms should be and how they should be handled. I think it entails a lack of trust in the teachers by these authorities, and I think it's passed on to the public by the authorities. A lot of things have been blamed on teachers which were very likely economic and social problems of our society. It's easy to start pointing fingers, and it seems like when they point fingers they point them at us. Every time they start reforming education, they start reforming the teachers. For example, there's all the talk about competency testing and we're going to get rid of all the bad teachers. Teachers have the feeling that they're talking about all of us. We sometimes are used as public relations by authorities. And then often they take credit for what we do."

(Do you think raising salaries will help education?)

"Yes, I do, because you might draw in some good people who might then be tempted to teach rather than go somewhere else. You have a larger choice in people if you pay better. There's never enough money, and I think if you're going to get any more money it should go to, other than salaries, smaller class sizes. I have a small class this year and I cannot help but notice daily the difference in the way they work together and the way they work with me — their work habits, their social habits, their whole response is different than the class I had the year before. I have twenty-two this year, thirty last year."

(What would you say to people who say — one-room schoolhouses did a better job so why do we need small class size?)

"Can they honestly say that those children learned more and that their education was better? Did they learn all the things we cover today? But probably both the teacher and the parent had a stronger influence over the child than they have now. I don't mean this to be anybody's fault; parents are just these days more distracted — incomes are higher and they have to be busier and have their minds on other things.

"Education doesn't have an axe to grind. They're not trying to promote a single ideology; they're trying to give a good solid education."

Tape #208

> "At grade school level, you can run off an
> awful lot of word hunts."

I interviewed Ms. O. at her home, seated in her living room underneath the portraits of her three children. She was dressed in a red sweater and a skirt and looked a little cold. She was a teacher who believed that the majority of teachers were not very good — she argued cogently and she sounded like she knew her stuff. She, herself, taught learning disabled grade schoolers, grades five and six, though she had taught regular grade school classes also, as well as a stint in a private school.

She was forty, divorced, and had completed seven years of teaching. She now worked in a fairly rural area outside a large Midwestern city.

"I went into teaching by accident. I was a math and physics major and I went into teaching because I needed a job immediately. And this was at a time when they needed teachers really bad. If you could just say your name, you were hired immediately. They just wanted a warm body. So I taught double sessions there as they were on a double shift. Then after the initial period where I was merely teaching to earn money, as soon as I no longer needed to . . . I wasn't teaching. I had children and a family and I did not work for those ten years.

"Then later I went to the university and I asked, where will I most likely be hired, as there was no longer a teacher shortage, and they said — special education. And since I was more interested in psychology, I went into the behavior disabled end of it. And I'm glad I went into it. I like it. I like to be able to arrange my own work, to feel responsible for what I'm doing daily. I like the progress that I see; I like to see behavior changes; it really thrills me to death. And I do see behavior changes.

"But believe me, I taught in a building in '68 where people who were teachers should never have been teachers. They were very poor at what they were doing; they simply didn't care at all. I can see that type of situation coming again, and it would be very sad. I think they hired people then because they needed them; people decided on teaching because they couldn't or didn't decide on anything else. It was something that they were steered into at undergraduate level because they were not good students. Like I said, I was in math and physics and I was a good math and physics student. So when I went to a counselor in college and said, 'I need to teach because I need a job right away,' they laughed and said, 'You're crazy. You're going to sit in how to teach reading classes and be bored stiff,' and I was. But that was no problem; I could take twenty-two to twenty-five hours of education classes at a time and get through. And they were right. I sat in there with the bottom of the barrel. Those people are forty now — and they're still teaching. To me, that's part of the problem."

(How did they stick it out when teaching can be such a hard job for people?)

"They don't work at it; it isn't a hard job for *them*. Teachers can get in their cars at 3:00; they can have lesson plans from one year to the next; they can get into a groove of one way of doing things. They can have those dittos ready to pass out and they get into a pattern that just keeps their noses above water. At the grade school level you can run off an awful lot of word hunts. You can keep those kiddos busy and things really look good . . . and not really have to be accountable about how you're spending your time. You still have a lot of paper work to grade and everything, record everything. But if you're fairly neat and have a fairly pleasant personality and come to work on time and that sort of thing . . . you can get by very well in teaching. And that's very sad. With no innovation, creativity, intelligence, drive to work, need to change — there's none of that. Or not enough of that."

(What do you think can be done to get better people into teaching?)

"Well, everybody else says money, but I'm not convinced of that. People go into other professions not necessarily for money but because they feel a calling, a need, a mission — they see themselves as a certain kind of person. It's an identity kind of thing. I mean, when I die, I expect it to say on my tombstone — TEACHER. It sounds strange, but that's what I am. And that's the kind of person you want to look for in teaching, a person who has that identity, who gets a real kick out of — teaching.

"An example of not good teaching? Ridicule, berating the student . . . boring, just being boring, not covering enough material fast enough, not attempting to make anything interesting, reading from books — using a manufactured text and saying now we're going to do the questions, running off the manufacturer's dittos and passing them out. I mean the janitors can do that, right? And the bus drivers . . . and that's what I see a lot of. That can be very easily done, but I don't call that teaching. That's what you see; that's what's seen so many times. Parents are many times, oddly enough, very impressed by this; they think this is just the thing to do. I mean, 'He covered the entire textbook and used all the dittos in these packets,' and so the parents are very impressed by that. And that's sad. It's easy to fool a parent.

"Children can be challenged but there's a fine line between challenged and pushed, I mean literally pushed. It can be almost fighting — 'I told you to do chapter nine and I don't think you've done it.' It should be more — 'let's see what we can do together. What do you see for yourself?' I do more of that because the children are very limited when they come to me; they're worn out; they're scared to death.

"I'm not a very warm and loving person. And I think my learning disabled students see me as rather hard. I don't hear many compliments. I told my principal the other day I was really shocked because the other day I was just sitting in my chair and one of them came up and hugged me. And I hadn't particularly motivated him in any way; I'm not particularly nice to that person. But it was Valentine's Day and he was leaving me for that particular day — and I was quite shocked by that. But some of them will talk about teachers they like and so I go and visit their room and the reason they like them is that not much work is being done. And I'm being very tough and they must get a certain amount of work done and be busy at it all the time. And they don't like that very much. It's a big adjustment, but that's what I see that they need. Because then they smile . . . they smile when they're done with something. And I point that out to them: 'That's what made you feel good, accomplishing something worthwhile. You got a 90 on it; you got a 75 on it — whatever — you did it well; how does that make you feel?' 'It makes me feel good.' See, they've had so little of that, that they put no value on grades or succeeding at all. You have to really feed that. Twenty years ago these kids would have been in mentally retarded classes. But then the public laws came out and changed all of that. And you couldn't put a child with above an 80 I.Q. in a class for the mentally retarded. Now you've got all these kids, about ten percent of the school population that the teachers swore up and down were mentally retarded . . . now what do you do with them? Well, that's why this category was designed — I think in '67 or so . . . for them with learning disabilities.

"I think it's good; I think I save children from being problems for society. I think I save them from being juvenile delinquents or psychotic. That's why I'm able to sleep soundly at night! (Laughter) I mean, I can't come home and look in the mirror and say, gee, at least he learned to read — although to tell you the truth, a lot of them do read well once they're taught one on one — but many of them just weren't getting anywhere in the regular classroom. They just did not have that one-on-one relationship. It's like a little preschooler. You put him in day care at eighteen months . . . If he isn't talked to daily by another adult, he'll not learn to talk from the other eighteen month olds. He can't, you know, come up. It's one of the problems I see in my own seven year old, because that's where he went. And his vocabulary suffered so tremendously. There was no adult speaking to him. When she was speaking, who was she speaking to? She wasn't speaking to an individual eighteen months old or three years old; she was talking to at least three or four or five of them at once. And I can remember my son coming home and I said, 'Did your teacher talk to you?' 'Oh, no, she doesn't talk to me ever. She talks to the class, but not to me.' She's just talking; it doesn't *mean* anything. When you get right down to it, education can only be done one at a time, one at a time. I mean, Montessori had some really good ideas about teaching children one at a time — little children. I don't know how it works in high school; I'm not a high school teacher. But I know for younger children, you need to divide and conquer. And divide them and conquer and divide again . . . even in the regular classroom. There are things you can do all at once — teaching a basic skill like silent Es or something and then you divide; you read at first grade level, you read at primer and so on . . .and we'll teach you what an A is — that's what they need to do. I do that every morning — teach something with everybody. But then, you need to divide it up and make sure everybody got that. The blessing of special ed. — I have eleven students. My eleven is not too many, but I promise you that any one of my eleven is worth two of regular children and three in some cases. And it takes time and planning because each one of those children has to be taught completely individually, different from his neighbor's books. And those books and things are different from the next person's things. His spelling words are for him. I can maybe team up a couple of them, but for the most part everything I do is individual. So it can really drive you nuts unless you're really well organized.

"I do feel like I'm not touching enough people, that I'm not reaching out there and doing enough, that I want to do more. But I serviced twenty-two kids last year and I really got tired; I was beginning to forget who was what. And it really doesn't have to do with how serious their problem is . . . it has to do with how many hours there are in the day, and how often I can get to each of them and have them read to me. They have to write every day and then read it to me, and that takes a lot of time."

(Would you become a teacher again?)

"Yes, even more so. I didn't know how great it was going to be, see? I fell into it. If I'd known I was going to like it this well, I'd have chosen it sooner. I guess it's the special kids that I deal with. I just see small successes. I had this one kid that was violent and all he did was throw things . . . I mean every single day. I remember from September to December 7th — and December 7th he did not fight! I remember that day. He didn't hit anybody, and I thought wow! December 8th rolled around — did not fight! Then for twelve straight school days he didn't and I thought wow! he must be on Thorazine! He didn't fight, you know, I can't figure this out. But basically he just decided it was more fun to be normal than to be violent. And then when he did 'fight' the next time, all he did was 'four-letter-word' somebody. Then instead of getting mad, I shook his hand and patted him on the back and said, 'Hey, you're learning to handle this with words instead of fists; that's amazing!' It was like finding some good. In other words, what thrills me is my ability to see that. And as long as I can keep seeing that, then I'll stay in this business and it'll feel good to me."

(Would you recommend teaching to others?)

"No — *they* have to know. It's an art; they'll know if it's for them. It's like would you recommend concert piano for someone? You can't recommend that for people, can you? It's just not done. You don't recommend that someone paint Picassos."

Tape #212

> "I put in forty hours a week of overtime . . ."

Ms. F. had taught for eight years . . . in three different school districts, two different states. She had seen a lot in those eight years, but she remained dedicated to public education. She was currently teaching English and journalism at a large high school in the Midwest with a very diverse student population. As both yearbook and newspaper advisor, she told me she put in those forty hours a week almost every week in an attempt to get the work done on those two publications. Next year, she said, there had to be some changes made or at least a supplemental salary, which this year she did not receive.

Ms. F. had long blonde hair. A gold locket hung from her neck and she sat through the entire interview with her hands folded in her lap. She was thirty-four and single. Her hobbies included music, painting, needlework, antiques, and writing. Her heroes were John Kennedy, King Arthur and St. John Bosco.

"I spend about forty additional hours a week putting the school newspaper and the school yearbook together. I don't get paid extra for those because I teach three journalism courses . . . it's called stupidity. (Smile) I taught English last year, and I was hired with the idea that I would take over this program. The person who did the program was close to retirement, but he had a stroke during the summer and had to leave suddenly so — surprise! But he had release time; he only taught one class a day — he had independent study the rest of the day and thus only taught one or two kids in each class. He taught the journalism class that did the stories for the newspaper. We have a yearbook class of about fifteen kids, and they're very good kids, but in fifty-five minute periods you don't always get a lot done by the time you get set up and put everything away — not many layouts can get done. Some kids volunteer to stay after to help; they're good kids and they worry about me a lot because they can see what it's doing to me this year. I teach five classes altogether along with that forty extra hours a week . . ."

(What is that doing to you?)

"It's pretty well ruined my health for this year."

(Do you intend to do this next year also?)

"Not without some changes. I would like to see a free period for publications where I would not have any students and I could do some of the telephoning to advertisers. That's something I can't do during the daytime. I would like to see a supplemental contract if I'm going to have to continue to do a good bit of the work after school. I hear lots of promises . . . nothing's come through yet. First they promised that they'd take away one class this year . . . they didn't do that. Then they said they would get me a supplemental contract since technically they changed the salary since last year the advisor was getting five-sixths of his salary to do the yearbook and newspaper. That was a supplemental contract really. But that hasn't come through either. I have two English classes and three journalism classes so I have the full five class schedule.

"In the three journalism classes, we get all of the writing for the newspaper done, and the editors do the editing — I just check it for grammar. Because in the past — both of them had become more and more 'advisor publications.' It goes a lot faster if you do it yourself! But I'm trying to move away from that because the paper was at the point where nobody read it. It's given out free. And so they would give it out and at the end of the day, you would find the halls covered with it. So we've changed that this year; they're at least reading the newspaper. It's a result of the kids and giving them a little bit more freedom. And so they care a little bit more . . . and they have good ideas for stories. And I'm willing to try them, though I tell them ahead of time if I think we're going to get into hot water about it . . . and sometimes we decide to go ahead anyway."

(Would you become a teacher again?)

Yes — on my good days, I think that.

(Not when you're here at 8:00 at night, huh?)

No, the times when I think about quitting teaching are when I'm here at 2:30 in the morning.

(I found out months later that Ms. F. was released at the end of that school year.)

Tape #88

"One of my daughters was over here the other night with her little four year old son, and I had some papers that had to be graded. So I just sort of set myself off in a corner. I mean, I even sit on only half the chair, back in a corner of the kitchen. I really concentrate as I've learned to do teaching with five kids of my own around. But I heard my daughter saying to her little boy, 'Justin, look at Grandma now. See that look on her face; that's all I remember ever seeing of Grandma when I grew up. Look at her now, Justin. You can say anything and Grandma won't hear you. She's too busy concentrating on her papers. She doesn't even hear us; she doesn't even know we're here.' And I looked up at that, with a horrible look on my face, and told her to come back and talk to me when she had a job and five children to raise . . . then we'll talk."

Ms. C. was fifty-two. She'd had her ups and downs in life. She'd been divorced for the last five years after twenty some years of marriage. She'd raised five children and had taught now for sixteen years at the elementary level. We sat in her den to do the interview, and the wall across from us was covered with pictures in a montage effect — all of her family and grandchildren. She had just had her hair done, but nothing could hide the aging, the wrinkles that were new, the weight that was newer. Even her glasses made her look older . . . and very tired. What vivaciousness was gone was made up for by her sincerity about teaching.

After the tape was off she told me stories about teaching . . . stories that for whatever reason she wouldn't commit to tape, gentle stories, funny stories . . . stories of perseverance.

"When I came into teaching, and where I came in, their attitude about any kind of creative writing . . . actually any kind of writing was — don't touch it, put a positive remark on the top of it. Do not correct spelling. Do not change any punctuation. Do not deal with any kind of errors at all. Say it's a wonderful idea — da da da. *I did that!* For four months — I said then, I can't stand this. I cannot do this. I got . . . I got — 'Don't ever use your horrible red marker on anything.' And I do all this now *initially* in creative writing. 'It sounds good' or 'I like this idea' or 'wonderful thoughts.' I don't really correct it. But then after this quarter I do. We're just getting into the grammar and punctuation. And then I expect them to edit it. They're going to have to catch up to it sometime, before they get to the people who are hiring them. The people who are still making the decisions about business or anything else are still the kind that want the grammatical things right, the punctuation right. They still want that red pen used. I mean, it's our people and we were raised with that. Now maybe in twenty years when people who have had these experiences are hiring, then —

then maybe the secretaries will be the only ones who have to bone up on all this . . . I think it's ludicrous.

"But I'm less enthusiastic as a teacher now than when I first started, though I really think I'm more involved with the curriculum. I think I was out there to entertain. And I wanted the kids to like me. I wanted to have them love school. I was told by my first principal — what you are above everything else is a motivator. You make these kids feel so good about themselves. You make them feel good about school. Even if they're the lowest group — good about themselves. But what I did meanwhile called curriculum — I just never dealt with that too much. I'd think of things that never ended in my plan book. The first couple of years I'm sure I put everything in my plan book, but after that I kind of just sketched a skeleton thing and then I'd put in what I did. I had a lot of creative juices flowing. Now I'm not so creative. I guess I'm still creative, but I'm not as fired up as I used to be. So I think it's like I sort of grew up in the profession.

"A kid last year in my reading team said, Ms. C., when my teacher is gone next week we're going to have Ms. Smith. And I said, 'Great! that'll be nice, Matt.' He then said, 'I was talking to one of my friends who's in her class, and he said she always says, "Try to do your best." And I said, 'Matt, if your teacher were going away, and somebody told you I was going to be your replacement, what would you say that I say?' And he shouted, 'DO IT OVER!' I mean, he raised his voice: 'DO IT OVER!' I said, 'Do I do that a lot?' 'Oh, yeah!'

"So I started off school with a new image this year. I decided I wasn't going to yell; I was going to talk very quietly. Because — if you go around to those teachers who talk very quietly, their classes talk very quietly too. My kids are all loud and I'm loud.

"When I was directing student plays at _____, I felt so involved. I always said I was about a six at home, a seven and a half in the classroom, and when I'm directing a play I'm about a ten. And it must have shown, that — six . . . 'It's a little bit over half of mother we're getting.' I really come alive when I'm in front of a group or an audience. I was going to be a nun when I was in college, but I was going to be a teaching nun. I feel fulfilled. I feel each year I get another chance to prove that I can be an effective part of education. I miss teaching in the summertime. I go around and when I'm in some place, shopping or eating, I think — oh, I'd hate to be a waitress, oh, I'd hate to be the hostess, oh, I'd hate to be the people waiting on me . . . I always sort of reinforce in myself the positive kind of things I'm doing. I really think that it's a service.

"I guess people respect teachers in retrospect. But they don't think enough to raise the salaries or fix the schools up. There's just not enough physical evidence that they do care about teachers. I think everybody feels very mellow towards one teacher. And I think all lawyers and doctors and engineers, etc., all owe their skills to a teacher."

Tape #15

A male kindergarten teacher? I was curious to meet him. And he was almost what you would expect — completely unique and verbally eclectic! He was forty-three and had taught for seventeen years, coming to teach after military service. He smoked nonstop through the interview, held in a crummy union hall for the local association, but he was delightful. He was married with two children.

(Can you define "good teacher"?)

"I — that's an interesting question, because it's an unanswerable question. I think there are different combinations. You know, one guy can be very outgoing and be a good teacher and so the inclination would be to say, well, you've got to be outgoing. And the next guy could be a real introvert and be as good or better. And so then you end up arguing that, well, you've got to be an introvert."

(You could generalize that a good teacher is someone who takes his own talents and somehow molds — his own uniqueness and uses that in his teaching?)

"I've never thought of that. I've got to believe you're right."

(It's just the next step in what you're saying?)

"Yes, it is, and it's a step that I've never made. And you've got to be right. You brought that to my mind — good teachers are those who have their own thing . . . Good teachers are unique. Yes, they are themselves. Yes. And they are a very strong David or John, good teachers are. Yeah. If someone is going to role model off of you, you have to be someone they can do that with.

"You really have to be — you said *weird* or *odd*. Or maybe you said *odd* and I said *weird*. But one of the theories I have about teaching and teachers and education is that you have to hope. Do you have kids? Are you married? It will be fun for you when you start sending your own, because it's hard to . . . you start seeing things a little bit differently. You have to hope.

You have to hope you gave something to somebody in your class. And maybe you're right. Maybe you have to be so weird or so odd or whatever that you're not — to everybody. But you have to hope that you are for some. I mean, otherwise there is no point to your being there...if you're not going to get to any [students]. And then you have to hope that the guy next year — I mean it could be a woman — guy next year is a nonsexist term in this case — could hit some of the other ones.

I happen to think I'm a pretty good math teacher. I'm not bad in reading. I'm ok in science. I'm God awful in social studies. I hope next year's teacher is good in social studies. And that's also true of personality . . . you just have to hope.

Tape #215

"Education is a neurotic situation."

Ms. D. spoke with me in the speech and debate office of a large suburban high school. She had taught English for twelve years, two in a Brazilian school. She was married with one child of her own. She admitted that there were questions about education to which she didn't know the answers . . . and that bothered her.

"I think about getting out, mainly because of burnout. I also like variety and I've now seen other things that I would like to do. Money is a very small part of that decision. And I think that there's a general attitude that if you became a teacher, it's because you couldn't do anything else. When I went back to graduate school and I had to take the Miller Analogy Test, I was appalled to find that one of the lowest scores that you could get is for a teacher. If you were going into psychology, you had to score like a 75; if you were going into education you had to score 25 or 26. And I just think there's a general attitude that you're civil servants and [there's] not much respect for the product and the end that you supposedly produce, which is the youth. My husband and I taught out of the country for a couple of years and found a totally different attitude in the status and prestige of being a teacher. We taught in Brazil and there was a great deal of respect and, number one, we did make more money than the majority of the populace there. But we were considered intelligent which I don't think is true in the United States.

"I think in our country education has never been held in high esteem just for education itself. It was looked on as a way to get more money, unlike other countries, like in Brazil where education was seen as being important. But we went through that period of time here where even having a college degree didn't mean you'd get a good job, and I think they lost some of their respect for us at that point. I don't think that we do teach that we educate for education itself. We teach for some sort of end product of a job. And if you can't see that, it has very little value. I think we're reaping that attitude now.

"I think most teachers like kids; being in education, you have to like kids or you do burn out. But I think there are some teachers where this really is secondary to everything else they're doing. But I still think that the majority of the people who are in it are in it because they like kids. They *mean* to do well, but I personally think education is a neurotic situation. I think there are goals that you may have in mind that, because of the overload, because of social situations, because of the administration demands — you can't do it. It's frustrating; you're working with environments that are not conducive to teaching, so a lot of it is hitting your head against the wall.

"I think the discipline here is about like what I hear about in other schools. I think drugs and alcohol are problems but I don't see it overtly. It's there in the way the kids talk and act. It's a major part of their daily discussion. I think the schools say they are doing a lot to deal with that, but I don't think they are. And I don't think I'm trained well enough to know what to do. There are situations that come up and you don't know what you're supposed to say or how you're supposed to respond. I think that's frustration a lot of us feel. Sometimes you want to go overboard and think that every child is doing drugs, but I don't think that's true. But I don't think we offer enough to those kids who don't know what to do with [drugs]. And I don't know what to do."

(Is that part of the school's role?)

"I don't know. At this point if you asked me what role the schools are supposed to have, I think that's another major problem. I don't think we have any idea. I think you get caught up in it because it's just too much of the environment that you're in. I'm not sure what I'm supposed to be doing. Am I the social worker; am I the educator? Sometimes I feel really silly jumping all over these kids when they didn't get their homework in the night before when I know they have problems in their lives. And yet on the other hand, I get angry and want to say — well, this is your ticket out. And if this is the ticket out, what am I doing; is this really going to make a difference for them? And I don't know . . . education is neurotic. . . .

"Sex is a major problem in this school; the hormones are going constantly. But I guess the major problem of public education is that it doesn't know its own direction. And I think that's maybe why I think we're trying to do too many things, and we don't do any of them well because we're not sure what our focus is supposed to be. But if I knew, it would make a difference to me where my energies were supposed to go. But I personally see that as a big problem . . . and nobody tells you either. In this particular school district . . . they want to keep their reputation. I think what they really want is that if you have academic students, you are as academic as you can be. If you have students that aren't academic, they want you to discipline them. That's about as cut and dry as it is. I feel like there's not a real emphasis on the social work, changing the lives, nor necessarily getting these kids what they need. The lower levels are pretty much lost in the shuffle. And I'm sensitive to their needs because the majority of the kids I have been teaching since I have been working here have been lower level kids.

"You know if I had to think about my *best* experiences in teaching, probably a lot of them would be because of the extracurricular. It's a different relationship; I mean, those are the kids that you have over to your house. It's not tied up with academics; and that's why I've hung in there.

"Last summer my husband and I were invited to a wedding of a student we both had about ten years ago. He was on the speech team but didn't really ever do anything. So we went but we weren't sure we were going to recognize him since we hadn't seen him in so long. Yet when he introduced us to people . . . they all knew who we were. And his parents said, the greatest thrill he had was when we came to the wedding. We just could not get over [it] — and they said you have no idea what an impact you had on his life. And considering we hadn't talked to him in so long, it was just amazing . . . and yet there are still teachers that I can think of who had a tremendous effect on me and on my life. Hopefully, someday I'll have the opportunity to say something to them."

(Do you think public education really works?)

"I think it needs to be overhauled."

(If you had to take a yes or no at that, which would you more likely take?)

"Well, in the direction we seem to be going, I'd say no. I think the size needs to be looked at; I think what the priorities are need to be looked at, as far as where the emphasis should be. I think the whole concept of what should be taught and when and at what age and how long a child needs to stay in school — I think the time spent needs to really be looked at; [there is] a lot of wasted time, a lot of repetition. Every now and then these kids just really turn on . . . and you wonder where did it all go the rest of the time. And again, if I were teaching all upper level kids, I might have a totally different perspective, but I feel like I teach the majority of the world. They're burnt out someplace and I don't know if it's us; I don't know if it's their environment. And I think we kind of have to know where that is too. Because when those sparks happen and they're interested . . . I mean, I still think inherently they want to learn and they want to know. I think there's stuff that we're doing that just kills it and deadens it . . . and I don't know what it is."

(Would you become a teacher again?)

"Yeah . . . still . . ."

Tape #156

Before the tape started, Mr. B. told me about a boy in his senior "less-than-completely-academic" English class who asked him what he would get out of reading the classic English literature they were doing in class. Mr. B. said he knew the kid was looking for an argument so he looked at him, thought a minute, shook his head and said, "Well, quite frankly, I don't think you *will get a single thing out of any of this literature."*

"And you know," he said to me, "I doubt a kid like that will."

When he sat down, he said he needed to hurry to get home to grade papers. Throughout the interview he acted antsy and rubbed his balding head continually. He looked the picture of an English schoolmaster, Mister Chips — middle-aged. And he spoke of poetry and drama, and novels as if they were — something more. He was a real English *teacher.*

Mr. B. was fifty-five and had been teaching English at the high and junior high school levels for twenty-six years. He had taught at a predominately black high school in a large Midwestern city and he'd taught (for the most part) at a suburban, middle class school. He was married with one child of his own. His hobbies were travel, chess, and photography, reading, and biking. He wanted to take early retirement this year. He had wanted to take it last year. He got it this year.

"At one time I wanted to be an aviator, but I proved to be color-blind so that ruled that out. But beyond that, I never really thought of any other career than teaching. Why English? Oh, well — because I've always loved poetry, and reading plays and short stories . . ."

(Do you think that's what you deal with the majority of the time in teaching English?)

"Yeah — once I get past the administrative crap. Especially now that I'm doing twelfth grade stuff."

(Do you think most of your seniors get something out of the English curriculum?)

"Well, as the curriculum is structured right now — no, I don't. We have this really beautiful new book which I myself like — but unfortunately most of that book is poetry. And I think we should get more into plays, short stories, and novels. I think kids take more to those things, particularly I have found that they enjoy plays. And it's not just because you read aloud or any of that, but because they can really get into it and realize the situation and the characters and all that stuff. But no — I'm not saying that poetry doesn't have a lot to offer; and I'm not saying that it isn't a wonderful way to — learn about yourself and the world and so forth. But I really don't think that as the twelfth grade curriculum is structured right now it's as beneficial as it could be.

"My kids like to argue with me about all that too. You know, their objection is one I've heard over and over again. 'Why should we know about the past? This is 1987 and why should we care what those old bastards did back in the 1600s, and so forth.' Well, I really think there are lessons to learn back then. But if you're not going to allow yourself to learn them, then no, I don't think it is going to be beneficial. But I think that all that comes with maturity. I think we try to push a lot of things on the kids before they're ready for it. I think that's one of the main things wrong with the English curriculum: we try to push things on to them long before they're ready. Now some kids will be ready for certain things — as everybody knows; I'm not saying anything brilliant — I mean, you can have two fourteen year olds and one will be ready for any number of things and the other may not be much beyond Pooh Bear. But I think it takes a mature mind to understand much of the poetry that we present to kids in the twelfth grade. And it takes a lot of experience; it takes a lot of thought. It takes a lot of having read widely and deeply for years before you're going to understand some of what you see in John Donne or Dryden.

"And I think some kids are right when they say, 'I feel like this is never going to help me.' I think they're right. We've made this mistake historically. Part of it is due to the fact that it's a democracy and blah de blah. I just think that a lot of those kids would be a lot happier — and I'm not necessarily talking about trade schools or things like that — but I think they would be a lot happier doing something else, and preparing for something else would be quite practical and quite useful to them. I certainly have no objection to the guy who says, 'Look, you may find Samuel Pepys fascinating, but personally I think he's a bore; and I don't see how he's ever going to help me. My interest lies elsewhere, and why can't I pursue that interest?' I'm perfectly willing to accept that, and I think he should be able to. In the long run I think it's far more beneficial for him, and it's more beneficial to the country as a whole because I think we're wasting a lot of people by trying to jam them full of things they don't find to be particularly interesting or very helpful."

(How many of your students, or even students across the board, will do much "mature" reading once they are out of school?)

"Very few. Very few. Even the kids who seem to have some interest don't carry books. And please, I don't want to sound like the old man — I hate that kind of stuff. But I will say — for one thing, I don't think kids are terribly different than in the past, but one thing I have noticed is — that when I started as a teacher (and even then, I complained) — but there were far, far more people who carried books that they were reading. They'd come in and they would have novels or they would have short stories, or they would have this or that. They may not always have been very good, but at least they carried them. And over the years I have noticed that it has just dropped, and dropped, and dropped, until now you just barely see kids carrying books. And — I can remember when they even exchanged books. I'm not saying that this was a widespread practice or anything, but there were just more people who seemed to do that. I don't think kids read very much today. They just don't seem to have an interest."

(If a parent came to you and wanted to know what they could do at home to make their kid better in English, what would you suggest to them?)

"Well, I would suggest what I do with my own daughter. I'm not bragging, but she is an honor student and she ranks very high on those state tests, and it's because I read to her from the time she was six months old. *Six months* — that's right! When she could not apparently understand a word, I read to her. I read to her tiny, tiny little things. The first thing I read to her was about farm animals and her eyes would just shine and she would point and I read that to her and then other little things. All were just extremely simple. And, you know, today, she's an absolutely voracious reader. She loves to read. It's just an immense part of her life. And I think there's just no other way. You've got to start them young. You've got to make sure they have books, and not only that but you have to like books and you have to like talking about them. She and I and her mother — we always talk about books, and things that we've read. And we all have them; we have a house full of them. I think . . . you've got to start young. You can't just let some kid drift along until he's ten or eleven years old and try — it's impossible. So seniors . . . ?"

(What do you think is the major thing wrong with public education?)

"Well, that's easy for me because I have felt this from the very beginning. That is, it belongs in the hands of teachers and not — not administrators. And I am not making a blanket condemnation of administrators. I have known many fine ones. But, I think this is true — if you go back historically, they are people who were hired to handle the tasks that teachers couldn't find time to do. And somehow the thing got perverted and the power swung around and they've gotten it into their hands. We've lost it and gotten into this subservient position and I think it's all wrong. I still feel that there ought to be people who should handle all these damn forms and things, but I don't think the *power* ought to rest with them. Because we don't have time to do those things, I think they ought to do them, but I don't think they ought to have the power. We ought to have the higher power. I think we're the ones that know better than they do. And I particularly resent, though I don't have anybody particular in mine, administrators who have maybe spent six years in the classroom and then who tell me that they are going to drop by one day and help me do this and that or maybe point out some of the things that I'm not doing that maybe I ought to be doing, etc., etc., etc. That is not to say that I think I'm perfect; I know damn well I'm not. And I think there are qualified people someplace who could probably tell me a whole lot, but I don't think they are currently among the ranks of administrators that I know or have known. Seriously!

"Think of some things that have come down from — 'on high.' Mastery learning — which I have no objection to in theory; or competency testing, again I have no objection to the theory. But you know, just this year when I dragged out some of those competency tests, the more I see those things, the more I realize how absolutely shallow and how absolutely meaning-less they are. So I would definitely have to say that competency as it is now structured is one of the biggest farces of all time. It was done by the — 'on high.' Though — we were in on it. But we had tasks *assigned* to us. They'd say, now today we're going to do this, this, and this. It's just a situation where administrators think they know best."

(What could the district do to make you a happier teacher?)

"Well, they could cut my classload down to four classes. And then give me more time at school to work. And they could just do away with a lot of this stuff that does not amount to a damn, such as pointless meetings, tapes by some broad out in Los Angeles who always teaches to this classroom full of just perfect people! They could supply me with more materials. I would like to think that things were not so rigid that if I wanted to spend two or three days on something, I could do it. I could proceed at a more leisurely pace. I could go more deeply into this or that thing, or at least as deeply as I'm capable with these students, whereas with another thing I could just do it or forget it depending on how the class responds. I think we could pretty safely do away with lesson plans. I really do; I just think they're an insult. We still have to list little numbered objectives at the top. I think a competent teacher would know what had to be done and would go and do it. And as I say — he would do it at his own pace. He would not necessarily be hide-bound to 'this has got to come after that' and 'that's got to come after this,' and blah blah blah. He would be able to draw on things as he felt they were necessary. I just hate this thing of having to turn those damn lesson plans in all the time. And we still have potty patrol . . ."

(What do you say if a parent or somebody says education is crummy, what do you say in defense of it?)

"Well, I'd have to know what they are saying because I think some parts of it *are* crummy. (Laughter) No, really, seriously! But I think that every time something horrible happens, there's somebody out there who says, 'Well, this wouldn't happen if they were only teaching — you know — kids in the public schools to do this or that or the other thing.' And —

I don't care whether it's pregnancy [or] use of condoms [or] AIDS. We're now going to teach them all about AIDS. And I'm not making this up; I think it was either this week or last I heard somebody say, 'Well, it's time for us to educate kids about the street. These kids were going out to live in the streets; they need an education.' So it just seems to be like every time a really hideous thing comes up, it's something for the public schools to take up. And I'm not trying to get off the hook or anything, but you're only capable of so much. And not only that, a few years ago they got the idea that we should be doing all this career education, and this and the other thing. So if you're going to have to spend more and more time on that kind of thing and less and less time on your subject — well, then sure, there're going to be problems. There's probably no question about it. And if you're just going to give them a little of that and a little of this and never get into anything very deeply then, sure, it's going to get kind of 'crummy.' But I feel that where you don't have the terrible racial issues tearing you to pieces, I would say schools are probably still doing just about the same job they always have. They could do better . . ."

(Do you think teachers really are that important?)

"I do, I really do. Because I think so many of these kids don't have anybody else. I think they have absolutely horrible parents, people who tell them to shut up and get lost all the time. They don't pay attention to them, and I think a lot of these kids really look forward to coming to school and seeing certain teachers . . . maybe not all of them. But I really do think so. It's just a matter of confidence and helping them to understand that they can do it. I think that's the problem with most problem students in school. They come from homes where probably nobody hardly ever asks them . . . how are you doing or have you had any tests, or what did you get on the test, or what do you think about this or that. Or they come from homes where nobody *ever* asks them or where nobody even cares. All some care [about] is that they don't get into any trouble or they get a C or a D or just enough to get them through. I think a lot of our children lack confidence and are afraid to speak up. They're afraid because they think they're ugly or their hair's not nice or their nose is too big or they're afraid because people are going to laugh at them . . . and in many cases they're absolutely right. People *are* going to laugh at them. And make fun of them — that's part of being teenagers. . . ."

"Do I have any heroes? Well, again, I don't live as much in the present as I should. (Laughter) I would say — amongst the living, I can't put a specific name. I know it's going to sound weird, but my heroes and the people I really respect are the people who dedicated their lives to finding things like cures for diseases and things like that. And I don't have to know their names. I *know* there are people out there doing those sorts of things. And there are people out there dedicating their lives to helping the sick and the oppressed and the afflicted and things like that. And I don't even have to know their names. It's just the fact that they're out there. Those are my heroes. It's not the people who make the big name and reputation and not the people who make the millions of dollars, but the people who are just quietly working and dedicating their lives to serving their fellow man."

(Do you think teachers somehow fit into that category?)

"Absolutely. Oh, by all means."

(And is that a part of the reason you're a teacher, not just because you're good at explaining things?)

"Well, sure — well, I'd like to think that I had contributed toward somebody's understanding or enjoyment or helping them grow. And I can say without hesitation that I think it's true. I don't think I've helped maybe in every single case, but I know I've had some sort of moderate success along the line."

(If you were back in college and you knew then what you know now, would you go into teaching again?)

"I would have to say no. The reason? Ahhh, let's put it this way. If a lot of these changes were made, these changes that I've been talking about, then I would definitely consider doing it all over again. But I would not come back if I knew I was going to have to fight all of this foolishness . . . all these things that we've talked about. And knowing that I was going to have to play second fiddle to Neanderthal coaches and that sort of thing — no, I wouldn't do it. If some of those things could be effectively changed, then I would; I really would. I think I've had some of my finest moments in the classroom.

"I've had some things happen that in fact I couldn't talk about now — because I know I'd burst into tears. Just some really, really wonderful things . . . oh, I had a really, really slow class at the inner city high school. I mean, these were people who were just so painfully, painfully slow. And I just threw the curriculum out; I just said the hell with it. We're not going to read this, we're not going to read that. I mean, I didn't tell them. I just tailored it to try and fit them, and I'd bring in things I thought they were interested in. And we had some really great sessions together and we all got to know one another and when the school year was over, on the very last day (begins to cry) — I'll never get through this. They lined up clear around the room and every person shook my hand on the way out. To me, I mean, that says it. I mean, that's it — right there."

Tape #80

"We give the resources of the future."

I would have probably enjoyed socializing with Mr. B. He had a warm smile and liked biking, reading, and swimming — all my favorites. He was also my age at the time, thirty-five, another one of the '60s generation who had gone into teaching. His mod thin tie was but one illustration of his being well dressed in a fashionable way. He sat cross-legged, smoking, and gesturing with his hands. His hair was thinning and there was quite a bald spot on the top . . . after twelve years of teaching seventh graders U.S. history. He had also been a local association president.

He spoke for me; he spoke for a lot of teachers.

(Why did you become a teacher?)

"Because I wanted to do something that I thought could help other people. And this was an area that I was interested in. The subject that I teach is something that I enjoy. And I like kids and I like working with them so it was the perfect opportunity for me. I think at the time I was growing up, there was a feeling that you wanted to help do something, you wanted to help others, make the world a better place, or maybe give others opportunities that maybe you didn't have while you were growing up, and to share and to build a better world. You'd do what you could to have a part in that."

(Do you think it's different today?)

"I think in some cases I do. A lot of people who enter this profession with more a — *what can they get for themselves* idea without realizing it's more of a *you have to give so much* type of deal. I think a lot of people in the world are out to make a fast buck; let me get myself straight and maybe then worry about other people. If you enter this profession, you've got to realize from the start, that you're not going to be a wealthy person. So yeah, I think it's changed somewhat. I think there's a real trend to go into positions where you can make more money and more personal success, achievement on a more individual basis than working with a group where you didn't necessarily go into it to be the number one person in the crowd.

"But I think the older teachers at least from my experience, tend to be more restrictive, more regimented in their approaches to dealing with the students. They tend to deal with them as a full group instead of dealing with them in many cases as individuals. That was a big hurdle for a lot of people to get over, and I think there are still some older teachers who haven't gotten over the fact that you have to take each kid for what his abilities are and to go from there. They tend instead to just approach the general. You sink or swim whether or not you're in that middle area. And that middle area is becoming so much more gray with mainstreaming and the differing abilities. I teach a history class which is not ability grouped, and so I run the gamut as far as students' abilities go. I would prefer ability grouping because you would have kids of similar ability progressing at the same rate. Now the situation I have, I've got different students doing different things and with the ones that are a little bit slow, I try to work with them individually, a one on one basis in many cases or in a group basis where they can work with each other or with some of the better students. But with these kids, at their age level, those who are much faster tend to lord it over the other kids at times. It is true sometimes that the higher level kids pull up the lower ones. I had a class once that had a large number of gifted kids in it and there were two LD kids and they did do better out of a desire to be a part of what was going on in there. But I don't see that as something in all cases, as a general kind of rule. I think it's a good idea, but I'm not certain it really works the way it's supposed to."

(Have you lost any of your idealism from when you first started teaching?)

"Yes. I think a lot of times it is the administrative rules and regulations that you've got to follow and that you don't a lot of times feel are compatible to what you see as what you need to do with your class for the students. There's the paperwork that continually mounts up even though there are people who say, 'Oh, we're going to reduce the amount of paperwork that you have.' And then they just slide in all these other things that have to be done. Also — not recognizing the fact that we are highly trained professional people. And I think you begin to think — 'what am I doing?' when that's not recognized, not just by administrators but by members of the public at large who sometimes come in and think that they know how to run your classroom even though they only have one child in that classroom. You tend to see that the job is not all it's cracked up to be. You think you're going to be helping kids and bringing them on, and then you still have to deal with their own personal problems at home, especially at this age level.

"Kids are very social; everything is changing for them — bodies, the whole deal. They're going from little kids to young adults. What's my identity; where do I belong? All that pressure is coming in on them from older kids and from parents and, I think, teachers. You know — you're thirteen now, you have to act more adult. But inside they're still not sure what that is. You often find that subject matter falls by the wayside when those types of problems become pervasive. One student with a real problem can create some real problems within a class that need to be worked out in order for that class to function right. You go in and you think you're going to teach these kids the world. I'm going to make them see that history is the greatest thing since sliced bread. They're going to go out of here loving it. But you're not always successful, and that's a hard thing for some people to accept. It takes time.

"You think — oh, I'm going to be wonderful; I'm going to be great, and you plan all these great ideas and then you don't do all that well. That can be pretty devastating inside. And when you first start[ed], I can think of plenty of times when I stayed up late and planned this certain type of activity, and I just knew that it was going to fly perfectly, but it didn't. Last night on the news, this guy was introducing a story that you could just see he was just all prepared for, and then they put on the tape and it was a whole different story. Well, in teaching, there's a lot of that. You get all pumped up and ready to go and then someone comes on the speaker and says — send this kid down, or do that, or we're going to have an assembly today — pictures have to be made up today; forget everything you're doing. So you've got that kind of stuff going on. We've got some schools that are not air conditioned. And you have your plans all set up and then you get to school and find you're going to be dismissed early. Well, there goes all that. So there are so many things that go on — yes, it does tend to knock down your idealism. And maybe that's good, because you've got to be realistic if you're going to be in the classroom. You can't be talking about a world that really isn't there and expect these kids to grow up into a world of tomorrow, a world that they're going to have to create, if they don't deal with reality.

"I think kids today are a little more hopeless. Some of them tend to see school as something they have to exist through. It's something they just have to live through without realizing what kind of benefits they can get from it. I don't know; maybe it was just my idealism, but it seems like when I first started teaching, everybody knew that education was a way to a better future. But the kids I have today are much more aware than my peers and I were. They're more 'streetwise' about all kinds of issues that when I was in seventh grade, kids just really didn't know about. It wasn't so much that we were so sheltered; it's just that our opportunities to do certain things were more limited. Today, their freedom is so much greater. A lot of them come from families where both parents work and they've had to fend for themselves in many cases and take care of younger brothers and sisters, which I think gives them an increasing level of maturity. When I was a kid, mother was home; we didn't have as many working mothers.

"So when society has demands, too many times they say the schools can handle it. And they don't stop and count up everything that schools are having to do. And teachers just become more and more frustrated. You've got to do this and you've got to do that . . . standards of learning tests, basic skills tests, minimum competency tests — I'm sure they're all nice things in helping to fix the students' ability of what they're doing at a certain point in time. But what effect that that has on a teacher is simply adding more paperwork. When there's time that you could be working with this kid, instead you've got to be filling out folders that record his standards of learning tests, competency tests, minimum skills tests, checking this out and filling that out. And we have to collect money for this and that. You know, in college, they don't tell you that some days you're going to have to go in there and collect money, and it may take you all bell to take everybody's money and give them all a receipt so that everything is accurate. Well, that puts you a day behind in your lessons. And then they bring an evaluator in and they say, 'This is where you're at? You haven't done this material yet?' And you say, 'But you understand, I had to [collect] these picture moneys and I had to do these projects' — their expectations aren't realistic with what's going on in a classroom.

"And in this area class size is a problem — there are too many kids in too few classrooms. You asked the question of whether teachers should have their own classrooms — absolutely. We're professionals and that classroom is where we do our work. To put a teacher in a closet, in a hallway, in a van, in a foyer of a building — is an insult. It's not only an insult to that professional educator; it's an insult to those students. And class size? When you have mixed ability groupings, if I could have five to ten less in a class it would make a big difference in what I could accomplish with them. But when you have thirty-two, thirty-five in a classroom and that's a fifty minute bell — you don't even have two minutes per kid!

"I think education needs some understanding and patience . . . and that doesn't cost people a lot of money. Understanding and patience on the part of the public, on the part of the administrators, and a lot of time on the part of teachers who expect things to get done the minute they think things should be done, not realizing it takes time. Every decision is a political decision in education. And that takes some time. Maybe it's a way of looking at education as a process, as a good process.

"I've thought about getting out of teaching. Money was the first reason — to make more money. To get out from under the pressures that are put on you when you have 150 to 275 kids a day. And though you want to do the best that you can do, you can't always reach all those kids. Then you feel like you've failed. What have I done wrong? There may be one kid out of all those kids who may not make it and you feel like you should have done something a little bit more. That's a big drain on you. You put up with that year after year and day after day. There're lots of — 'why didn't you listen' or 'I could have done this'; 'I could have saved this child,' and that's a lot of pressure. But I haven't gotten out . . . because of the kids; I love the kids. I like the variety; I like the change each day. We've got a great faculty at my school; we get along fairly well. I like the situation and I like working with the kids. To me, it's rewarding. I mean, I know that there are some that I'm not going to be real effective with. I'll do my best to try, but I know that sometimes it's just not going to work out; yet for the most part, I just enjoy what I'm doing.

(What does that mean — reward or satisfaction from teaching?)

"We prepare students for a world that is constantly changing. We give them skills and abilities to make decisions in their own lives, hopefully the right decisions. We offer them a variety of areas to spark their interests, not just in academic subjects but in vocational subjects. We give them a chance to build for themselves a life that they can dream about. If they take advantage of what's available, there's no limit to what they can do. We give to this country . . . we give the resources of the future. And I think that's our best contribution."

Tape #283

Mr. G. had taught high school English for twelve years at a suburban high school. He had been described by one central administrator he

worked under as crude and obnoxious; the administrator, as usual, was
wrong. Mr. G. was a bundle of sensitivities, hidden by a brash, quick-
witted exterior. And he was a fairly popular teacher who had been dedi-
cated to teaching.

At the time of this talk, he was also a fairly content man as he had, a few
months before, gotten back together with a past lover but was not em-
ployed to teach for the next year.

A week later (in August) he landed a high school position at a very tony
suburban high school.

"I don't remember ever actually making a conscious decision — I'll be
a teacher. I fear I may have fallen into it like so many teachers have, an
easy place to do good and still have time to yourself. What else could I do
with a BA in English? One of my brothers suggested I get a job at P&G
reciting Shakespeare at lunch in the cafeteria. I decided to teach. A year
and two summers of grad school and I was certified and had my master's
degree in education — it wasn't much effort.

"But I did have dreams. I wanted to help — in some way. I wanted to
do something job-wise where I wouldn't be just making money. You have
to make a commitment to someone besides yourself and something besides money or — what are you? Over-commitment may be making
yourself a slave to a cause, but no commitment is turning yourself into a
robot. A commitment to educating teenagers with the luxury of summers
off — it seemed just the right proportions. People smile indulgently at you
a lot today when you say you went into teaching because you believed in
helping the world, but I'm still proud to be a child of the '60s. And I'm still
committed, believe it or not. Doing what you can for your corner of the
world is what gives life purpose and meaning; and life without meaning 'is
the torture of restlessness and vague desire' (Edgar Lee Masters). Become
a business executive or an insurance salesman or a stockbroker if you
want, but you'll never know the satisfaction of having taught. Teachers
may very well touch eternity, but they definitely mold the here and now.

"What's wrong with public education? From writing this book, I've
come to see three major problems. Largest among these is the society in
which that educational system exists. As most people understand, a school
system merely reflects the society in which it works. If we live in a society
where a parent will call in and lie about her son or daughter being sick
when they're not but just want to skip school, how efficient can we expect
that school system to be? I called a parent once about his son who was
doing poorly in my class, was about to fail if something didn't change.

The parent's response was: 'If he fails another class, I'm kicking him out of this house.' I had another father call me and tell me I couldn't give his son a detention for walking out of my class because his son had a bad bladder and he just had to go . . . the son could be heard over the phone laughing in the background. At a party in our district the police came and sent everybody home because it had gotten so out of hand; the mother of the host was found locked in the attic of the house where she'd gone because all of the ruckus so frightened her . . . she had not called the police. Unemployment for young blacks is around forty percent right now; you think that doesn't affect how they work in school?

"It's a cruel, weak society. This is what teachers have to function in. And remember, teachers are products of that society too. I've heard, from a student undergoing psychiatric therapy, about the teacher who said anyone who sees a psychiatrist is a fruitcake. Or from a young and very frightened gay student — his teacher lectured the class on how all homo-sexuals are going to hell . . . that in an English class, no less. It would be nice to think that our teachers are better than the rest of society, but it would be naive. It's a terrible world out there, and the schools are just a part of that terrible world. We try to do what we can, but we have insurmountable odds.

"Think of all that people want the schools to do today that schools never had to worry about in the past — from driver's training to rape assemblies — no, not to teach them how to but how to not be. We have sex education, AIDS education, values clarification, LD tutors, psychology classes, drug testing, family living courses, and on and on and on. I'm for all of this, but you're going to have to come up with some new tests to see if we're doing the job well. How many SATs or ACTs measure how well we teach kids how to drive or deal with sex or learn about themselves? Maybe we're not doing as badly as tests say we are; maybe we've just learned to teach more important things than the meaning of the word *dross*. I'd rather my son or daughter knew how to prevent AIDS then memorized the dates for the Civil War. I don't give a lot of objective tests, though God knows they're easier to grade. I make my students write essays which make them think — do you agree with what the author is saying and why or why not? Try to measure what my kids learn by giving them some sort of objective tests . . . it won't show up. Does that make it less valuable than the equation for pi? To me, this new push for competency testing reflects society perfectly, a society obsessed with trivia.

"Parents reading this will say, 'Don't blame us; I'm not responsible; I raise my kids well.' And they probably do . . . the lousy parents don't read books like this. And the good parents aren't aware of just how awful a mother or father can be . . . I've seen too many abused children; I've seen too many ignored children.

Another problem with education today is administration. If education is so bad off, why aren't people placing the blame on the people who have control of it. That isn't the teachers. If a business goes bankrupt, it's rare that they blame it on the workers in the factory. And believe me, I've seen too much incompetence in administration to not believe that this is a major problem. Me? I'd fire them all and let the teachers run the district on reduced class schedules. Think of the money that could be saved if we didn't have to pay all those high salaries to people who quit teaching! I can still hear one principal at an in-service telling wide-eyed teachers that putting marbles in a clear jar when kids were good and taking them out when they were bad was a good way of disciplining students . . . even at the high school level. I kept waiting for the punch line; there wasn't one. This guy had been out of education for years and had come back in as an administrator — just what we need, more non-teachers telling us professionals what to do.

"If you want to see a really bad teacher, go look at a central administrator. I still remember seeing my name on a list of teachers who hadn't given competency tests that year. We had been promised by the central administration that individual teachers would not be checked, that these tests were not to test the teachers. Then, a list comes out listing who had given or not given what tests. I was livid; I had been out on sick leave for almost two months. What was I supposed to do? Give them from my hospital bed? Central administrators told my principal to lecture me on being a better team player. I had visions of what I could do to them with my IV's.

"And believe me, I've been lucky. I've gotten along with and liked the vast majority of building administrators with whom I've worked. They've been nice guys, not particularly great educators, but nice guys. I've had all excellent evaluations. I've really got no gripe towards them. But just once I'd like to be observed by an English teacher, a peer, and given some specific suggestions on how to make this lesson better or a clever idea for the lesson I have written down to do next week. I mean, it's nice to be told what a fine teacher you are and all that, but it would be nicer to talk to someone who knew something about teaching English.

"Unfortunately too many administrators, particularly at the central level, think there [is] 'one way' of doing things . . . and there isn't in education. We're dealing with people, not products. There are many different kinds of students who learn in many different kinds of ways; the more kinds of teaching techniques used in a school, the better it is as it gives each individual student more of a chance of learning from — somebody! Anyone who insists on one way of teaching . . . is a factory manager, not an educator.

And the final major problem in education today — class size. It would cost a lot of money to lower all class sizes, but it should be done, especially in the primary grades. Grades K though three should have no more than fifteen to a class. Catch those kids when you can do something about it. Spend your money on the schools; we'll deal with so many problems that you won't have to be spending your money on the prisons. I truly believe that education is the solution to most of this country's problems today. Give good teachers a small enough group of kids to work with and we can get the majority of them drug free, alcohol free, full of values and respect and mentally healthy . . . then what would we need prisons for? Spend federal money on this country, not on the defense of this country, or you're not going to have a country worth defending.

"What else would make me a better teacher? You could get rid of all those demeaning duties that they order a teacher to do . . . I don't think anyone with a college degree should be asked to stand in restrooms and watch young boys piss. I was tempted to tell them I was gay, hoping that would get me out of that duty, but I was afraid they'd just put me in the girls' restrooms. So I just didn't do it, period. Every year, they'd put out a schedule of teachers who were to walk the halls during exams . . . during their free periods. I had papers to grade; besides, I figured if all teachers just kept all their kids in their classrooms where they belonged, what was the point of patrolling? I never did that either — for twelve years. Lesson plans! What a silly thing to ask a professional to do, put numbers out of a book on pages that no one is going to read anyway. The state decided that this was how to check competency — to check the numbers on lesson plans . . . makes you sort of wonder what state legislators smoke, doesn't it?

"And teachers must have control of what is taught and how it's taught. The working professional is the one who has the experience to know what has to be done and how best to do it. I'm sick of hearing administrator and college professors (and even businessmen now!) talk about this global view they have of education which is so much better than the isolated view of the individual classroom teacher. Change *global* to *idealistic, naive, inexperienced, no contact with reality, educationese, ivory tower* — and you're closer to the truth. Honestly now, who do you want operating on your child, the doctor who's been in the operating room for the last ten years or the one who's been sitting in his office theorizing about the human body?

"I might also add that I could stand to be seen and treated as a professional; it's the least people could do if they're not going to pay me like one. A teacher is deserving of respect; what more important profession is there for a society? But I can understand why the teaching profession isn't respected as it should be. There *are* a lot of bad teachers. It was hard to decide that, but I think it's true. I'd say forty percent of the teachers out there in public schools aren't very good and twenty percent of those are awful. Why? One reason is bad administration again. First, they do nothing to help train a new teacher. I've seen too many first year teachers handed their books and a schedule — two days before classes start — and told to teach. I was hired the week before classes started; so was one of my best friends. You can't tell me that school districts couldn't be run well enough to know how many teachers they needed at least by the middle of July!

"And do administrators fire teachers ever? No, you can get away with doing nothing in education. I taught in a building where there were dumb teachers, cruel teachers, lazy teachers, and burnt-out ones. I still had respect for the burnt out ones, but the others? There were some ex-coaches who taught twenty-five minute classes. I had a student who would walk out and drive home ... twenty-five minutes into the one coach's class ... because he'd stop teaching then and not care what his students did. These people should have their case histories documented and then fired after going through the proper due process. But administrators are too lazy or too incompetent to do it. And don't blame the associations and unions; they don't protect incompetent teachers. They merely insure that each teacher gets his due process; if the district can prove incompetence, that teacher could be a goner and no decent teacher union or association is going to argue to keep a bad teacher. They hurt all of us.

"Why are teachers deserving of respect then? It's like the president — you respect the office if not the man or woman. I think a few teachers are horrible human beings, but the job itself — well, that's another question. Nothing is more important to insuring the survival of our society than teachers. If we could deal with small enough numbers of kids, we could eliminate the vast majority of problems that aren't caused by our economic system ... and a lot of those too. Teachers are *that* important. And considering the number of excellent teachers out there, it's time they were listened to. Believe me, no one wants to get bad teachers out of teaching more than good teachers. We all get paid on the same pay scale. The only difference is that the really bad teachers who have some ambition — go into administration and make more money.

"You know, sometimes I wonder if I *am* a very good teacher. I have a lot of students who tell me I am, and I've formed a lot of great relationships with a lot of ex-students, but sometimes I still wonder. I remember the bored students; I remember the ones who yelled things at my door when it was closed; I remember the ones I had to punish; I remember all those hundreds of kids who sat through my classes for twelve weeks, eighteen weeks, a year, and who seemed to say nothing, do nothing, enjoy nothing, gain nothing from me. I can list more students I was a failure with than I was a success with.

"And yet I cared. That's what always saves me when I think about this. It isn't always how well you succeed, but how sincerely you try. One teacher may get stuck with all low level classes where the chance of success is already much lower; the cards are stacked. Another may get all honors classes. I know I was more successful in those. I got to know a heck of a lot of students on a personal level . . . I cared enough about them to do that when I could, when the numbers weren't too exorbitant, when I could get clearance from them to land inside their brain and stimulate them for a while before I took off again.

"How do you motivate a student. Get to know him. What can parents do to help their kids be better students? Get to know them. What can you do about discipline problems? Get to know your students . . . what it doesn't eliminate, it helps you know how to deal with. Does public education really work? Yes, if teachers know their students — if they know their subject matter, can communicate well, and they care enough to do it.

"I lost my job in teaching the spring after I researched this book. I was ten days late in getting a letter of intent back to my district office to let them know I'd be coming back from a leave of absence I'd taken to write this book. Nothing's accomplished without taking risks and I felt this year off had not only taught me a lot about teaching but also had renewed my commitment to it. I didn't work for a year and luckily I profited from it. I chose that risk. I'd never had a negative evaluation. All of the building principals I'd worked for, except the one who was only there for the last year I taught, offered me letters of recommendation. I was popular with most of the kids and most of the parents with whom I'd dealt. I'd worked overtime every year to put out the student newspaper. I have a master's degree in education. Both of the last two men who observed and evaluated me called me one of the finest teachers they'd worked with. There was a job opening in the district a week later for exactly what I taught. I cost

$30,000 a year on their pay scale; a new teacher cost about $18,000. I was active in curriculum and argued my case, usually supported by my whole department who were oftentimes too hesitant or too afraid to speak out themselves. Central administrators are often a very insecure lot . . . they don't want anyone to disagree with the company line. And yet most of the things I argued against, they later changed.

"What happened to me this past spring was just the perfect symbol for what's wrong with public education — money, incompetent administrators with no connection to the real classroom . . . a good teacher treated unprofessionally and unethically. Members of the community and teaching staff told me I was lucky to be out of there. In fact, my ex-students had often told me I'd be a fool to go back. 'You're too good to be a teacher!' 'You could do so many great things; why be a teacher?' And yet, as misguided as some of them were, it was my ex-students who made me feel good about being terminated unfairly and by men whose kids I'd taught and by men who were completely lacking in educational knowledge. These were the people who made you think poorly of education, dumb men who had quit teaching because they were no good at it and too lazy to improve.

"But the week I found out that my school district didn't want me, I was inundated with activities with ex-students, and I realized that those twelve years in my suburban school district were nowhere near a loss; I had all these people to validate it. It just happened that two called from their respective colleges (both out of state) to ask me for some help on papers they were writing. One I helped move into a new apartment here in town. One called just to talk about his senior year ending at the high school where I used to teach and prom and graduation and those kinds of things. Another called to give me some addresses of school districts to apply to since I had given her all of the ones I had . . . and we were both applying for the same position — English teacher at the high school level. Another student from two years ago stopped by while she was in town before leaving for her summer job. She just wanted to chat and let me know what was going on and what I thought of it and how I was doing — two hugs, one when she came in and one when she left. It made me feel so good. And one former student from ten years ago called because she was in from California where she's lived for the last five years — just to say hello. 'I couldn't come into the city without at least saying hi.' Amazingly enough, I didn't hear from my suicide case that week. But I talked to an ex-student I talk to almost every week and got two other letters from ex-students. My old school district didn't want me; my students still did. And I'd rather have it that way than the opposite. I have more respect for my students.

"And it doesn't matter if people disagree with me, with my ideas. It isn't the conclusions that are important . . . but the commitment. That's why I became enthusiastic again after spending a year traveling the country and talking to teacher after teacher after teacher; that's why I really wanted to return to teaching — I met some fantastic, intelligent people who were wonderfully committed to teaching. It made me feel good about teaching, and I hope this book will make other people feel good about teaching. For commitment will make most education programs successful; it's just that it requires the commitment of the teachers, the parents, the community, and the students themselves.

"It's funny but in good teaching the initial impact is so small that a teacher can hardly see it. Like I said, we're not dealing with a product; we're dealing with human beings. At the end of the year, we can't point at any part of them and say, 'Look at that, I did that. I made that kneecap; I molded that ear.' Our end results may be years away. And yet looking back at that week . . . I feel the impact in a very powerful way. A district can terminate a good teacher; a student can't. I may not have reached and affected in any great way but twenty percent of all the students I dealt with, but how many people can say they affected the lives of that many hundreds of people? To me there are three things a person wants to attempt in life — attempt to form relationships, attempt to live according to what you believe, and attempt to teach."